Taxploitation

The Case for Income Tax Reform

Taxploitation

The Case for Income Tax Reform

Edited by Peter Saunders

CIS Readings 11

THE CENTRE FOR INDEPENDENT STUDIES

2006

Published 2006 by The Centre for Independent Studies Limited.

National Library of Australia
Cataloguing-in-Publication Data:

Taxploitation : the case for income tax reform.

Includes index.
ISBN 1 86432 114 8.

1. Income tax - Australia. 2. Tax reform - Australia. I. Saunders, Peter (Peter Gordon), 1948- . II. Centre for Independent Studies (Australia). (Series : CIS readings ; 11).

336.24150994

Copyediting by April Palmerlee and Dominic Rolfe
Design and layout by Sophia Austin

Artwork on front cover:
'Tax Collector' (1542) by Alte Pinakothek,
photo © Blauel/Gnamm – ARTOTHEK,
reproduced with permission of the Alte Pinakothek Museum, Munich

Printed by Griffin Press
Typeset in AGaramond

PO Box 92, St Leonards, NSW, 1590
cis@cis.org.au
www.cis.org.au

Contents

Introduction
What We Need To Do And Why We Need To Do It

In an interview with *The Sydney Morning Herald* on 7 August 2004, the Prime Minister was asked about any plans he might have for reforming Australia's income tax system. He replied: 'I think we've been very generous in relation to tax. You never say never in this business, but I think it is fair to assume that we feel we have done quite a lot on tax.' Having successfully introduced a new Goods and Services Tax (GST) in 2000, John Howard saw no compelling case for further major tax reform.

The Treasurer, Peter Costello, seems to agree, for he has repeatedly rejected calls for income tax reform. He was critical of a Liberal backbench 'ginger group' when it began to push for radical changes following the October 2004 election, and he was scathing when prominent Liberal backbencher Malcolm Turnbull published an array of costed options for reforming income tax in September 2005. Eventually forced to do something by a growing groundswell of opinion demanding reform, he established an inquiry into Australia's tax system in February 2006, but coming after ten years in office, and being given just five weeks to report, this initiative looked more like a way of defusing the tax issue than promoting it.[1]

Both the Prime Minister and the Treasurer are happy to make electorally popular tax cuts when the budget allows, but neither sees much advantage in a more fundamental restructuring of the income tax system which is likely to produce losers as well as winners. As John Howard put it in March 2006, 'Tax cuts is what people want. Commentators are interested in tax reform. The public out there is interested in the tax burden.'[2]

This antipathy to radical reform is unfortunate, for our income tax system is riddled with distortions and disincentive effects that cry out for serious attention. The top rate of almost 50 cents in every dollar is increasingly out of line with most other Western countries which have been moving to lower and flatter rates. The top personal income tax rate is also out of kilter with the company rate, and most really high earners are in consequence paying a lower rate of income tax than workers earning little more than average income. There are so many special allowances, exemptions, credits, offsets and write-offs that tax law has become almost indecipherable, and gross amounts of money and time are spent on wasteful forms of investment designed purely to reduce liability to tax. Retirement savings are viciously taxed (Australia is the only country in the world that taxes superannuation savings when the money is put into a fund, when it earns profit while it is in a fund, and when it is withdrawn). The threshold at which people start to pay tax (an income of just $6,000 per year) is well below subsistence income, so people are taxed before they have earned enough to keep body and soul together. This in turn contributes to a high level of 'churning' of tax and welfare payments, for having taken money away from low-income families, the government has to give it back again. Churning then results in dispiritingly high 'effective (or equivalent) marginal tax rates' which deter people on welfare from looking for work and penalise low-wage families whenever they try to increase their take-home pay. And because tax brackets are not indexed to inflation, the total tax-take increases year by year without anybody even realising it.

Outside of the federal government there is a mounting recognition that something radical needs to be done to tackle these problems. Among those who have called publicly for fundamental change to our increasingly irrational income tax system are specialist taxation groups such as Taxpayers Australia and the Certified Practicing Accountants; business groups including the Business Council of Australia, the Australian Industry Group and the Australian Chamber of Commerce and Industry; academic tax experts like Neil Warren (author of *Tax: Facts, fiction and reform*) and Melbourne Institute director John Freebairn; and media commentators led by *The Australian* newspaper (which has run a long campaign demanding tax reform). The Australian Council of Social Service wants taxes lowered at the bottom end of the income distribution, and trade unionists and the Labor Party have begun to complain about the high taxes being levied on lower- and middle-income workers. Prominent politicians from both sides of politics have also become increasingly vociferous in calling for change. They include Liberals like Malcolm Turnbull and Sophie Panopolous (founder of the backbench ginger group), and Labor members such as Craig Emerson and Lindsay Tanner. But despite the growing momentum for reform, the government has so far remained resolute in its conviction that nothing much needs to be done.

Notwithstanding John Howard's claim that his government has been 'generous' when it comes to taxation, federal government spending as a proportion of GDP is as high as it has ever been, and taxes have been getting more onerous. Back in 1901, total tax revenue per person as a percentage of per capita GDP was just 6.3%. It reached double digits in the 1920s, crashed through 20% at the time of World War II, and has gone past 30% during the Howard years.[3] According to the Australian Bureau of Statistics, the total gross incomes of Australians rose by 33% between 1998–99 and 2003–04, but total income tax revenues accruing to the Commonwealth government rose by 36%, or nearly $40 billion, during the same six-year period.[4] This has been a period of unprecedented economic boom, when we might have thought that the need for government spending should have been falling, yet government has gone on a spending spree.

Every year the Centre for Independent Studies calculates 'Tax Freedom Day,' the day in the year when Australians have collectively generated enough money to cover the government's annual spending so that they can start to earn money for themselves. In 2005, Tax Freedom Day fell on 26th April.[5] In other words, we are working nearly four months of every year to pay for the government's programmes before we start to earn a cent that we can spend on ourselves. If this is 'tax generosity' one shudders to think what 'tax exploitation' might look like.

How big is the tax burden?

Some academics and journalists believe the current tax burden is acceptable. Some even argue it is too low and should be increased in order to give the Government yet more money to spend. Among them is the former Secretary to the Department of Prime Minister and Cabinet, Michael Keating, who claims that tax in Australia is too low and that 'the Australian economy could tolerate a significant increase in the ratio of taxation to GDP without great difficulty'.[6]

Those arguing for higher taxes and more government spending generally rest their case on comparisons between the level of taxation in Australia and the average level of taxation across all the OECD countries. When this simple comparison is made, it seems that, although our government soaks up over 30% of all the wealth we produce each year, other governments are taking even more. Compared with the OECD average, Australians do appear to enjoy a 'low' tax regime.

Statistics, however, are slippery things, and simple averaging can conceal more than it reveals. In chapter 1, Peter Burn points out that the OECD consists of a large number of relatively small European countries and a small number of much larger non-European ones, of which Japan and the USA are the prime examples. The European nations account for 76% of the OECD's member nations, but for only 35% of the OECD's total GDP. Of the 30 countries in the OECD, 23 are in Europe, yet even when they are all put together they have a lower total GDP than the United States on its own.

Use of simple unweighted averages to compare Australia's tax burden with that of the rest of the OECD is therefore hugely misleading, for it takes no account of the size of different countries. A simple average will always over-emphasise the European pattern at the expense of the big non-European economies, because it treats a country like Luxembourg as the equivalent of a country like the United States. As Burn puts it, 'The only possible basis for the claim that Australia is a relatively low-taxing country is a Eurocentric one. While doubtless not deliberate, the use of the simple average of all OECD countries institutionalises the Eurocentric perspective and gives a distorted impression.'

Clearly, then, we need to take account of the size of different countries before we calculate average tax levels, and this is what Peter Burn does in his chapter. The results show that, weighting for the size of the GDP of the different countries, the average tax level across the OECD nations is roughly the same as that found in Australia. Our tax level is lower than in most of Europe, but is higher than in the American and Pacific OECD countries. The countries with which Australia carries out most of its trade tend to have lower tax levels than we do, which suggests that we are over-taxed in comparison with our major economic competitors.

That's not all. While our overall tax burden is roughly comparable to that of other OECD countries, our levels of income tax are way out of line. Burn looks at the composition of Australian tax revenue compared with other OECD countries, and he finds that Australia relies much more on personal and corporate income taxes than most other countries do. Not only are we taxed more heavily than other non-European countries, therefore, but we overburden our income earners. Claims that we are a low taxed country compared with the OECD average are spurious, and there is an obvious and strong case for reducing the burden of income tax.

The inefficiency of high income tax

Does it matter if Australians are suffering a heavier tax burden than their American or Japanese equivalents? Commentators like Michael Keating believe not. They think that middle- and higher-income Australians could easily afford to pay more tax on their earnings than they currently do, and they deny that this would have any serious adverse consequences. In particular, they insist that a heavy income tax burden need not undermine the incentive to work, and that the government could therefore squeeze more tax out of the workforce to spend on 'socially useful' things without doing any real damage to output or productivity.

In chapter 2, Alex Robson accepts that much of the money the government spends each year does *some* good, but he points out that the key question we have to ask is whether the good it is achieving outweighs the harm it is causing by the increased burden of taxation. The issue is not whether more spending could do some good, but is whether the relentless increase in the personal tax burden needed to finance higher spending costs more in lost enterprise and effort than it brings in added benefits.

Politicians rarely stop to consider this basic question of 'tax efficiency', but as Alex Robson reminds us, every extra dollar raised in tax has a cost. Taxation does not simply redirect resources from the private sector to the government—it destroys resources along the way.

Obviously, a dollar going to the Treasury is a dollar lost to the private sector of the economy, but the cost of tax is nearly always much higher than just a one-to-one substitution. Robson identifies a number of different ways in which tax imposes costs on individuals, irrespective of whether they gain from the way government chooses to spend it. These include enforcement costs, evasion costs, compliance costs (which are particularly high in Australia given the extraordinary complexity of our tax system) and administration costs (borne not only by the ATO but also by thousands of employers acting as unpaid agents of government by processing income tax deductions and GST returns). He also identifies what he calls the 'rent-seeking costs' of taxation, which are incurred whenever one sector of the population devotes time and money to influencing the government to divert resources to it from other people.

All of these costs mount up, but in his chapter, Robson focuses mainly on one other, crucial cost of taxation: 'deadweight losses'. Deadweight losses arise when individuals change their behaviour in response to higher taxes, substituting one kind of behaviour for another which would have been preferred had the tax increase not occurred. For example, if income taxes rise, some people might decide to work fewer hours, or they might conclude it is not worthwhile training for an additional qualification, or they might stay on welfare rather than look for a job, or be deterred from the risk of setting up a company of their own. Deadweight losses, in other words, represent the disincentive costs of tax. They are the value of all the work and output that we lose as a result of taxing people's incomes.

It is extremely difficult to calculate these deadweight costs of tax with any accuracy (and governments rarely even try). However, drawing on a variety of OECD research, Robson estimates the Marginal Cost of Funds—that is, the wealth destroyed for each extra dollar we raise in income tax—at between 1.2 and 1.3. If this is right, it means that each extra dollar of income tax raised by Peter Costello is costing the economy at least $1.20 and perhaps $1.30, even without counting the costs of administration and enforcement.

The Treasurer raises more than $200 billion in tax each year. About half of this comes from tax on personal incomes, and a further one-fifth from tax on company incomes.[7] Even on a conservative estimate, this means that personal income tax alone is costing the economy at least $20 billion per year in lost output. Robson believes the actual figure could be as high as $60 billion.

In light of this, it would not be unreasonable to require of government that any new policy should generate at least $1.20 worth of benefits for every extra $1 it would cost in tax revenue, otherwise it should not go ahead. But our politicians in Canberra rarely consider such cost-benefit calculations when making their spending promises. One suspects that few of the new spending projects they come up with would get anywhere near meeting this rate of return benchmark. Robson points out that no country anywhere in the world has ever achieved a 4% annual growth rate once its tax-take exceeded 40% of GDP. The probable reason is that, once the basics have been put in place, each new item of government provision costs the economy more in tax than it creates in benefits, and therefore depresses the rate of economic growth.

Alex Robson's evidence alerts us to how much the failure to reform our income tax system is costing us. His analysis is technical, but the basic message is very simple: we are killing the goose that lays the golden eggs.

High income taxes undermine incentives

A key reason why higher income taxes destroy wealth is that they reduce the incentive for people to work hard and build their own, and the country's, prosperity.

Some economists challenge this. They suggest that lowering taxes might induce people to work *less* rather than more, for leaving more money in workers' pockets means they can attain a satisfactory income with less effort than before. Sinclair Davidson discusses the evidence in chapter 3.

The issue of whether lower tax increases or decreases work incentives turns on the balance between what economists call the 'substitution effect' (higher taxes deter workers from working harder and encourage them to spend their time on leisure instead) and the 'income effect' (higher taxes lead workers to intensify their working effort in order to achieve the net income that they desire). Davidson reviews a number of studies which try to determine which of these effects is stronger. Although the evidence is not clear cut, he finds that workers on higher incomes who can control their hours of work often respond to the prospect of higher net earnings by working harder. Self-employed physicians, for example, tend to work harder if there is the chance to make more money. He also finds that people work longer in countries with lower taxes while they take more leisure (or accept higher unemployment) in countries with high taxes. Entrepreneurial activity, such as new business start-ups, is also stronger when taxes are lower. Overall, therefore, it does seem that lower taxes promote greater economic activity.

If this is the case, then it has important implications for governments seeking to maximise their tax revenues. On the face of it, we would imagine that tax cuts will reduce government revenues. This is why advocates of higher public spending routinely oppose tax cuts, for they assume that lower taxes will reduce the amount of money available for spending on public services. But if lower taxes generate more output, then it is at least possible that cutting taxes could stimulate so much additional economic activity that total tax revenues actually rise as a result.

The American economist Arthur Laffer famously outlined the theory behind this. He reasoned that if marginal tax rates are set at zero, government will get no revenue, but that this must also be logically true if marginal tax rates are set at 100% (for nobody will then bother working). It must, therefore, logically be the case that, somewhere between 0% and 100% there is an income tax rate which maximises revenue, and that *either* side of this point, revenue will be lower than it could be. The key question is where this point falls, and whether current Australian tax rates are above or below it.

Laffer provides evidence, reviewed by Davidson, of occasions when big tax cuts in the USA resulted in increased rather than decreased government revenues, but there are also contrary examples where big tax cuts appear to have triggered big budget deficits.[8] As with data on the substitution versus income effect of tax cuts, so too with evidence on the so-called 'Laffer curve', Davidson finds there is no conclusive answer, but he finds indications that current Australian tax rates may be on the high side of the Laffer optimal point. Certainly our experience with corporate income tax reform in recent years demonstrates how dramatically reduced tax rates can lead to increased rather than reduced government revenues, for when the corporate rate was reduced from 36% to 30%, total corporate tax revenues expanded to record levels.[9]

A fair go for all taxpayers

Australia operates what its defenders like to call a 'progressive' income tax system. This means that higher earners not only pay more tax than lower earners, but they pay a higher *rate* of tax. At the time of writing (early 2006), there are five different tax rates applicable at different levels of income. Up to $6,000 per year the tax rate is zero. We then pay 15% on every dollar earned between $6,001 and $21,600; 30% on every dollar between $21,601 and $63,000 (rising to $70,000 after July 2006); 42% on every dollar between $63,001 and $95,000 (rising to $125,000 after July 2006); and 47% on every dollar earned above that.[10] The more you earn, the smaller the proportion of your income you are allowed to keep.

In the second of his two chapters (chapter 4), Sinclair Davidson shows that this 'progressive' system of taxation results in higher income earners paying a lot more than their 'fair share' of income tax. Indeed, the great bulk of income tax receipts come from a relatively small minority of taxpayers. Davidson calculates that three-quarters of the population is paying less than its proportionate share in tax while one quarter is paying more. The popular idea that 'the rich' are getting away with paying very little while low- and middle-income earners are being left to shoulder the burden is thus entirely false. Many people are paying little or nothing, and a few people are paying a lot.

Davidson also shows that in recent years, the tax burden has shifted increasingly onto higher-income earners. Although political activists and pundits commonly assert that higher income earners have done better than anybody else as a result of tax changes during the Howard years, Davidson shows the reverse is the case. In 1996–97, the top quarter of income earners paid 61% of total net tax; by 2000–01 they were paying 64% of it.

One reason why many Australians apparently believe that the rich have benefited most from recent tax changes is that, in a progressive system, tax cuts will tend to favour higher earners because they pay most of the tax. For example, the 2005 federal budget raised the top rate income tax threshold from $70,000 to $125,000 over two years. This provoked a storm of protest from the Labor Party, the trade unions and the welfare lobby complaining that the Coalition government was 'unfairly' favouring the rich. But as Davidson explains, with 63% of all personal income tax revenue coming from just one quarter of taxpayers (and with the bottom quarter paying just 3% of it), higher earners are almost bound to benefit disproportionately when taxes are reduced. Just as an aspirin will bring more relief to somebody with a bad headache than to someone suffering only mild discomfort, so a tax cut will bring more relief to somebody paying a greater chunk of their income in tax than to somebody paying only a small proportion.

It is an unfortunate feature of electoral democracy that the majority of the population will always be tempted to push an ever-increasing share of taxation onto a minority, and that politicians seeking votes will therefore exploit the more affluent minority while bestowing their beneficence on the majority of voters lower down the income scale. As a politician, you don't risk many votes when you 'hit the rich', but you can buy a lot of popularity when you distribute the proceeds to everybody else. This is precisely what has been happening.

Put in these terms, our 'progressive' tax system does not sound particularly fair or just. Classical economists and philosophers like Adam Smith, John Stuart Mill and Friedrich Hayek all argued that fair taxation must be *proportionate* to people's means. In other words, in a fair income tax system, everybody pays the same proportion of their income in tax. Defenders of so-called 'progressive' taxation have advanced all sorts of arguments and propositions to try to demolish this fundamental principle, but Davidson finds they are all flawed or fallacious. He concludes that the main reason we have progressive taxation has nothing to do with principle of fairness; it is simply because it allows politicians to squeeze more revenue out of the population by targeting the relatively better-off minority of voters.

Lauchlan Chipman agrees, and in chapter 5 he reinforces Davidson's call for a move towards more proportionate taxation by setting out the moral case for a 'flat' income tax.

Chipman acknowledges that most people nowadays believe that 'progressive' taxation is fair, and that 'flat taxes' are impractical, unethical, or both. But these judgments simply reflect our familiarity with progressive taxation. We assume this is the fairest way of taxing people because this is what we are used to. On both sides of politics, politicians recoil from the idea of a flat tax because they assume it would be 'regressive' and 'unfair', but Chipman shows these judgements are mistaken.[11]

Under a 'progressive' tax regime, people lose an increasingly large proportion of their income as their earnings rise, whereas with a flat tax, higher earners still pay more tax than lower earners, but everyone pays the same *proportion* of their income in taxes. Under a flat tax system, the different tax bands would be scrapped (although we might retain an initial zero-rate [tax-free] income threshold). Everyone would then pay tax at the same rate on all of their taxable income. If the rate were 30%, for example, somebody with a taxable income of $30,000 per annum would pay $9,000 tax, and somebody with a taxable income of $60,000 would pay $18,000.

A flat tax is therefore neither 'regressive' nor 'progressive.' It is neutral, applying exactly the same rule to everybody rather than taking proportionately more from person and less from another. This neutrality is precisely why a flat tax is more 'just' than a 'progressive' tax, for it alone complies with the basic principle of the Rule of Law.

Anticipating Geoffrey Walker's analysis in chapter 6, Chipman explains that the Rule of Law demands that people in similar situations should be treated in similar ways, while those who are in different situations should be treated in a way that is proportional to the relevant differences between them. It is this principle that distinguishes Law from the mere exercise of arbitrary power. Applied to the question of taxation, it means that taxes should be *proportional* to people's incomes, rather than being levied at different rates on different levels of income. A flat tax, in other words, is the only just form of income tax.

Could a flat tax work? In principle there is no reason why not, for as Chipman points out, some Eastern European countries are already operating such a system. Latvia has a flat personal income tax rate of 25% with no tax-free threshold; Estonia has a flat personal income tax rate of 26% with a small tax-free threshold; and Russia has a flat rate of 13% on most categories of income. The trend in many Western countries has also been towards flatter rates, and with increasing mobility of professional labour between countries, this trend is likely to strengthen in the future.

Could a flat tax ever get introduced in Australia? Chipman suggests that a radical innovation like this would have to form part of a broader tax reform strategy which includes winding back some of the special deductions, rebates, credits and offsets that clutter up the current system, increasing GST with the increased revenue being retained by the federal government, and cutting total federal spending. A move to a flat tax would therefore have to form part of a broader reform strategy involving a radical simplification of taxation.

Does anybody understand the income tax system?

Our current income tax system is not only unfair; its unfathomable complexity is also eroding the fundamental principle of the Rule of Law on which our whole society depends.

In chapter 6, Geoffrey Walker identifies the two fundamental principles underpinning the Rule of Law. First, rules and sanctions must be clearly specified in advance so that everyone knows how they are supposed to behave and what will happen if they do not. Secondly, all rules must apply equally to everybody (including the government). He explains that the rule of law is the crucial linchpin of any liberal democracy, for it is the citizens' primary safeguard against the arbitrary and capricious use of political power by rulers.

Walker's concern is that, as the burden of taxation has inexorably increased in Australia, so the rules governing tax liabilities have become increasingly tangled and complex with the result that nobody any longer can be sure what the rules say or how they will apply in any given case. We live, he says, in 'an anomic state in which the law has lost its intelligibility, certainty and predictability'. The Australian Tax Office (ATO) has come to enjoy huge discretionary powers in the way it interprets these complex rules. It no longer simply implements a known set of rules, but rather is in the business of developing and amending the rules case by case. 'The tax system', says Walker, 'can hardly be called "law" at all rather than direct bureaucratic rule.'

The combined effect of ever-rising taxes and the increasingly arbitrary interpretation of tax rules has also eroded the moral basis of taxation. Walker recognises that nobody ever enjoys paying taxes but he points out that in the 1950s and 1960s, relatively low taxation and a comparatively simple set of tax rules meant that most people paid what was due without too much complaint or ill will. Today, however, the ATO (and behind it, the government) finds itself locked into a destructive relationship of repression and resistance with ordinary taxpayers. Where they can avoid tax (for example, by exploiting loopholes, or by gravitating to the cash economy), people increasingly do so; where they cannot (the PAYG taxpayers who have tax deducted by their employers before they ever get to see the money), people just get resentful at the unfairness of it all.

The importance of Walker's chapter is that it shows the less tangible, non-economic price we are paying as a nation for our government's failure to keep its tax demands within reasonable bounds. It is bad enough that escalating taxation is undermining enterprise, penalising initiative and destroying the will to work. When we add to this the corrosive effects it is having on the fundamental principle of the Rule of Law, and on the moral relationship between the State and its citizens, the case for fundamental reform becomes compelling.

Restoring personal responsibility

The amount of tax individuals pay on their income depends on two things: marginal tax rates and tax thresholds. Although tax rates have been reduced in Australia over the last 20 years, most of us are losing a bigger slice of our incomes in tax than before because tax thresholds have not kept up with inflation. We are therefore paying a lower rate of tax, but on a much larger sum of money.

One particular tax threshold has hardly changed in value in quarter of a century. This is the 'tax-free' or zero-rate threshold – the point at which people start to pay tax. As Barry Maley and I point out in chapter 7, its value has been eroding at an alarming rate.

In 1980, an individual did not pay any income tax until he or she earned $4,041 per year, which at that time was one-third of average earnings. Wages have gone up by more than 350% since then, but the tax-free earnings threshold has risen by less than 50%, to just $6,000. This represents around one-ninth of today's average earnings, and it means that workers now pay tax on a much larger proportion of their total earnings than they used to. Had the 1980 personal threshold of $4,041 kept pace with earnings, nobody would pay any tax on the first $14,000 of earnings.

There is both a principled and a pragmatic argument for restoring the value of the tax-free threshold to something like its 1980 level. The principled argument is that people should not be taxed until they have at least earned enough to support themselves (that is, until they have earned a 'subsistence income'). If the 'subsistence level' is defined as the minimum amount an unemployed person living wholly on welfare benefits would receive, then the subsistence income for a single person was almost $13,000 per annum at the end of 2005. It follows that, if we want to allow people to earn and retain their own subsistence income before they start to pay tax, the tax-free threshold should be raised to at least $13,000. It should also be indexed to the CPI to ensure it does not fall below the subsistence level in future.

The pragmatic argument for substantially increasing the tax-free threshold is that it would reduce (or possibly even eliminate) the problem of tax-welfare churning. The government tops up low-income families with welfare payments, but it also taxes them on everything they earn above $6,000. It therefore takes money away with one hand (as tax) and then gives it back to the same people with the other (as welfare benefits). This 'churning' is expensive, and it creates huge work disincentives,[12] for as people move from welfare into work, or from part-time into full-time employment, so they have to pay more tax at the same time as they lose their means-tested welfare entitlements. In some cases, the result can be that they lose three-quarters or more of every extra dollar they earn (an 'effective marginal tax rate' in excess of 75%).

Maley and I argue that raising the tax-free threshold above the welfare floor is an essential first step in reducing this churning and restoring incentives and the principle of self-reliance to the income tax system. But on its own, it is not enough, for even a tax-free income of $13,000 or $14,000 is insufficient to maintain more than one person. Clearly, where workers are earning a wage or salary which is supporting more than one person, be it a spouse and/or dependent children, a more generous tax-free threshold is required if they and the rest of their family are to achieve a subsistence income without recourse to welfare payments. But for this to happen, the tax system would need to take account of family circumstances.

Currently, the welfare system recognises that households of different sizes need different levels of income in order to attain comparable living standards. Welfare benefits are therefore adjusted to take account of needs assessed at a family or household level (for example, an unemployed single man receives around $13,000 while an unemployed couple gets more than $21,000). The tax system, however, treats individuals as distinct income units, for earners are taxed separately, irrespective of how many other people might need to share that income. A single person pays the same tax as someone who is earning for two people.

In chapter 8, Terry Dwyer argues this is both inequitable and inefficient. It is inequitable because it ignores the question of how many people have to be supported from any one individual's earnings. A single earner in a family of four starts to pay tax on earnings beyond $6,000, just as a single earner living on his or her own does.[13] But the former is sharing his or her income with three other people—his or her other family members are the ultimate recipients of a large chunk of the income, but they are not recognised for tax purposes. The earner therefore carries the cost of supporting four people, but can claim only one tax-free threshold.

Dwyer points out that this situation is also inefficient, because it skews people's preferences and behaviour. For example, the tax system creates an incentive for both partners in a family to go out to work, even if one would prefer to stay home. This is because it makes more sense for two people each to earn an average income than for one to earn a high income and share it with his/her spouse. Two earners will each receive a tax-free threshold and will only pay a basic rate of tax on the remainder, but a single earner will receive only one threshold and will get taxed at higher marginal rates on the additional income earned.

In recent years, the Federal government has tried to counter some of the inequity and inefficiency in the income tax system by giving certain categories of families with children a welfare top-up. Family Tax Benefit, Part B, for example, is paid to families where there is only one earner to try to compensate them for the disadvantages they suffer through the tax system. The result, however, is a tangle of money transfers in which people get tax taken from them only to have some or all of the cash returned in the form of welfare payments. This is not only costly, it is also wrong in principle. We should not be taxing families until they have secured their own subsistence, and a family's subsistence level will be higher than it is for single people or couples without dependent children.

Dwyer explores various ways in which the tax system could be reformed to recognise shared family incomes. He comes down in favour of a voluntary system in which family members can choose whether or not to pool part or all of their incomes for tax purposes, and he lists various ways in which this might be done in practice. Under his proposals, many working couples would probably prefer to continue filing separate tax returns so that each can retain their own tax-free threshold. They would be free to do so. Couples where there is only one earner, however (and especially those who also have dependent children) might prefer to transfer part of the threshold of the non-working partner to the working partner.

Dwyer also recommends that children should be given their own thresholds which could be transferred to their working parent/s. Again, the parallel with the welfare system is instructive. In early 2006, the minimum welfare income for a couple was over $21,000, but two adults with two children would receive more than $30,000. Translated into the tax system, this means that a family of two adults and two children should be able to claim a total tax-free threshold of around $30,000 before any of its members start to pay tax (in addition to the $21,000 couple allowance, this means they should be allowed to claim an average $4,500 of tax-free income for each of their two children). Under current arrangements, however, we tax such a family on every dollar earned over $6,000 and then compensate them through the Family Tax Benefit system. It would make more sense to allow them to keep more of their own money so they can take full responsibility for their own maintenance.

In chapter 9, however, John Humphreys turns Dwyer's argument on its head. Rather than recognising family liabilities in the tax system, he thinks we should individualise the welfare system.

Although he concedes in the Appendix to his chapter that parents could be given a higher tax-free threshold to take account of the costs they incur in raising their children, Humphreys thinks people should ideally be taxed without regard to their family circumstances. Every individual worker would therefore continue to have his or her own tax-free income allowance, just as they do at the moment. But in Humphreys's proposal, this allowance would be much greater than it is at the moment.

Humphreys argues that the tax-free threshold should be set at $30,000 per year. This is a large enough sum to ensure that nobody earning above it would need any financial top-ups from the government. Any income earned from any source in excess of $30,000 per year would be taxed at a flat rate of 30%. Anybody earning below that annual threshold, on the other hand, would receive top-ups (a so-called 'negative income tax', or NIT) worth 30% of the shortfall. Somebody earning $20,000, for example, would pay no tax but would receive a NIT payment of $3,000 (30% of the $10,000 shortfall). The NIT would replace all existing welfare and family payments.

A non-working adult would therefore receive a basic Negative Income Tax payment irrespective of whether or not he or she had a partner, and each partner in a jobless couple would receive his or her own full NIT allowance. This contrasts with the current welfare system which offers a couple living together less than it gives two single people living alone because their needs are less (two can live cheaper than one). Humphreys is perfectly happy with this, arguing that a couple should be allowed to reap the economies of scale that arise from living under one roof.[14]

Humphreys's proposal offers the prospect of a simultaneous reform of both the tax and welfare systems that goes to the heart of the problems in both. We have seen that our over-complex and burdensome tax system is eroding work incentives, and that this is compounded at the lower end of the income distribution by a tightly means-tested welfare system which sharply withdraws benefits as soon as people begin to take responsibility for earning their own money. The only real solution to this is to disentangle the tax and welfare systems completely so that no worker receives welfare at the same time as he or she is paying tax, and no claimant pays tax at the same time as he or she is receiving welfare. Raising the tax-free threshold to the welfare subsistence level, as advocated in chapter 7 by Maley and me, goes part the way there, but it would still mean that some low-income earners (notably part-time workers) would pay tax at the same time as they receive welfare payments. Humphreys's reform goes all the way, for those above the $30,000 threshold pay tax at 30%, and those below it receive

NIT top-ups of 30%. Nobody pays tax at the same time as they get top-ups under this system, and what is even better, nobody loses more than 30% of the next dollar they earn.

A reform like this would massively strengthen work incentives by reducing tax-welfare churning and slashing 'effective marginal tax rates'. It would also go a long way to meeting other reform objectives discussed in this book. It would make for a much simpler, more transparent and less dishonest tax system, for example, for Humphreys would wipe out virtually all tax exemptions and allowances (although he recognises that expenses necessarily incurred in generating an income would still have to be allowable against tax).[15] It also offers potentially huge efficiency gains by stimulating economic activity while cutting back on administration and compliance costs. And because it would introduce a flat tax, it would meet the criteria of fairness laid down by Chipman in chapter 4. The big question, however, is affordability.

Raising the tax-free threshold to $30,000 while lowering the tax rate to 30% threatens to take a huge bite out of the federal government's current tax revenue. Moreover, a 30% NIT would increase spending on top-ups to many working families, even though it would reduce the basic level of welfare benefits.

As we saw in Davidson's discussion of the Laffer curve in chapter 6, estimates of likely revenue gains and losses from tax and welfare reforms are notoriously unreliable, especially when analysts try to factor in possible behavioural responses such as the impact of tax cuts on people's willingness to work. When change on the scale envisaged by Humphreys is proposed, figures inevitably become highly speculative, for there are bound to be knock-on effects that no model can reliably predict. Humphreys does, nevertheless, attempt to gauge the likely fiscal impact of his reforms, and he concludes that, over the medium term, they could well pay for themselves. Whether he could convince Peter Costello of that is another matter.

The politics of tax reform

This book sets out a number of powerful arguments for cutting taxes and allowing people to retain more of their own money. Against this, however, are social affairs commentators in the media, the universities and the pressure group world who keep telling us that the public mood in Australia is shifting against tax cuts and in favour of yet higher levels of government spending. If this is really the case, the arguments outlined by the various contributors to this book will presumably attract little public backing. In chapter 10, Andrew Norton analyses the opinion poll evidence to see whether it really is true that taxpayers prefer politicians to spend their money for them.

Norton points out that the results of opinion polls depend crucially on the way the questions get asked. If you tell people that higher taxes will be used to fund better health care, you find substantial numbers of voters apparently prepared to pay up. But if you ask people whether the current level of taxation is too high or too low, you find very few arguing for an increase (most people think that even relatively high salary earners are already paying enough or too much tax). Opinion poll findings thus commonly contradict each other. Voters tell pollsters they are willing to pay higher taxes yet still complain that taxation is too high!

Nevertheless, while casting doubt on the validity of some individual polls, Norton accepts that the *trend* in opinion polls seems to indicate a growing willingness among voters to countenance higher taxes in order to pay for better health and education services. He sees this mainly as the product of rising prosperity. As in the 1960s, so too today, a long period of rising real wages has increased voters' willingness to sacrifice some of their earnings in order to get better quality provisions from government.

Having said that, Norton also adds some heavy provisos. For a start, what people say is not necessarily indicative of what they actually believe. People who tell pollsters that taxes should rise to pay for better services will also say in the next breath that they personally stand to gain more from tax cuts. It is also well known that respondents' answers to questions about tax and services are often influenced by their desire not to appear 'selfish' (that is, they say what they think they are expected to say rather than what they really want). Furthermore, many of those saying they favour higher taxes do not expect to have to pay themselves and think other people will pick up the tab. Left-wing commentators who interpret the opinion poll data on tax and spending as evidence of a renewed spirit of public altruism may be misreading the signs.

There is also the problem of what Norton calls the 'tax trap'. What are you to do if you are a low- or medium-income voter who wants better health care than you are currently getting? Private health insurance may appear an unattractive option, for you are already paying for the government system and the extra cost of going private will be substantial. The cheaper option is therefore to opt for a marginal tax increase in the hope that it will produce a better outcome, even though past experience suggests you are likely to be disappointed.

Norton's review of the evidence does not indicate the existence of a population keen to pay more tax. Politicians know this, which is why the

Coalition has delivered limited tax cuts (as well as a lot more spending) at successive budgets while the Labor opposition has announced its support for cutting taxes even further. What the evidence reveals is a population that feels more prosperous after years of sustained economic growth, and that wants to use some of this prosperity to buy better health care (and to a lesser extent, better quality schooling too). When pollsters ask them whether the government's budget surplus should be spent on improving the health system or on tax cuts, many opt for the former. But this does not mean we have suddenly turned into a nation keen to increase an already onerous tax burden, despite what some commentators would have us believe. There is nothing in the opinion poll data to suggest that a radical but coherent programme of tax reform could not capture widespread voter support—especially if it then leaves people with more money in their pockets to buy the better quality services they crave.

Conclusion: Eight steps to genuine tax reform

The basic message from the chapters in this book is that Australia's income tax system needs a radical overhaul to increase efficiency, reduce complexity, improve fairness, reward effort and encourage people to accept more responsibility for their own lives. The government's current preference for tinkering—tweaking a rate here, fiddling with a threshold there—does not begin to recognise the scale of what needs to be done. Tax reform does not mean building up revenue surpluses and then squandering them in an orgy of vote-buying at election time. Nor does it mean taxing one section of the population heavily in order to give another enhanced transfer payments. Rather, it means establishing a set of clear criteria for a good tax system and then working out methodically how to realise them in practice. There are at least eight such criteria:

1) Reduce taxes by keeping spending in check.

Politicians must resist the urge to keep increasing spending in response to each new demand that surfaces from this or that section of the electorate. If it is not parents of pre-school children demanding subsidies for childcare places, then it's farmers wanting special treatment because of the drought, or it's age pensioners expecting more financial aid with their health care costs. Voter demands are infinite, but buying off voters and pressure groups means that politicians spend all their time robbing Peter to pay Paul, and then having to mug Paul to pay back Peter, hoping all the time that neither Peter nor Paul twigs what is going on. The result is that taxes go ever higher as everyone ends up cross-subsidising everyone else.

Politicians must remember that every dollar they spend takes at least $1.20 out of the real economy, and they should not embark on any new spending programme unless it replaces an existing programme of comparable cost. The Commonwealth government should at the very least make a public commitment to get its level of expenditure as a proportion of GDP back to its 1996 level, and not to allow it to go above this level in the future.

2) Scrap as many special allowances and rebates as possible.

Since the Coalition government came to power in 1996, it has created 100 new tax breaks. Most tax concessions distort market behaviour (a classic example is negative gearing and Capital Gains Tax concessions which have together encouraged over-investment in rental property and helped stoke the recent house price explosion),[16] and they all make the system more complex and opaque. The total cost of tax breaks now amounts to $39 billion, or 4% of GDP, and this massive level of 'tax expenditure' leads to higher taxes as government tries to claw back lost revenue.[17] The government has therefore locked itself into a vicious circle: tax rates are high because there are so many exemptions, and the pressure to create more exemptions keeps building because tax rates are so high. This vicious circle has to be turned back on itself by broadening the tax base and starting to reduce the rates.[18]

3) Index tax brackets.

A fundamental requirement of an honest tax system is that any increase in taxation should be debated and resolved in Parliament so that all taxpayers are aware that the government intends to take more money from them. This does not happen in Australia because tax brackets are not indexed to inflation as they are in Canada and the UK.[19] The result is taxation by stealth through 'bracket creep'. Government revenues increase each year without any change in rates or thresholds being announced, because as inflation pushes up nominal wages, an ever-bigger proportion of people's incomes falls into higher tax brackets. This increases the real (inflation-adjusted) revenues flowing to Government while reducing the real take-home incomes of workers. To stop this, the Government should introduce a law requiring all tax brackets to be revised upwards annually in line with average wage inflation.

4) Align company and personal income tax rates.

Competition between countries has driven down rates of corporate taxation across the world (although the total tax raised from companies has often risen as a result of increased output). In Australia, the corporate rate of income tax is now 30%, which is 17 percentage points lower than the top personal rate. This gap between the corporate and personal rates has opened up opportunities for arbitrage, and few really wealthy people pay the 47% top personal rate. In 2005, the top 2% of wealth holders in Australia were on average officially earning only $112,000 per annum and were paying income tax amounting to just $28,000 per year. This was substantially less than the tax liability of many far less wealthy PAYG employees being taxed at the 47% top personal rate.[20] The Treasurer has resisted cutting the top rate on the grounds that it would give huge tax cuts to the wealthiest Australians, but this is clearly fallacious given that the wealthiest Australians are not paying the top rate. The Government should immediately abolish the 47% and 42% income tax bands. As an interim measure it could replace them with a top rate no higher than 40%, but the longer-term aim should be to align them with the company rate.[21]

5) Move toward a proportional ('flat') tax.

Introduction of a 40% top rate could be the first step in a coordinated move towards an eventual two-band income tax system consisting of a zero rate (the tax-free threshold) and a flat 30% rate above that. A flat tax of 30% would increase output and would reduce tax avoidance and evasion by negating the usefulness of many of the existing exemptions and allowances that people use to reduce their exposure to current confiscatory tax rates. It would also, crucially, be fairer than the existing system, where three-quarters of the taxpaying population pays less than their proportionate share in income tax. Instead of pandering to the politics of envy, ministers and Opposition leaders should start to explain to voters why flatter taxes are fairer. They should announce a sequence of steps taking us towards a 30% flat rate, and as this policy is implemented they should monitor its impact on employment and output levels (and hence on net government revenues). This would enable the country to exploit Laffer curve efficiencies without risking a major budget blow-out.

6) Increase the tax-free threshold above subsistence.

At the same time as the top marginal rate is reduced, the tax-free threshold should be raised to a level above the welfare minimum (subsistence) level—currently about $13,000 per annum for a single person and $20,000 for a couple. Linked to corresponding changes in the system of family payments (point 7, below), this would ensure that no worker pays tax before they have earned enough to take care of themselves and their dependants at a minimal standard. It would also provide a significant incentive for second earners (usually women) who are not currently in the labour force to get a job.[22] Such a change would halve the total income tax paid by the bottom 60% of income earners, so if it were introduced at the same time as the reduction in the top tax rate, it would mean that all taxpayers enjoyed a substantial tax cut, thereby ensuring widespread electoral popularity for the measure.

7) Reform the family support payments system.

The most difficult, but crucial, task for tax reform is to disentangle the tax and welfare systems in order to reduce the high effective marginal tax rates that lower income families encounter when they try to increase their earnings. The cleanest solution, advocated by Humphreys in chapter 9, is to replace all welfare and family payments with a negative income tax and to raise the tax-free threshold to $30,000. A less dramatic answer could be to augment people's tax-free earnings allowances by allowing them to claim for partners and children, as advocated in chapter 8 by Dwyer. These are complex issues, and we need to get them right. The government should therefore ask Treasury and the Department of Family and Community Services to model these proposals and evaluate their likely outcomes with a view to developing a specific set of proposals for reforming the family tax and welfare support system in such a way that the problem of high effective marginal tax rates is satisfactorily resolved.

8) Leave people to spend their own money.

Longer term, there needs to be a concerted attempt to scale back the extensive tax-welfare churning that has built up over the years. High taxes have reduced people's capacity to pay their own way. The result is that pressures have grown for the government to provide things that we should be organising for ourselves. The welfare state (which includes government health and education, as well as social security, expenditures) has blown out to soak up more than two-thirds of everything the government spends. Until this is brought back under control, the tax burden cannot significantly be reduced. At least half of all this welfare state spending goes back to the same people who provided the money in the first place. Reducing this $85 billion churn will be the central task facing governments in the future. This means the tax reform agenda must evolve to address the question of how to restore self-reliance and reduce widespread dependency on government payments and services.[23]

Renewal of the Australian economy is needed to ensure our competitiveness and vibrancy in the 21st century and to ensure continued growth as the population ages. We need labour market reform (to generate more jobs), welfare reform (to get more people off benefits and into work), and tax reform (to make it worthwhile for people to work). Since winning control of the Senate at the 2004 election, the Coalition government has moved on the first two, but seems to have a blind spot when it comes to the third.

There will never be a better time than now to improve the tax system. With a booming economy and buoyant government receipts, we have an opportunity today that may not come round again for a generation or more. Reforms such as those outlined in the various chapters in this book would re-energise the Australian economy and make this country an exemplar for governments around the world.

Professor Peter Saunders
Social Research Director
The Centre for Independent Studies

Chapter 1

How Highly Taxed Are We?

Peter Burn

In recent years Australia's level of taxation has fluctuated within a range between 29.8% and 32.1% of Gross Domestic Product (GDP). There is an underlying upwards trend (Table 1.1).

Table 1.1: Total Taxation[1] as a Proportion of GDP Australia 1995-6 to 2003-04

1995–6	1996–7	1997–8	1998–9	1999–0	2000–1	2001–2	2002–3	2003–4
29.8%	30.4%	30.2%	30.9%	31.6%	32.1%	30.5%	31.4%	31.6%

Source: OECD, *2005 Revenue Statistics, 1965–2004*, 68.

Current levels of taxation can be contrasted with total revenue collections over the years since 1965–6. Figure 1.1 shows that since 1965, the share of total Australian taxation in GDP has grown on average by slightly more than a quarter of a percentage point of GDP per year. This growth of the share of taxation in GDP comes on top of the solid growth of GDP which increased by around 300% in real terms between 1965 and mid 2004.[2] In real terms, the amount of tax paid per person[3] grew by over 200%.

Comparisons between OECD countries based on unweighted averages

Despite the increase in taxation over the years, it is often claimed that Australia is relatively lightly taxed. These claims almost invariably involve a comparison of Australian taxation levels with those of other members of the Organisation for Economic Co-operation and Development (OECD). In a recent article, for instance, the respected policy economist Michael Keating described Australia as 'being low-taxed relative to most other developed market economies'.[4] In its analysis of taxation, the Australian Council of Trade Unions (ACTU) put forward the proposition that:

> OECD data shows that Australia is a low tax country. The latest available figures (for 2000) show total tax revenue in Australia amounting to 31.5% of GDP. By comparison the OECD average is 37.2% of GDP, Canada has a total tax revenue equal to 38.7% of GDP, and Sweden has a total tax revenue equal to 52.2% of GDP.[5]

Similar claims have been made by the Australian Council of Social Service (ACOSS) which suggests that, 'By OECD standards, Australia is a low tax country.'[6]

Figure1.1: Total Australian Taxation as a Proportion of GDP 1965–6 to 2003–4

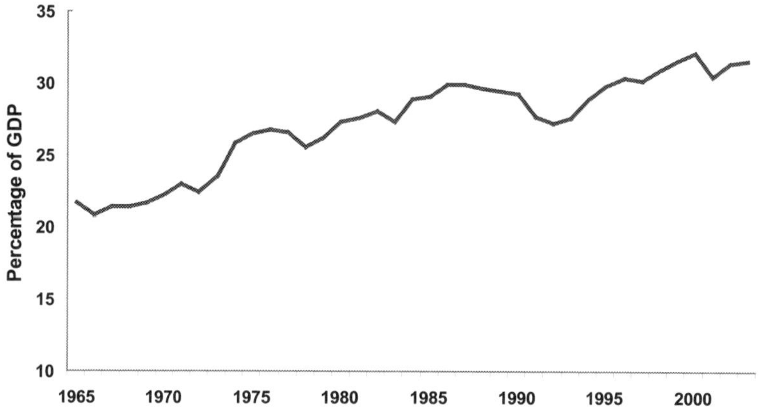

Source: OECD, 2005, *Revenue Statistics 1965–2004*, 67–8.

Figure 1.2 sets out the comparative national tax data on which claims that Australia is a low-taxing country are based. It shows that in 2003 (the most recent year for which complete comparisons of OECD countries can be made) Australia was the eighth-lowest taxing of the 30 OECD countries. At 31.6% of GDP, Australia's level of taxation in that year was substantially lower than the simple (that is, unweighted) average for all OECD countries, which stood at 36.3%. It is this sort of comparison that lies behind assertions such as Michael Keating's that Australia 'could tolerate a significant increase in the ratio of taxation to GDP without great difficulty'.[7]

One obvious shortcoming with this and similar claims is that the OECD is a sample of only 30 countries. Thailand, India, Indonesia, Malaysia and Singapore, for instance, are not part of the OECD. China, as Australia's fastest growing and perhaps most challenging trading partner, is also left out of the comparison. Given that around 40% of Australia's trade is conducted with non-OECD countries, conclusions about Australia's relative level of taxation based only on OECD comparisons should be treated with caution.

Further inspection of Figure 1.2 reveals additional grounds for caution due to the clear differences between clusters of OECD countries.[8] Most (four out of seven) of the OECD countries with lower levels of taxation than Australia also have a Pacific coastline (the United States, Japan, Korea and Mexico). The only other countries with a Pacific coastline (Canada and New Zealand) also have levels of taxation below the unweighted average for all OECD countries. The highest-ranking of the seven non-European countries (New Zealand) ranks as the 12th lowest taxing of the 30 member countries.

Reflecting the regional differences within its membership, the OECD publishes data relating to three major OECD sub-groups: OECD Europe, OECD Americas, and OECD Pacific. Table 1.2 contrasts the unweighted average level of taxation for the OECD as a whole with the unweighted average levels of the sub-groups. It shows that taxation levels in the OECD Americas group (the US, Canada and Mexico) and the OECD Pacific

Figure 1.2: Share of Total Taxation in GDP in 2003 (Australia 2003–04), All OECD Countries

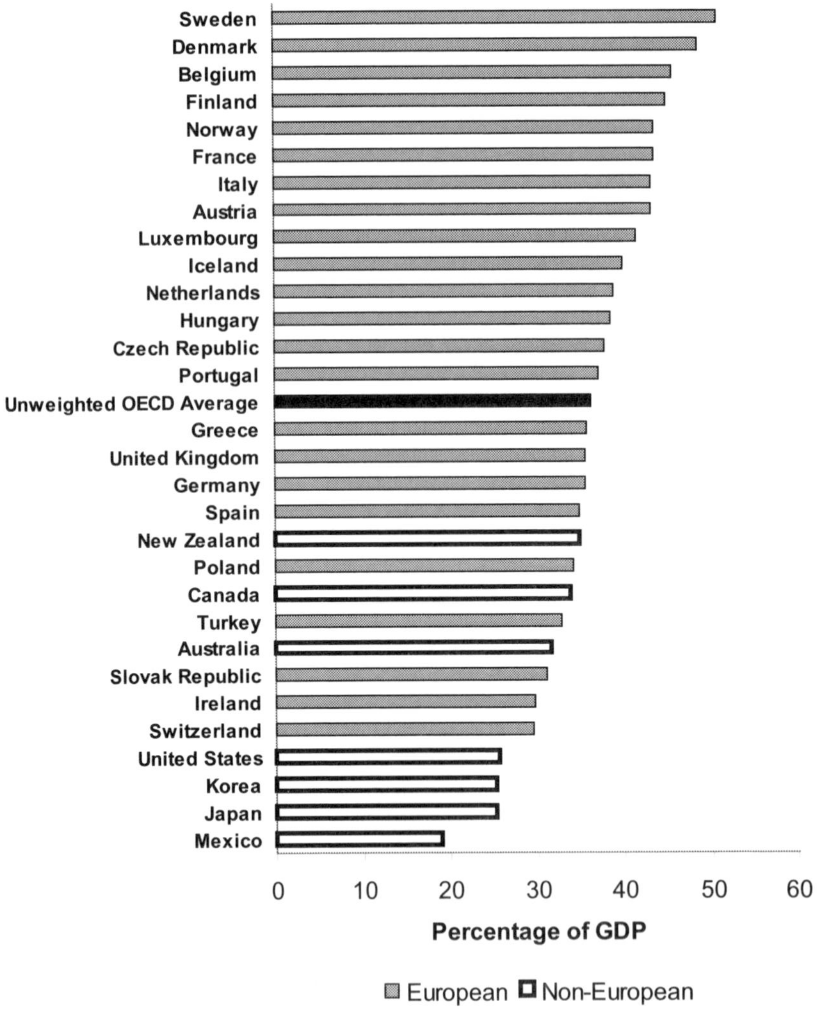

Source: OECD, 2005, *Revenue Statistics 1965–2004*, 68.

group (Japan, Korea, Australia and New Zealand) are well below the unweighted average level of taxation among the European OECD members. The European countries, in other words, are high taxing compared with everybody else. Australia's level of taxation as a share of GDP is higher than the unweighted averages of both the non-European sub-groups.

In recent decades, these regional patterns have been fairly stable. This is clear from the unweighted average taxation levels between 1965 and 2002 presented in Figure 1.3. This demonstrates that the Pacific countries have consistently levied lower taxes than the Europeans, and that the Americas bloc has converged towards the Pacific pattern since the mid-1970s.[9]

Table 1.2: Total Taxation as a Proportion of GDP (2003) Unweighted Averages for OECD and OECD Sub-Groups

	Share of Tax in GDP *(unweighted averages)*
OECD Total	36.3%
OECD Americas	26.1%
OECD Pacific	29.3%
OECD Europe	38.9%

Source: OECD, 2005, *Revenue Statistics 1965–2004*, 68.

The evidence presented in Table 1.2 and in Figure 1.3 lends strong support to the view that, as far as taxation levels are concerned, there are two OECDs: a European group and a non-European group. Countries in the latter group, which includes Australia, have been, and remain, consistently lower taxing than their European counterparts.

Figure 1.3: Total Taxation as a Proportion of GDP 1965–2003 Unweighted averages for OECD sub-groups

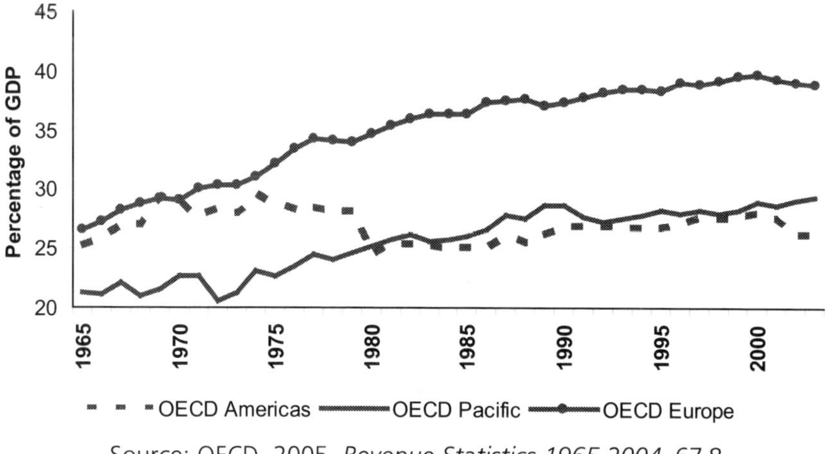

Source: OECD, 2005, *Revenue Statistics 1965-2004*,.67-8.

OECD comparisons using weighted averages

The use of unweighted averages to compare tax levels across OECD nations and sub-groups makes no allowance for the vast differences in size and economic significance of different countries. To illustrate with reference to the extremes: the US, which accounts for approximately 37% of the total GDP of all OECD countries, is over 400 times larger than Luxembourg (approximately 0.09% of total GDP of OECD countries). As far as international comparisons are concerned, the overall level of taxation in the US (25.6%) is of far greater significance than that of Luxembourg (41.3%), yet an unweighted average will treat them as equivalent.

Unweighted averages also take no account of the significance of different OECD countries as trading partners. When comparing the competitiveness of Australia's level of taxation with that of other countries, for example, it can be inappropriate to give equal weight to Japan and Mexico. Japan (with a tax to GDP ratio of 25.3%) accounts for over a quarter of Australia's trade with OECD countries. Mexico (which collects a level of tax equivalent to 19% of GDP) does not trade enough with Australia to register on its Trade Weighted Index.

While not without their own difficulties, various approaches to weighting can attenuate these shortcomings. Two methods of weighting the raw tax data are used in this chapter.

- A weighting by the relative size of different economies with weights set according to the proportion of individual countries' GDP to the GDP of all OECD countries (see the Technical Appendix for a discussion of data sources and methodology).
- Weighting according to the relative shares of Australian trade with OECD countries with individual proportions related to the shares of OECD countries in the Australian Trade Weighted Index (TWI) (see the Technical Appendix for a discussion of data sources and methodology).

The GDP-based measure gives the greatest weights to levels of taxation in the largest economies. The two largest OECD countries account for around 51% of the total GDP of all OECD countries.[10] Both are non-European and both are lightly taxed relative to other OECD countries. It is therefore not surprising that weighting by relative economic importance has a noticeable impact on the measurement of the average level of taxation raised in OECD countries. As shown in Table 1.3, the average level of taxation for the OECD when adjusted for economic size is 31.0% of GDP compared with the unweighted average of 36.3%.

The second weighting method, also recorded in Table 1.3, is based on countries' relative importance in Australia's trade. The OECD accounts for about 62% of all Australia's trade. The trade-weighted approach provides a measure of the competitiveness of the Australian tax level relative to the level of taxation imposed in those OECD countries with which we trade. The weighted average level of taxation among OECD countries based on this measure is 30.6%.

Is Australia really a 'low-tax country'?

Table 1.3: Total Taxation as a Proportion of GDP (2002)
Comparison of Unweighted and Weighted Averages

	Unweighted Average	Weighted Averages	
		(by GDP)	*(by TWI)*
OECD Total	36.3%	31.0%	30.6%
OECD Americas	26.1%	25.8%	26.5%
OECD Pacific	29.3%	26.0%	27.3%
OECD Europe	38.9%	38.8%	38.4%

Sources: See the Technical Appendix.

The analysis to date suggests strongly that Australia is not a low-tax country relative to other OECD members. In fact, with a level of taxation to total GDP that trended upwards within a range between 30% and 32% in recent years, Australia's total level of taxation is slightly above the weighted average level of taxation of the OECD as a whole. It is however distinctly higher than the weighted averages of both non-European sub-groups.

- At 31.6% of GDP, Australia's overall level of taxation in 2003–04 was higher than the weighted average of all OECD countries by 0.6 of a percentage point on a GDP basis and by a full percentage point (or 3.3%) on a trade weighted basis.

- Relative to the weighted average based on GDP, Australia's overall level of taxation was 5.8 percentage points (or 22%) higher than the OECD Americas sub-group.

- Australia's level of taxation was 5.6 percentage points, or 21.5% higher than the GDP-based weighted average for the OECD Pacific sub-group.

- Under these measures, Australia was lower taxing than the OECD European countries by around 7 percentage points.

The only possible basis for the claim that Australia is a relatively low-taxing country is a Eurocentric one. The use of the simple average of all OECD countries entrenches the Eurocentric perspective and gives a distorted impression.

- Although 23 of the 30 OECD countries (76% of the members) are in Europe, the European countries only account for around 40% of the GDP of all OECD countries.

- These countries together account for only around 20% of Australian trade. This is less than half of the share of Australia's trade accounted for by the non-European OECD countries (close to 43%).

When measured on a weighted basis, therefore, the OECD data do not provide empirical support for the frequently repeated claim that Australia is relatively low taxing. Rather, Australia's level of taxation is slightly above the weighted average level of taxation of all OECD countries, and it is considerably higher taxing than the two largest OECD countries.[11] These countries—the United States and Japan—rank prominently among Australia's trading partners as does Korea which is also lower taxing than Australia.

There is certainly no support here for Michael Keating's claim (referred to earlier) that international comparisons suggest that Australia could 'Tolerate a significant increase in the ratio of taxation to GDP without great difficulty'. On the contrary, a leading risk of a significant rise in the overall level of taxation in Australia is an adverse shift in Australia's competitiveness relative to other developed countries and relative to our largest and closest trading partners.[12]

The composition of taxation in Australia

Just as the level of taxation impacts on international competitiveness, the composition of taxation is also significant. Different kinds of taxes have varying impacts on commercial decisions and behaviour and therefore also on general economic efficiency.

In a global context, the international mobility of tax bases is particularly important.[13] Income, particularly investment income, is the most mobile of tax bases both because financial markets are increasingly global in orientation and because decisions relating to physical investments are taken in an environment of expanding opportunities for alternative locations.

Labour markets, while less global than capital markets, are also increasingly subject to international mobility. The international mobility of senior executives, business service providers, scientists and technologists is well-known. There are also increasing international opportunities for people in occupations as diverse as nursing, teaching and truck driving to shift across countries in pursuit of higher net incomes.

Comparisons of the composition of taxation in OECD countries are clouded by the OECD's treatment of social security levies as a separate category of taxation. These contributions are levied either on an income tax base or on a payroll tax base.[14] For the purposes of the analysis that follows, social security contributions for member countries are incorporated into their constituent income and payroll tax bases (the data sources and methodology employed are discussed in the Technical Appendix).

The composition of Australian and OECD taxation is summarised in Figure 1.4. The measures for the OECD as a whole are the weighted averages (on a GDP basis) of the degree of reliance on various tax bases.

This comparison reveals clear disparities between the composition of Australian taxation and that of other OECD countries.

- The level of income taxation in Australia is about 58% higher than the weighted average for all OECD countries.
- Australia's reliance on the payroll tax base is around 20% of the weighted average level for the OECD.

This difference relates in part to the role of social security taxes in most OECD countries. These taxes are levied overwhelmingly on a payroll base. (Note the Australian measure does not include the Superannuation Guarantee Charge (SGC). The SGC is, nevertheless tax-like in that it is a compulsory charge on employers. It is also levied on a payroll base.)

Figure 1.4: Composition of Taxation 2003
Australia and OECD Weighted Averages (GDP basis)

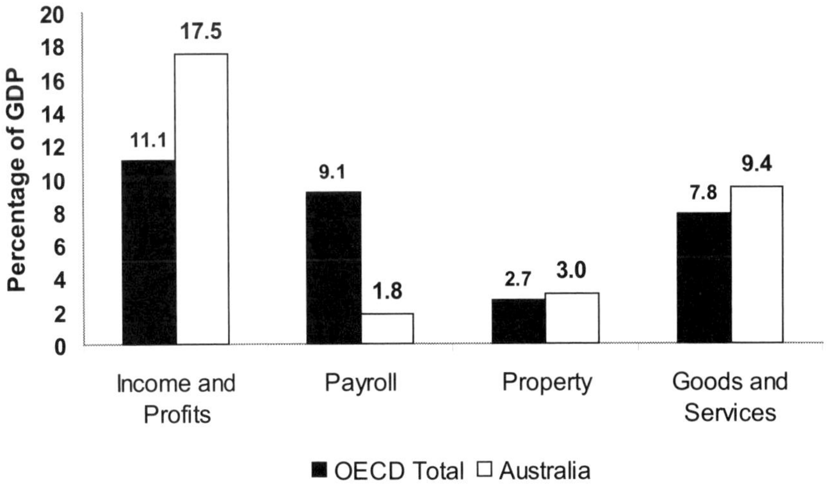

Source: OECD, 2005, *Revenue Statistics 1965–2004*. See also the Technical Appendix.

- The level of property taxation in Australia is noticeably higher in proportional terms than the OECD weighted average.
- The level of consumption taxation in Australia is distinctly higher than the OECD weighted average (by around 20%).

Table 1.4 shows the composition of taxation varies significantly among the three OECD sub-groups.

- Australia's level of income taxation is distinctly higher than for any of the sub-groups and is almost double the weighted average of the OECD Pacific sub-group (dominated by Japan).
- Consumption taxes figure more prominently in Europe than among the non-European OECD countries.
- Relative to the OECD Americas sub-group, Australia's lower level of payroll tax is almost offset by the higher level of consumption taxation. Australia has a similar reliance on property taxation.
- The OECD Pacific as a whole has a heavier use of payroll tax and a lesser use of consumption taxation than Australia.

Table 1.4: Composition of Taxation: Australia, OECD and OECD Sub-groups Weighted Average (GDP Basis) 2003

	Australia	**OECD Average**	**OECD Americas**	**OECD Pacific**	**OECD Europe**
		Weighted Average (% of GDP)			
Total Income Taxation	**17.5**	11.1	11.1	8.8	12.2
Individual income	***12.2***	*8.5*	*8.9*	*5.2*	*9.6*
Corporate income	***5.3***	*2.6*	*2.1*	*3.6*	*2.6*
Consumption Taxation	**9.4**	7.8	5.2	6.1	11.3
Payroll Taxation	**1.8**	9.1	6.5	8.3	12.2
Property Taxation	**3.0**	2.7	3.0	2.7	2.3

Source: OECD, 2005, *Revenue Statistics 1965–2004* and the Technical Appendix.

Australia's relatively heavy reliance on the personal and corporate income tax bases

Australia's comparatively heavy use of the income tax base applies to both the taxation of personal income and the taxation of corporate income. Relatively high tax burdens are imposed on both of these tax bases. This heavy recourse to income taxation occurs despite Australia having an overall level of taxation that is only slightly above the OECD average.

Figure 1.5 below contrasts Australia's level of taxation on personal and corporate income with the weighted average for all OECD countries. It shows:

- Australia's level of personal income taxation is around 44% higher than the weighted average of all OECD countries.
- The level of taxation on corporate income in Australia is around 104% higher than the weighted average of OCED countries. To some extent the high level of taxation on corporate income in Australia reflects the incentives built into the imputation system. About one third of OECD countries have imputation systems and several others have other forms of relief from the double taxation of corporate income (Greece for instance exempts individuals from tax on dividends). Other factors, such as the role given to flow-through business entities and the relative size of the incorporated sector can also impact on the differences in the distribution of income and income tax between the company and personal levels.[15]

Figure 1.5: Personal and Corporate Taxation (2003)
OECD Weighted Averages (GDP basis) and Australia

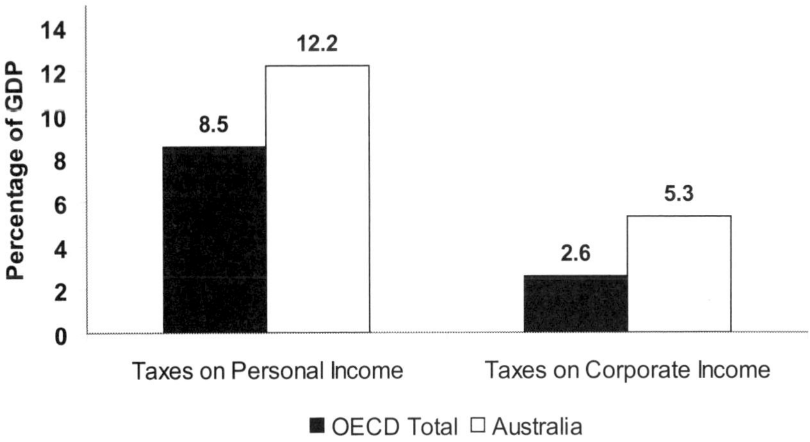

Source: OECD, 2005, *Revenue Statistics 1965–2004*. See also the Technical Appendix.

These factors mean that direct comparison of corporate income taxation is somewhat hazardous. While the level of corporate taxation is clearly relevant to international competitiveness, in some respects the total level of income taxation is the more revealing measure. In 2003, Australia's total level of income tax was around 58% higher than the OECD weighted average.

Australia's high reliance on income taxation is a challenge to international competitiveness and to domestic economic efficiency.

- In an increasingly integrated global economy, relatively high income taxation is a barrier to inbound investment.[16]
- Just as importantly, given the growth in opportunities abroad for Australian business, high levels of income taxation are an impediment to outbound investment from an Australian base.[17]
- High levels of income taxation are barriers to attracting skilled migration. Similarly, high personal income taxation is an obstacle to the retention of highly sought-after Australian talent.
- High reliance on income taxation dictates recourse to high marginal rates of income tax and thereby implies relatively high distortions to work, investment and saving decisions.
- When, as is the case in Australia, a high proportion of individual taxpayers face marginal tax rates on income well in excess of the company tax rate, further distortions are imposed on decisions relating to business structure.
- High rates of income tax also create incentives to under-report income and otherwise minimise tax liabilities.
- High income taxation, particularly of companies, adds disproportionate costs and difficulties to administration and compliance.[18]

These disadvantages of Australia's high income taxation present substantial challenges to policy makers. There is clearly solid comparative evidence to suggest the Australian tax system needs to move away from its high reliance on income taxation.

Conclusion

Broad comparisons with tax collection in other developed countries reveal two general facts about Australia's pattern of taxation:

- The level of Australian taxation is slightly above the weighted average level of tax in all OECD countries. Australia is, however, more heavily taxed than our most important OECD trading partners.
- Australia has an unusually high level of income taxation. This bias is shared between the personal and corporate tax bases. Australia's recourse to both these tax bases is distinctly higher than OECD averages.

This pattern of taxation is a serious flaw in Australia's social infrastructure. In an increasingly global operating environment, an excessive reliance on the most mobile tax base—the income tax base—is a competitive disadvantage.

There is, therefore, considerable scope for further improvement to the structure of Australian taxation. The central focus of further reforms should be a reduction in the entrenched over-reliance on income taxation.

TECHNICAL APPENDIX

1. Taxes and Tax-Like Charges[19]

To some extent international comparison of taxation is a matter of apples and oranges. The OECD itself notes that 'proper comparisons require detailed analysis of the nature of countries' tax systems'.[20] The data should therefore be regarded somewhat tentatively and the discussion in the present paper, like any involving these data, must also be treated cautiously.

A limitation of particular relevance to Australia is the treatment of social security contributions and tax-like charges. Taxes are defined by the OECD as 'compulsory unrequited payments to general government.' 'Unrequited' in this context means that benefits available to taxpayers are not normally in proportion to contributions.[21]

Compulsory social security contributions are generally included in the OECD revenue statistics. There is some hesitation surrounding this and separate summary tables excluding these contributions are also presented. Australia, along with New Zealand, does not levy social security contributions. Whether it is more appropriate to compare countries with or without the social security contributions is something of a thorny issue.[22] In 2003 social security contributions for OECD countries averaged of 9.5% of GDP and 26.1% of total taxation on an unweighted basis.[23]

The picture is clouded further by the fact that the Australian Superannuation Guarantee Charge (levied at 9% on a payroll tax base and paid by employers) is not included as a tax and therefore not reflected in the OECD revenue statistics. Although compulsory, the SGC is not paid to general government revenue and benefits available to taxpayers are related to contributions.

Neil Warren includes the SGC in total taxation and calculates the SGC at 11.4% of all taxation revenue in 2001–2. This translated to 3.8% of GDP. If the SGC were included Australia's level of taxation in 2001–2 would have been 34.3% of GDP instead of 30.1%. If this 3.8% level remained constant into 2003–4 the ratio of taxation to GDP would have been 35.5% as opposed to the 31.6% reported by the OECD. As the comparisons in the present paper do not include the SGC they could be seen as understating the level of Australian taxation.

Similar complications arise in relation to workers' compensation premiums. In Australia, these are not paid into general government revenue and therefore are not treated as taxes. Some of the OECD countries include premiums for workers injury insurance as part of their social security contributions.

Clearly tax-like charges are relevant to a broader consideration of cost competitiveness and, when equivalent charges are treated as taxes in some jurisdictions, they are also relevant to international comparisons of levels of taxation. The focus on taxation and, in particular, the use of the OECD definition of taxes limits the comprehensiveness of comparisons such as undertaken in this paper.

2. Weighted Averages Based On Gross Domestic Product

Calculation of the weighted averages for OECD countries is based on the OECD data on tax revenue for each country in US dollars and proportions of revenue to GDP.[24]

The weighted average proportion of taxation to GDP (W_{OECD}) is calculated as:

A_i	=	Proportion of revenue to GDP for each country
B_i	=	Tax revenue in US dollars for each country
$GDP_{i\ (in\ \$US)}$	=	B_i / A_i
$GDP_{OECD\ (in\ \$US)}$	=	$GDP_1 + GDP_2 + \ldots + GDP_n$
C_i	=	GDP_i / GDP_{OECD} (GDP Weights)
$\mathbf{W_{OECD}}$	**=**	$\mathbf{(A_1 \times C_1) + (A_2 \times C_2) + \ldots + (A_n \times C_n)}$

This general approach is used to calculate all the weighted averages of tax revenues expressed as a proportion of GDP. The weighted averages for each of the sub-groups are calculated with reference to the total GDP of the members of the sub-group.

The GDP weights (C_i) used in all of the calculations are shown in Table 1.5.

An important caveat is that this approach is sensitive to the exchange rate used in the conversion of national taxation collections levels into United States dollars. This limitation implies that the weighted averages calculated on this basis need to be regarded with some caution.

The present paper perseveres with this approach to the weighted averages and the results should be seen as indicative rather than definitive. Nevertheless, as a correction to the limitations of the use of unweighted averages discussed at the outset of this paper, the weighted averages employed here retain clear advantages.

Table 1.6 summarises the OECD data sources used in the calculation of the weighted averages. For the weighted averages relating to the composition of taxation, the OECD compositional data are used in conjunction with the allocation of social security contributions between the income and payroll tax bases (discussed below).

Table 1.5: GDP Weights used in Calculation of Weighted Averages OECD Countries and OECD Sub-groups (2003)

	Total OECD	OECD Americas	OECD Pacific	OECD Europe
Canada	0.0293	0.0702		
Mexico	0.0215	0.0514		
United States	0.3668	0.8785		
Australia	0.0177		0.0952	
Japan	0.1451		0.7802	
Korea	0.0204		0.1099	
New Zealand	0.0027		0.0147	
Austria	0.0086			0.0216
Belgium	0.0102			0.0257
Czech Republic	0.0030			0.0077
Denmark	0.0071			0.0179
Finland	0.0054			0.0137
France	0.0599			0.1512
Germany	0.0819			0.2066
Greece	0.0058			0.0146
Hungary	0.0028			0.0069
Iceland	0.0003			0.0009
Ireland	0.0051			0.0129
Italy	0.0492			0.1241
Luxembourg	0.0009			0.0023
Netherlands	0.0172			0.0433
Norway	0.0074			0.0187
Poland	0.0070			0.0177
Portugal	0.0049			0.0124
Slovak Republic	0.0011			0.0028
Spain	0.0295			0.0744
Sweden	0.0101			0.0255
Switzerland	0.0108			0.0272
Turkey	0.0080			0.0202
United Kingdom	0.0602			0.1518
TOTAL	**1**	**1**	**1**	**1**

Table 1.6: OECD Data Sources used in Calculating Weighted Averages

Total tax as a percentage of GDP	Table 3	pp.67–8
Tax revenue of main headings as a percentage of GDP	Table 6	p.70
Taxes on personal income as a percentage of GDP	Table 10	p.72
Taxes on corporate income as a percentage of GDP	Table 12	p.73
Social security contributions as a percentage of GDP	Table 14	p.74
Total tax revenue in millions of US dollars	Table 32	p.83
Exchange rates used, national current per US dollar	Table 37	p.85

All references to OECD, 2005, *Revenue Statistics 1965–2004*.

3. Weighted Averages Based On the Australian Trade Weighted Index

The Reserve Bank of Australia frequently publishes a Trade Weighted Index (TWI). The composition of the TWI reflects Australia's two-way trade with its major trading partners. The TWI data used align with the tax data used in the present paper (2003–4 for Australia).

The TWI-basis weighted averages are calculated in the same way as the GDP weighted averages outlined above.

Table 1.7: Weights Used in the Calculation Weighted Averages using the Trade Weighted Index Method

	TWI Weights (%)	All OECD Countries	OECD Americas	OECD Pacific	OECD Europe
Japan	16.06	0.2572		0.5753	
Euro Area	13.52	0.2165			0.6849
China	11.30				
United States	13.16	0.2108	0.8901		
South Korea	5.97	0.0957		0.2140	
New Zealand	5.88	0.0942		0.2106	
United Kingdom	4.73	0.0757			0.2395
Singapore	3.66				
Malaysia	3.10				
Taiwan	3.18				
Thailand	2.74				
India	2.62				
Indonesia	3.02				
Hong Kong	1.77				
Vietnam	1.13				
Canada	1.62	0.0260	0.1099		
Saudi Arabia	1.23				
South Africa	1.20				
Papua New Guinea	1.00				
Sweden	0.88	0.0141			0.0445
United Arab Emirates	0.86				
Switzerland	0.61	0.0098			0.0311
Philippines	0.76				
TOTAL	**100**	**1**	**1**	**1**	**1**

Source: Reserve Bank of Australia, 2005, 'Trade Weighted Index', Media Release 2005-12, 30 September 2005. The 2004 weights contained in this release are used.

4. Allocation of Social Security Contributions between the Income and Payroll Tax Bases

Because of their unique features, the OECD treats the social security contributions levied in most member countries as a separate tax category. This is done because social security contributions are related to taxpayers' future contingent benefits and therefore similar in some regards to Australia's Superannuation Guarantee Charge.

Social security contributions are levied on a combination of payroll and income tax bases and for comparative purposes can be allocated to these bases.[25] This chapter follows the OECD categorisation in the allocation of these taxes.

The difference between these two bases is that, regardless of whether the tax is levied on an employer or an employee, payroll taxes are those taxes levied on a gross earnings (or gross remuneration) basis and would normally be allowed as a deduction against income. Income taxes on the other hand, are levied on net income after deductions and exemptions.

For most countries, including all the large countries, the allocation is readily available from the detailed Country Tables.[26] The social security contributions levied on a payroll tax basis are categories 2110; 2210; 2310 and 2410 in the Country Tables. The income tax base is recorded in the categories 2120; 2220; 2320 and 2420.

For some countries either no breakdown or only a partial breakdown is available and for the purposes of this paper, the social security contributions are allocated in the same proportions as the averages for the countries for which breakdowns are available.

This element of the allocation is subject to error. However, the relatively small size of the countries involved implies only a small impact on the weighted average calculations.

Table 1.8: Allocation of Social Security Contributions between Income and Payroll Tax Bases (2003)

	All Social Security Contributions	Contributions levied on Payroll	Contributions levied on Income *(all on personal income)*
	Proportion of GDP (%)		
Canada	5.20	5.14	0.06
Mexico	3.20	3.20	0.00
United States	6.70	6.70	0.00
Australia	0.00	0.00	0.00
Japan	9.70	9.70	0.00
Korea	4.90	4.90	0.00
New Zealand	0.00	0.00	0.00
Austria	14.50	14.50	0.00
Belgium	14.40	14.40	0.00
Czech Republic	16.40	16.40	0.00
Denmark	1.20	1.14	0.06
Finland	12.00	11.30	0.70
France	16.40	16.40	0.00
Germany	14.40	14.40	0.00
Greece	12.90	12.39	0.51
Hungary	11.70	11.58	0.12
Iceland	3.40	3.39	0.01
Ireland	4.40	4.40	0.00
Italy	12.70	12.70	0.00
Luxembourg	11.50	11.50	0.00
Netherlands	14.10	6.13	7.97
Norway	10.00	10.00	0.00
Poland	14.10	13.62	0.48
Portugal	11.70	11.64	0.06
Slovak Republic	12.30	12.30	0.00
Spain	12.30	12.30	0.00
Sweden	14.70	14.70	0.00
Switzerland	7.50	7.50	0.00
Turkey	6.80	6.80	0.00
United Kingdom	6.60	6.60	0.00

Sources: Social security contributions as a proportion of GDP, OECD, 2005, *Revenue Statistics 1965–2004*, 70; other data derived from the Country Tables in that publication, 105–202.

Chapter 2

How High Taxation Makes Us Poorer

Alex Robson

If two or more individuals agree to exchange goods or services, then as long as the exchange is voluntary, both will be better off than if such exchange opportunities were not available. In an economy with free markets, the vast majority of exchanges are mutually beneficial—otherwise individuals would not conduct them. Individual pursuit of self interest—combined with institutions that facilitate voluntary exchange between individuals—tends to promote mutually beneficial outcomes, even though no single person consciously promotes this end. These mutually beneficial exchanges of goods and services lie at the heart of the creation of economic wealth and higher living standards.

In essence, taxes tend to discourage mutually beneficial exchanges by driving a wedge between the prices that suppliers wish to receive for their output, and the prices that consumers are willing to pay for these products. For example, income taxes drive a wedge between the wage that workers are willing to accept to supply labour, and the wage that employers are willing to pay them. Because of these wedges, some potential gains from mutually beneficial exchanges—which exist when demand prices exceed supply prices—are left unexploited. Agents instead are induced to conduct alternative exchanges which, while certainly involving mutually beneficial wealth creation, do not create *as much* wealth and are not *as* mutually beneficial. In summary, taxes, whilst raising revenue, also tend to divert economic resources from higher valued to lower valued economic uses. Economists generically refer to these unexploited gains from trade as the *deadweight loss* created by taxes.

Taxes therefore destroy economic wealth.[1] In 1819 the celebrated American jurist John Marshall noted that 'the power to tax involves the power to destroy'. Unfortunately, Marshall's wisdom regarding the nature of taxation continues to elude some economists.[2]

Another famous American jurist, Oliver Wendell Holmes, once remarked that 'taxation is the price we pay for civilized society'. This view is as popular among those in charge of raising tax revenue as it is among those responsible for spending it.[3] But the fact that a disbursement of funds may provide a benefit does *not* mean that the costs of raising those funds—the 'price', as Holmes put it—should be ignored or trivialised. What if the 'price' of a certain tax (in terms of its economic cost) exceeds the benefits that revenue allegedly provides? How are taxpayers supposed to know whether the gains from paying taxes are worth the costs?

Whether the benefits of government spending exceed the costs is a very different question from the questions of what exactly the costs are and why they exist. Once a full and proper discussion and assessment of the costs of taxation is completed, attention can then be turned towards the purported benefits of various spending proposals. It is then possible to examine whether the alleged economic benefit of the last dollar spent on a particular government programme more than offsets the economic cost of raising that last dollar from taxpayers. If costs are conflated with benefits, this is simply not possible.

A Taxonomy of Costs

In the *Wealth of Nations*, Adam Smith expounded some basic principles of taxation which provide an excellent introduction to some of the issues discussed in this paper. With regard to the costs of taxation and the design of the tax system, Smith's first principle was that:

> Every tax ought to be so contrived as both to take out and keep out of the pockets of the people as little as possible, over and above what it brings into the public treasury of the state.[4]

That is, Smith believed that taxes should be designed to minimise economic waste—or to 'take out and keep out of the pockets of the people as little as possible, over and above' what the tax raises in revenue. What kinds of costs did he have in mind?

Like many modern economists, Smith recognised that even if the tax system was simple, easy to comply with, and easy to administer, it could still have economic costs. He wrote:

> It (a tax) may obstruct the industry of the people, and discourage them from applying to certain branches of business which might give maintenance and unemployment to great multitudes. While it obliges the people to pay, it may thus diminish, or perhaps destroy, some of the funds which might enable them more easily to do so.

The modern microeconomic approach to measuring the pure economic or deadweight costs of taxation is based on Smith's observation and is discussed below. It is based on the observation that taxes raise revenue but also tend to divert economic resources from higher valued to lower valued economic uses.

Smith also noted that, in addition to these disincentive effects, taxation would have the following additional costs:

- Administrative and enforcement costs

  The levying of (a tax) may require a great number of officers, whose salaries may eat up the greater part of the produce of the tax, and whose perquisites may impose another additional tax upon the people.

- Evasion costs

  By the forfeitures and other penalties which those unfortunate individuals incur who attempt unsuccessfully to evade the tax, it may frequently ruin them, and thereby put an end to the benefit which the community might have received from the employment of their capitals. An injudicious tax offers a great temptation to smuggling. But the penalties of smuggling must rise in proportion to the temptation. The law, contrary to all the ordinary principles of justice, first creates the temptation, and then punishes those who yield to it; and it commonly enhances the punishment, too, in proportion to the very circumstance which ought certainly to alleviate it, the temptation to commit the crime.

- Compliance costs

  By subjecting the people to the frequent visits and the odious examination of the tax-gatherers, it may expose them to much unnecessary trouble, vexation, and oppression; and though vexation is not, strictly speaking, expense, it is certainly equivalent to the expense at which every man would be willing to redeem himself from it.

All of these costs are as easily recognisable today as they were in 1776, when Smith wrote the *Wealth of Nations*. Today's taxation systems not only require 'a great number of officers' (the ATO currently employs over 21,000 people, and its expenses from ordinary activities in 2002–03 amounted to over $2.3 billion)[5], but many of the administrative costs have been transferred from the 'great number of officers' to taxpayers themselves or to employers. In many cases the administrative costs and compliance costs of taxation have become indistinguishable from one another because responsibility for administration has been transferred to the private sector. For example, when employers withhold income taxes from employees, they are performing more of an administrative function than a compliance function. They are, in effect, collecting taxes on the government's behalf.

The primary reason for the growth in compliance costs and administrative costs is the increasing legal and economic complexity of the tax system. Legal complexity is best understood as the absence of simplicity. Simplicity tends to decrease with the sheer density of tax rules, their degree of technicality, the extent to which different tax laws apply to the same set of facts, and the degree of indeterminacy or uncertainty which they create.[6]

The growth of compliance costs manifests itself in a variety of obvious ways, including the growth in the number of accountants, tax specialists and tax lawyers employed in the economy, many of whom do not create any new wealth but are employed to prevent the government acquiring the wealth of their clients. To illustrate this trend for the United States, Richard Vedder of Ohio University[7] compares the size of the 'tax army' (one quarter of all lawyers, one half of all accountants, and all officers employed by the US Internal Revenue Service), with the size of the 'real army' (permanent US Army forces), and finds that the former easily exceeds the latter, with the gap growing over the last two decades.

Figure 2.1: The 'Tax Army' and the 'Real Army', 2001-02

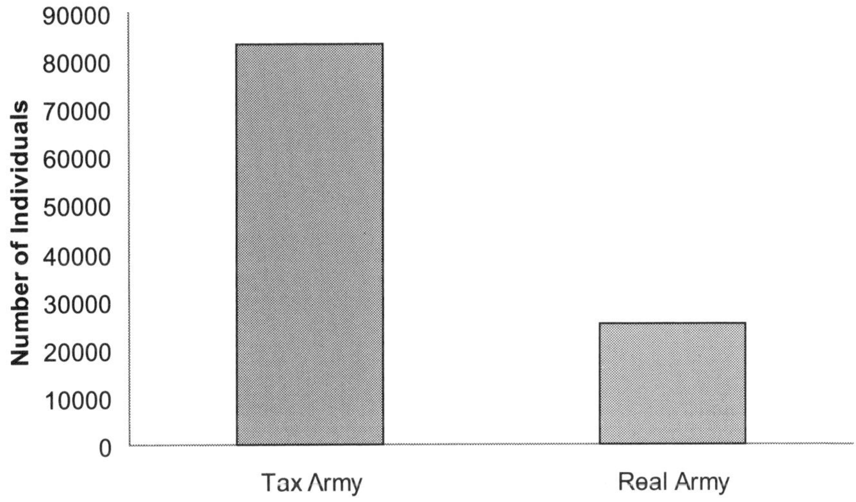

Sources: Australian Taxation Office and Department of Defence Annual Reports 2001-02; Australian Bureau of Statistics Cat No. 8668.0 *Accounting Practices 2001-02, Australia* Australian Bureau of Statistics Cat No. 8667.0 *Legal Practices 2001-02, Australia*

Figure 2.1 uses Vedder's methodology to make the same comparison for Australia in 2001-02. It shows that our 'tax army' was more than three times the size of the 'real army' (permanent Australian Army forces) for that year.

At the margin, higher administrative, evasion, enforcement and compliance costs will be associated with lower levels of economic activity, and perhaps even lower *rates* of economic growth, depending on how the costs change with changes in the level of economic activity. The existence of complexity is itself an obstacle to tax reform and lower levels of taxation. If nobody truly understands what the law means as it stands or to which situation it applies, how can intelligent reform proceed? The existence of complexity in the tax code is often the result of some interest group or another successfully lobbying for special deductions or treatment by the ATO. These special interest groups oppose reform because complexity in certain parts of the tax code benefits them.

This leads us to another cost of taxation: *revenue-seeking* or *rent-seeking costs.* These costs were not discussed by Smith but were first identified by Gordon Tullock of George Mason University.[8]

The revenues that governments raise from taxes represent lost consumption and profit opportunities for those who are taxed. However, taxes signify greater potential consumption and profit opportunities for those who gain access to this revenue by way of subsidies, direct transfers, or other redistributive government programmes. Thus, before taxes are raised and the proceeds redistributed, potential producers and consumers may lobby the government not to levy taxes, but other groups may lobby in favour of higher taxes in order to finance the greater spending that might be directed their way. Because these activities are directed at redistributing wealth rather than creating it, they represent an additional social cost of taxes and subsidies above and beyond the usual deadweight losses, because rent-seeking activity is not directed at creating extra production, but instead aims at reducing output below its competitive level in some markets and increasing it in other markets.

Any calculation of the full social costs of taxation and subsidies should therefore also include the resources aimed at influencing the distribution of wealth which do not (either directly or indirectly) create wealth.[9] These can be substantial, for existing distortions in the market caused by one set of taxes and subsidies may commonly get partially offset by the introduction of a new distortion in another related market. For example, if an existing tax on the consumption of butter induces consumers to switch to margarine, then introducing a new tax on margarine may partially offset the initial negative welfare effects of the butter tax. One set of rent-seeking costs thus begets another.[10]

Although this paper focuses on the pure economic or deadweight costs of taxation, all these other kinds of costs may be as important (or, in some cases, more important). For example, if a tax rate is very low, its deadweight costs may be very low in both a marginal and total sense, but the economic costs of enforcing, administering, avoiding and complying with the tax may be very high. While this chapter focuses on the deadweight costs of taxation, this should not imply that this narrow category of wealth destruction is the most important one.

The deadweight costs of personal income tax

The modern microeconomic approach to measuring the deadweight costs of taxation is based on Smith's observations. The approach proceeds by noting that when a government taxes a particular economic activity, it raises revenue but also alters individual economic incentives at the margin and 'obstructs the industry of the people'. The correct measurement of deadweight loss takes both of these effects into account (but it does not account for administrative, evasion, compliance, enforcement, or rent-seeking costs).

Higher income taxes reduce workers' after-tax wages. Lower after-tax wages make workers worse off, even if workers do not alter their behaviour. At the margin, reductions in after-tax wages make other kinds of economic activities more attractive. To mitigate partially the adverse effects of lower after-tax wages, workers substitute away from the taxed activity (work) into other activities. At the margin, they may increase time devoted to leisure or recreation, lower their work intensity (devote more time to 'on-the-job' leisure), pursue 'do-it-yourself' work, engage in home production for barter, or switch to activities or occupations with significant non-pecuniary (non-wage) benefits.

This is what meant by the observation that taxes drive economic resources from higher valued to lower valued uses. Higher personal income taxes encourage workers to substitute into economic activities which they otherwise would not have undertaken. These substitution effects never work in the same direction as the tax change. That is, higher personal income taxes never induce substitution towards more work.

Some commentators correctly point out that higher income taxes create disincentives and induce workers to substitute out of work, but then go on to claim that because leisure is valuable, income taxes should not be reduced or that they should even be increased.[11] This argument (which is discussed by Sinclair Davidson in chapter 3) misses the point regarding the nature of the disincentive effects of higher taxation. Leisure is indeed valuable—no economist has ever claimed that leisure has zero value or is a bad. The question is whether, at the margin, workers prefer to undertake more or less work. Higher income taxes alter the gains and losses involved in these marginal assessments and by themselves can never make workers better off than they otherwise would have been (otherwise, workers would tax themselves!). To claim that higher income taxes make workers better off by diverting their activities into leisure pursuits which are better for them is to take paternalism to an entirely new level.

Governments collect revenue from income taxes. The tax is said to create an *excess burden* or *deadweight loss*[12] if the revenue raised by the tax is less than the overall loss in worker wellbeing created by the fall in after-tax wages.[13] Correctly measured, the size of the deadweight loss is driven by the size of the tax and the size of substitution effects.[14] The steps involved in measuring the excess burden of personal income taxation are illustrated in Figure 2.2.

Figure 2.2: Computing the Excess Burden or Deadweight Loss of Personal Income Taxes

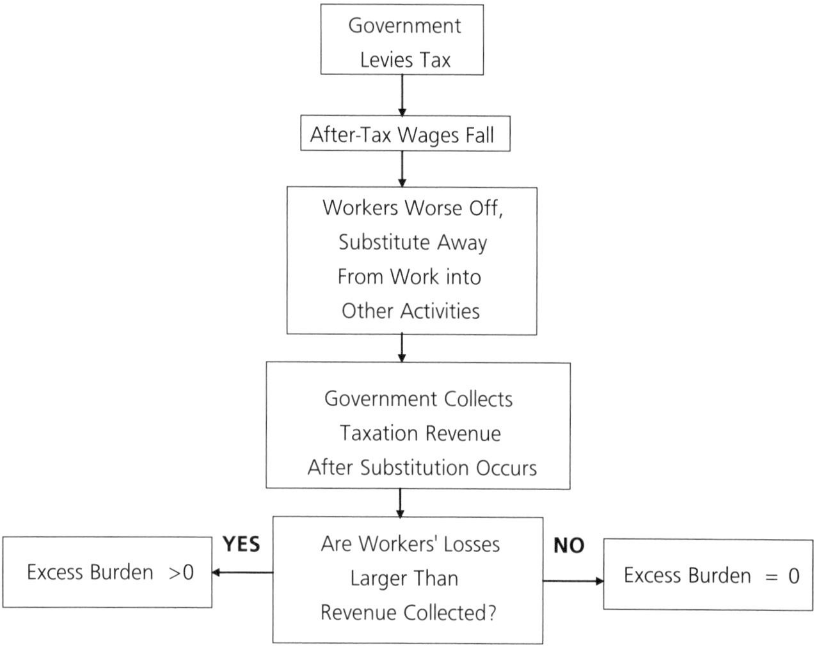

Those who ignore or seek to trivialise the deadweight costs of high marginal tax rates point to older literature on the effects of taxes on certain observable features of labour supply, and incorrectly infer from this literature that high marginal income tax rates create little or no deadweight costs. Some commentators go further and argue (for example) that 'cutting the top rate of tax might do nothing at all'.[15] But such views are misleading.

It is often suggested, for example, that changes in net wages may have little effect on the average labour force participation rates or average hours worked of adult males.[16] But these findings do *not* mean that taxing such activities creates no economically meaningful disincentives, because average participation rates and average hours worked provide extremely poor estimates of the true size of the substitution effect for individuals. For example, a finding of zero average effect on hours could mean that the majority of productive workers only slightly reduce their hours, whilst a minority of relatively unproductive workers increase their hours significantly. The efficiency consequences would then be quite large, even though average hours worked remain constant.

Moreover, individuals can vary their effective labour supply in many ways, none of which may involve reducing their actual hours worked or their decision to participate in the labour force. Indeed, in some workplaces individuals have very little freedom to vary their hours of work, particularly in jurisdictions with highly centralised and rigid industrial relations systems. In these circumstances workers can and do adjust to changes in after-tax wages along other margins.

Thus, for the purposes of meaningful policy analysis, the narrow focus on average measures of hours worked and participation rates is misplaced. For personal income taxes, a more accurate measure of the disincentive effects is the responsiveness of *taxable income* to changes in wages. Measuring taxable income is quite different from measuring hours worked or labour force participation rates, and is a more suitable way of picking up changes in work intensity or effort, shifts to home production or barter, or changes to occupations with significant non-pecuniary components.

Recent empirical evidence from the United States suggests that taxable income is quite sensitive to changes in after-tax wages. The key parameter is the *elasticity of taxable income* with respect to changes in tax rates, which measures the percentage change in taxable income when marginal tax rates change by one percent. Table 2.1 summarises some recent US studies of the absolute size of this parameter, with a higher number indicating a greater degree of responsiveness.

The most recent and most comprehensive study by Gruber and Saez estimates the elasticity of taxable income to be 0.4. They also find that the elasticity for taxpayers with annual incomes above $100,000 is 0.57, while for those on lower incomes it is much smaller.[17] As a general rule, the responsiveness of taxable income tends to be higher for higher income earners, indicating a very large economic cost per dollar of revenue raised for the most productive individuals. The notion that there are few or no economic costs associated with higher taxes on 'high income earners' may be popular, but it is wrong.[18]

Table 2.1: US Estimates of the Elasticity of Taxable Income with Respect to Tax Rates

Study	Estimate
Lindsey[19] (1987)	1.05–2.75
Auten and Carroll[20] (1987)	0.75
Feldstein[21] (1995)	1.1–3.05
Navratil[22] (1995)	0.8
Carroll[23] (1998)	0.5
Saez[24] (1999)	0.4
Gruber and Saez[25] (2002)	0.4

Measuring the costs of taxation

The pure economic (deadweight) costs of taxation can be measured in total and at the margin. The costs are typically normalised to allow for the fact that government collects revenue from taxation. The *average deadweight cost* of taxation or *average cost of funds* (ACF) computes the total deadweight loss created by a tax, and then divides it by the total amount of revenue collected by that tax.

Recent US studies (see Table 2.2) indicate that the ACF for all forms of taxation lies somewhere between 18% and 24% of total government revenue. This means that *on average* each dollar that the US government collects in revenue from all forms of taxation costs the private sector between $1.18 and $1.24.

Taxation revenue for all levels of government in Australia (combined

Table 2.2: US Estimates of the Average Deadweight Costs of All Taxes

Study	Estimate
Ballard et al (1985)[26]	23.8%
Jorgenson and Yun (1990)[27]	21.2%
Jorgenson and Yun (1991)[28]	18%

local, state, and federal) in 2003-04 was $257 billion.[29] Applying US estimates of the ACF to Australia suggests that the total excess burden of taxation in Australia in 2003-04 amounted to at least $46 billion and could be as large as $61 billion. To put this in perspective, in 2003-04 governments at all levels spent $51.5 billion on health.[30] Thus, the total deadweight loss from taxation in Australia, not including costs associated with administration, enforcement, compliance and evasion is approximately equal to the amount of public spending devoted to health.

The ACF can also be calculated for particular kinds of taxes. For example, there are several US estimates of the average cost of personal income taxation per dollar of revenue. These are reported in Table 2.3. These studies estimate that the ACF for personal income taxation in the United States is between 18% and 37% . In Australia, revenue from personal income taxation in 2003–04 amounted to $99 billion,[36] so applying the US estimates of the ACF to Australia yields a total annual

Table 2.3: US Estimates of the Average Deadweight Costs of Personal Income Taxes

Study	Estimate
Hausman[31] (1981)	18.4%–22.1%
Ballard et al[32] (1985)	37.4%
Jorgenson and Yun[33] (1990)	33.3%
Jorgenson and Yun[34] (1991)	18%
Feldstein[35] (1999)	32.2%

deadweight loss from personal income taxation of between $18 billion and $37 billion. To place this in context, the combined amount of spending on defence, public order and safety across all levels of government in 2003–04 was $26 billion.[37]

These estimates refer to the *total* deadweight losses from taxation. But most changes in economic policy are incremental. Taxes are usually increased or reduced incrementally, and each proposal for additional government spending or cutbacks is relatively small, compared with the overall size of the budget and economic activity. This means that, in addition to calculating total deadweight costs of taxes, we also need to know the marginal cost—how much is lost when one extra dollar of tax is raised.

Incrementally raising a tax may have a large additional deadweight cost, but may also raise a relatively large amount of additional revenue. Some sort of normalisation is required so that sensible comparisons of costs can be made between various taxes. The *marginal deadweight loss* (MDWL) of a tax does exactly this: it calculates the incremental cost of raising a particular tax, and then normalises this by dividing by the incremental change in revenue. The *marginal cost of funds* (MCF) is computed as one plus the MDWL. The MCF is a convenient summary measure of the pure economic cost of raising the last dollar in revenue from the private sector using any given tax. Raising a dollar by changing a particular tax reduces private sector wellbeing by at least one dollar, plus the additional pure economic costs of the tax increase.

The MCF gives a precise answer to the following question: At current levels of taxation, how much additional private wealth was destroyed when the government raised its last dollar of revenue? In addition, the MCF provides a benchmark with which to evaluate public projects or policy interventions. Specifically, any project or policy that does not provide a higher percentage return than the MCF should not go ahead, for it costs more wealth than it creates. The MCF can therefore be seen as a lower bound on the hurdle rate of return for public sector projects.[38]

The correct measurement and widespread publication of the MCF of taxation should be a fundamental part of the design of any public policy involving either taxation or spending. Even if the alleged public benefits of additional government spending exceed the *direct* production costs (say, of building a road or hospital), the extra spending may not be justified because private wealth was destroyed when those funds were raised via taxation. In other words, *to justify properly an additional dollar of government spending, the benefit of that extra dollar must be far more than a dollar, because the economic cost of raising that dollar is far more than a dollar to begin with.*

Interestingly, Australian governments and their agencies do not currently provide any official published estimates of the MCF or the total deadweight costs of taxation. For reasons that are probably not unrelated, they also fail to provide official published estimates of the alleged marginal or total benefits of public spending.

Estimates of the MCF for personal income taxation

The MCF can vary widely, depending on the nature of the tax in question. Since personal income taxation is the major single source (47.3% in 2003–04) of Federal government tax revenue in Australia, most analysts have focused on these particular taxes. For personal income taxes, older estimates for OECD countries are in the 1.2–1.3 range.[39] In other words, studies suggest that the last dollar of revenue raised through personal income taxation cost the private sector between $1.20 and $1.30.

For Australia, Campbell and Bond[40] estimate the MCF at between 1.19 and 1.24, while Findlay and Jones derive an estimate of between 1.23 and 1.65.[41] These estimates mean that to be economically justified, the last dollar of government spending should create an economic return of at least 19% (and perhaps as high as 65%), net of any direct administrative or production costs involved in that spending.

More recent evidence suggests that the MCF for personal income taxes may be much higher that these estimates. As discussed earlier, if income tax rates rise, then individuals and firms may respond by legally shifting part of the employee's compensation into non-pecuniary forms of earnings in order to reduce their tax liability. Thus, when income tax rates rise, observed hours may not change by much, but taxable income may fall substantially. But this implies that the additional revenue raised from a tax increase may also be very small. Indeed, there may actually be a *reduction* in tax revenue as workers accept more non-wage forms of compensation.[42]

All of this suggests that the traditional estimates of the MCF discussed earlier may be far too small. Feldstein[43] studies these issues in the light of the US 1986 Tax Reform Act, and finds substantially larger values of the MCF for income taxes than those obtained using traditional estimates. He estimates that the MCF may be larger than 2 for personal income taxes. In other words, Feldstein's estimates imply that the last dollar of revenue raised from personal income taxation in the US cost the private sector more than two dollars, and that the economic return from the last dollar of government spending should exceed 200%.

The MCF provides a *minimal* benchmark against which to measure public projects or policy interventions. From an efficiency point of view, any project or policy that fails to offset the cost of taxation (even if it would raise welfare in isolation) should not be undertaken. These costs should be taken into account when governments wish to levy taxes to redistribute wealth (that is, impose a system of direct cash transfers or government purchases of private goods) or to provide public goods. Expenditure on transfers, subsidies and public goods of course may produce their own (negative or positive) welfare effects, but these additional welfare effects of spending should not be confused with the economic costs of extracting the revenue in the first place.

Income Taxation and Economic Growth

The costs of high personal income taxation also show up in broader measures of economic activity. No economy in history has ever achieved per-capita GDP growth of 4% or more on a sustained basis once general government spending exceeds 40% of national product. Even though government spending may be productive, after it reaches a certain level it is not sufficiently productive to offset the distortionary effects of the high levels of taxation which are required to finance it. That is, once government reaches a certain size, any positive correlation that might exist gets swamped by the negative incentive effect of higher taxation.

From a microeconomic perspective, this is exactly what estimates of the marginal cost of funds tend to suggest—additional public projects should have a social return of at least or 20 and 30% (and perhaps higher) to have any chance of having a net overall positive economic effect. As government size increases and the average and marginal costs of taxation rise, there are fewer and fewer public projects or policies that possess such characteristics.

As discussed above, estimates of the MCF are driven by the fact that higher personal income taxes create significant work disincentives, and cause workers to substitute out of work into other activities. But the estimates are only a start—they assume that tax codes are easy to understand and easy to comply with.[44] Thus, they are far from being completely accurate summaries of the full costs of taxation, in the sense that they ignore some potentially important costs.

A key factor in determining long run growth rates is the *effective* supply of labour, which depends on productivity, skills, effort and so on. A worker who is more skilled will produce more output than a worker with fewer skills, even though each employee may work the same number of hours. By definition, personal income taxation induces individuals to substitute away from *any* activity which will earn them higher personal income, including investment in human capital. Human capital forms a significant part of Australia's wealth, and higher income taxes retard the accumulation of this wealth.[45] Again, the narrow focus on the effect of personal income taxation on hours worked or participation rates misses an important part of this story.

One problem with measuring the impact of tax changes on productivity levels across different countries is that international differences in institutions, legal regimes, and so on may swamp any effects that changes in taxes may have on economic growth. One way around this is to look for evidence of how variations in local and state taxes impact on economic growth *within* a particular country. There are several studies which do this, and most find negative correlations. Kleine,[46] Grierson,[47] and Grierson et al[48] report negative correlations between US state tax levels and state growth. Helms[49] uses a pooled time series and cross sectional data set from 48 US states, and finds that increases in property taxes, income taxes and user fees all tend to retard economic growth at the state level. Mofidi and Stone[50] find similar results.

The disincentive effects of taxation can also be analysed by tracking international data over long time periods.[51] The Fraser Institute reports on the structure of personal income tax systems for rich and poor countries since 1970, and derives a measure of the burden of taxation which takes into account the importance of high marginal tax rates and the level of income at which the highest marginal rate actually applies. Table 2.4 summarises their 0–10 rating scheme, where a higher number indicates a less burdensome personal income tax system. Tax systems receive a higher rating if they have low marginal rates, but also receive a high rating if the highest marginal rate does not apply to low income levels. Note also that the Fraser Institute measure controls for changes in nominal incomes across time and across countries by using 1982–84 US dollars.

Table 2.4: Measuring the Income Tax Burden (Fraser Institute Rating System)

	Income Threshold Level of Marginal Tax Rate			
	1982-84			
Top Marginal Tax Rate	**<25**	**25-50**	**50-150**	**>150**
<20%	10	10	10	10
21%-25%	9	9	10	10
26%-30%	8	8	9	9
31%-35%	7	7	8	9
36%-40%	5	6	7	8
41%-45%	4	5	6	7
46%-50%	3	4	5	6
51%-55%	2	3	4	4
56%-60%	1	2	3	3
61%-65%	0	1	2	2
66%-70%	0	0	2	1
>70%	0	0	0	0

Many countries in the Fraser Institute's sample have changed their personal tax systems in the last two decades, so it is straightforward to make long run comparisons of the effects of changing tax systems across countries. The change in income tax structures in OECD countries in the last two decades can be measured by the difference between their Fraser Institute ratings in 1980 and 2000. For example, Australia's measure only increased from a rating of 2 to a rating of 3, indicating that the Fraser Institute estimates that very little significant improvement occurred in our personal income tax system 1980 and 2000.

Average real per capita rates of economic growth over the same period are also available.[52] Figure 2.3 shows that OECD countries which significantly cut their taxes (meaning they increased their Fraser institute measure by four or more points) had an average per capita growth rate of over 3%, while those that increased taxes or reduced taxes only managed an average per capita economic growth rate of just 1.7%, almost *half* the rate enjoyed by significant tax-cutting nations. This strongly supports the proposition that lower marginal income tax rates are associated with higher per capita economic growth (although it does not provide conclusive evidence, for we would have to control for other factors that are important for growth). By examining all countries (including those outside the OECD) for which both sets of data are available (98 countries in total), we find that countries which increased their Fraser Institute measure by 4 or more points had an average per capita growth rate of 1.84%, while those that fell short of this managed a meagre average per capita economic growth rate of 0.66%. This is illustrated in Figure 2. 4. *On average, countries which significantly cut taxes between 1980 and 2000 enjoyed average per capita economic growth rates of nearly* ***three times*** *those that did not.*[53]

Figure 2.3: Income Tax Cuts and Per Capita Economic Growth Average Performance of OECD Countries, 1980-2000

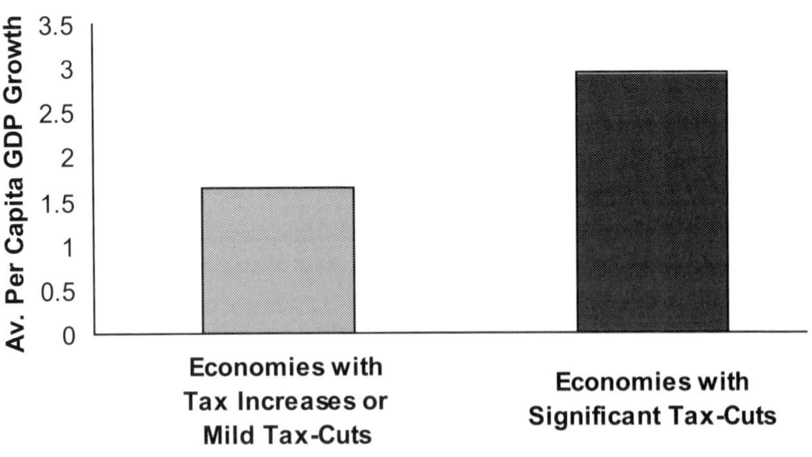

Figure 2.4: Income Tax Cuts and Per Capita Economic Growth Average Performance of 98 Countries, 1980-2000

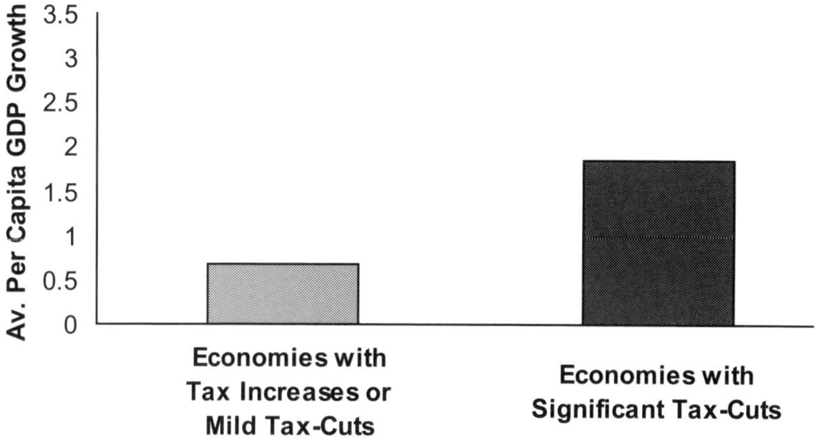

Sources: Fraser Institute, Economic Freedom in the World, Various Issues. Penn World Tables 6.1, Real GDP Per Capita 1980-2000 http://dc2.chass.utoronto.ca/pwt/

Conclusions

In this chapter we have seen that high personal income taxes not only reduce the ability of individuals to enjoy the fruits of their own labour, and therefore make workers worse off, but they also create significant disincentives. Because all forms of taxation alter economic choices and drive economic activity from high to low valued uses, a dollar increase in government revenue ends up costing the economy far more in real terms than the dollar that is actually paid in taxes. These harmful effects of taxation are present for all kinds of taxation and exist irrespective of whether tax revenue is spent productively or wasted.

Conflation of costs with benefits is a sure recipe for expanding the size of government over and above that which can be justified rigorously on economic grounds, and can lead to ruinous public policy decisions.[54] The MCF provides a dollar measure of the pure economic effects of a tax on the incentives to produce, work, save, invest or consume. It is important to note that it does *not* include the administrative costs of taxation, or the costs to business of filling out forms, or even the costs of avoiding taxes or evading taxes (this is not to say that these costs are not important or economically significant).

There is little evidence to suggest that higher taxation increases GDP growth rates, and much evidence to suggest that the opposite is true. Whatever view one takes of the merits or otherwise of higher taxes, it is simply erroneous to assert that, at current levels of taxation and spending, confiscating an additional dollar from individuals and transferring it to one's favourite bureaucrat or politician would have little or no effect on economic incentives.

Chapter 3

Cut Taxes To Raise More Revenue[1]

Sinclair Davidson

Defenders of high taxation and high levels of government spending like to pretend that high income tax does little or nothing to reduce work incentives. In chapter 2, however, Alex Robson showed this is mistaken, for in addition to creating additional administrative, evasion, compliance and rent-seeking costs, any rise in income tax also generates deadweight losses, which can be substantial.

Robson's analysis rests on the observation that workers typically reduce their efforts if they have to pay more tax. However, some defenders of high taxation argue that the reverse might actually be the case—that higher income taxes might lead people to work harder in order to recoup the extra money they have lost. I therefore begin this chapter with a review of the evidence indicating how workers respond to changes in their net incomes. This evidence shows that particular kinds of workers respond very positively to changes in top marginal tax rates: they put in more effort if they see opportunities to earn more, and less effort if they see rewards for their labour declining. This conclusion may not shock most people, but it evidently surprises some economists.

Having established that taxation does reduce the incentive to work, I then consider another common claim advanced by defenders of high taxation—that government revenues would be hard hit if tax rates were cut, and that this would then necessitate reductions in vital public services. Against this, I suggest that revenues do not necessarily fall if tax rates are cut. I argue that Australia is on the wrong side of the so-called 'Laffer curve', which means we could find total revenues rising if taxes were cut. However, the short-term costs of remedying this situation may be too high for politicians to accept.

Do tax cuts encourage people to work more? Income effects versus substitution effects

The common sense, intuitive understanding is that high taxes make people work less. After all, we are told that if we want less of an activity, say pollution, we should tax it. Why then should tax on work be any different?

According to the Australian Election Survey of 2004, most Australians (64%) believe that, 'High income tax makes people less willing to work hard' (see Table 3.1). Even among those voters who would prefer to increase government spending on social services rather than reduce taxes, most (56%) still recognise that high taxation undermines work incentives.[2] But pro-tax commentators think these people are wrong.

Table 3.1: Australian Public Opinion on the statement: 'High income tax makes people less willing to work hard'

	Number	Percentage
Strongly Agree	430	25.3
Agree	668	39.3
Neutral	336	19.8
Disagree	218	12.8
Strongly Disagree	47	2.8

Source: Australian Election Survey, 2004, Question: D.15.

For example, the economics editor of *The Sydney Morning Herald*, Ross Gittins, has written: 'You can understand why punters and business people see this as a self-evident truth requiring no further analysis but how a trained economist could fall into such sloppy thinking is beyond me—unless, of course, they're allowing their wallet to do their thinking.'[3]

To understand Gittins' argument, we need to recognise that an increase in income tax may have two different effects on the supply of labour. The *substitution effect* occurs when higher taxes reduce the opportunity cost of leisure, leading to greater consumption of leisure (that is, taxes lead to less work). On the other hand, a loss of income may cause an individual to work harder to maintain their lifestyle—the *income effect.*

In basic economic models individuals either work or engage in leisure.[4] These activities are mutually exclusive. The basic idea of a supply curve is that if price rises, more of a commodity will be offered for sale, and when price falls, less of that commodity will be offered for sale. If a tax cut results in the after-tax price of labour (wages) rising, we might expect more labour to be offered for sale. In this case, the substitution effect is operating. Conversely, a tax cut could result in individuals having to work less to maintain a given level of income. In this instance, the income effect dominates the substitution effect and the supply curve bends 'backwards'. The policy implication is that, at sufficiently high levels of income, an increase in wages (caused by reduced taxes) could lead to a decrease in labour supply.

Secondary earners, the self-employed and highly paid professionals

The incentive effects of tax cuts largely turn on which of the two effects dominates—the income effect or the substitution effect. Ross Gittins believes, 'There's no convincing empirical evidence of the substitution effect dominating the income effect in the case of primary earners.'[5] Most standard textbooks agree.[6] Gittins suggests there is little, or no, adverse relationship between hours worked and tax rates for employed men. But if true, this is not surprising, for the incentives for the 'principal earners' in households to participate in productive employment are fairly constant, irrespective of the marginal tax rates they face. Traditionally, most principal earners have been men, and they have had to keep working to pay for the household's living expenses whatever the tax authorities inflict upon them.

The impact of tax changes on secondary earners (generally partnered women), however, tends to be larger—especially in the decision over whether or not to participate in productive employment at all. Lowering marginal tax rates encourages more women into the work force.

Even in the case of principal earners, however, there are grounds for suspecting that tax plays a stronger role in discouraging work than Gittins and the conventional textbooks allow. Differences between the tax systems of the two countries suggest that people's responsiveness to high tax rates (what economists call their labour supply elasticity) may well be higher in Australia than in the US.

One issue that confounds the textbook analysis is the unit of taxation. In Australia partnered individuals are taxed separately, but in the US married couples are taxed as a single unit. The first dollar earned by the second wage earner in an American household is taxed at the first wage earner's top marginal rate. Furthermore, the average wage in the US is not subject to very high rates on income taxation, yet twice the average wage is known to be very responsive to tax effects. In Australia the top marginal rate (prior to 2005) applied to income only 1.3 times greater than average earnings.

The US textbook treatment of tax responsiveness does not therefore translate well to Australia. Partnered individuals are taxed separately, but individually face high marginal tax rates at lower incomes. Responsiveness to high tax rates may well be higher in Australia than in the US.

Another reason for suspecting that principal earners may be more sensitive to tax changes than Gittins imagines is that many salary earners have little control over their terms of employment, especially hours worked. This means any adverse impact of high marginal tax rates will not be found by looking at employees working average hours for average rates of pay. To gauge the impact of tax on work incentives, we really need to investigate professions where individuals are free to set their own hours, and/or where they can earn a very high hourly income. Given that nearly 20% of the Australian workforce are owner-managers in their own business, the number of people who could potentially have control over their own working conditions is high, and this means high marginal tax rates could be having a huge impact on our economy.[7]

Peter Martin, economics correspondent for SBS television, recently reviewed research evidence relating to New York taxi drivers and concluded that, although these workers can vary their hours in response to income incentives, they hardly respond at all to changes in financial incentives.[8] Martin suggests that, even when free to do so, workers do not respond much to changes in tax incentives. The evidence, however, is actually rather less clear-cut than Martin implies.

The key research on New York cabbies is by Henry Farber.[9] He concludes:

> There is an emerging literature on labor supply that … investigates labor supply responses in settings in which workers are free to set their hours of work. By and large, this literature finds substantial positive labor supply elasticities and evidence consistent with the standard neoclassical labor supply model. … My analysis shows that daily income effects are small, as one would expect in a standard intertemporal labor supply model, and that the decision to stop work at a particular point on a given day is primarily related to cumulative daily hours to that point.

In other words, taxi drivers work until they are tired, then they stop working. In contrast with Martin's interpretation, this actually supports the hypothesis for a substitution effect, for these drivers keep working to earn additional money until fatigue sets in. Farber contrasts this with an earlier study by Colin Camerer and others[10] that claimed that New York cabbies only work for as long as it takes to reach a desired income level:

> My findings are in direct contrast to those of Camerer et al. … They find that the daily wage elasticity of labor supply of New York City cabdrivers is substantially negative, implying large daily income effects that could be interpreted as target earnings behavior.

The Camerer team claimed that taxi drivers only worked until they achieve their desired income, and this is consistent with the 'income effect' hypothesis that Martin supports.

So which study should we believe? Farber investigates the difference between his results and the Camerer team's results, and it turns out the different findings reflect the different statistical methods employed. When Farber adopts the Camerer teams technique to analyse his own data, he comes up with results consistent with theirs. Conversely, when he analyses their data using his techniques he finds no strong income effects. In short, the backward bending supply curve result for taxi drivers is an artefact of the statistical technique employed.

Another group that is free to change its working hours in response to changing income incentives is self-employed physicians, and unlike New York taxi drivers, they tend to be highly paid. Mark Showalter and Norman Thurston[11] investigated their tax responsiveness by analysing data on their incomes, hours worked and demographic profile. Restricting their analysis to males under the age of 60 years, they found the tax responsiveness of physicians employed by hospitals and Health Maintenance Organisations was low. This appears consistent with the textbook literature suggesting that male principal earners are not responsive to tax changes. Self-employed physicians, however, were found to be very sensitive to tax changes, and solo physicians had an even greater tax response.[12]

Self-employed physicians work 22.2 minutes less per week for every percentage point increase in income tax. Assuming a 48-week year, this translates to 17.76 hours per annum per percentage point. If the top marginal tax rate were to fall from, say, 47% to 30 percent, this means self-employed physicians would be predicted to increase their working hours by 301.92 hours per annum.[13] Assuming a 7.2-hour workday, that amounts to 42 additional days of work. It seems from this that forty-two days worth of work could be 'lost' due to high progressive marginal tax rates. The effect for solo-physicians is 43.2 minutes per week—almost double.

Far from Gittins' belief that there is 'no convincing evidence' that high marginal income tax rates impact adversely on work incentives, there clearly is such evidence, but it relates mainly to workers in specific situations—second earners in households, self-employed people who can easily vary their hours, and highly-paid autonomous professionals.

High taxes destroy jobs and undermine entrepreneurship

There is also some evidence from cross-national comparative data that high income taxes reduce work effort. Edward Prescott—the 2004 economics Nobel Laureate—for example, has asked why Americans work so much more than Europeans do, and he thinks one key reason has to do with differences in tax incentives.[14]

Prescott derives a simple theoretical model that predicts labour supply (weekly hours worked) for the population aged 15–64. There are, of course, huge differences between the labour markets in Europe and the US (European labour markets are renowned for their 'rigidity' while US markets are said to be more 'flexible'), but Prescott sets up a deliberately simplified model in which country differences are assumed to be driven solely by tax rates and consumption-to-output ratios, and this generates predicted values for labour supply close to the actual values. In other words, the differences in labour supply across the G7 countries (and across time) can be explained largely by differences in their tax rates. Prescott reports:

> An important observation is that when European and U.S. tax rates are comparable, European and U.S. labor supplies were comparable. At the aggregate level, where idiosyncratic factors are averaged out, people are remarkably similar across countries. ... I am surprised that *virtually all the differences between U.S. labor supply and those of Germany and France are due to differences in tax systems.* I expected institutional constraints on the operation of labor markets and the nature of the unemployment benefit system to be of major importance.[15]

Prescott's research has not gone unchallenged. Alberto Alesina, Edward Glaeser and Bruce Sacerdote[16] suggest, 'Europeans have a cultural predilection for leisure' (translation, Europeans are naturally lazy). But this explanation is unsatisfactory. It is hard to believe Europeans suddenly became lazy over the past 30 years. Alesina et al., concede that hours worked may have initially declined due to tax policy (as Prescott suggests), but Europeans then realised that leisure was desirable and chose to consume even more leisure. They also investigate the impact of trade unionism on hours worked, arguing that strong trade unions (not high taxes) led to reduced hours, but they report that taxes still explain between a third and half of the difference in hours worked.

Prescott's evidence indicates that high taxes reduce labour supply, but that is only half the story. High tax rates can also introduce labour discrimination. There is evidence, for example, that high tax rates affect choices between participation in the legal economy and participation in the illegal, underground economy. Steven Davis and Magnus Henrekson derive a theory[17] which predicts that high tax rates reduce working hours, increase the size of the illegal underground economy, change industry mix, and (importantly) distort labour demand by 'amplify(ing) negative effects on market work and concentrat(ing) effects on the less skilled'. In other words, high tax rates, often justified on 'equity' grounds, lead to higher rates of unemployment among less-skilled workers.

They test their theory using a sample of OECD economies (including Australia). They find a tax increase of 12.8% (one standard deviation) would lead to 122 fewer market hours worked per adult per year, a 4.9% decline in the employment-population ratio, an increase in the underground economy, and a 10–30% decline in value add and employment share in those industries that rely on less-skilled labour. High tax rates lead skilled workers voluntarily to reduce their paid employment, while less skilled workers find their paid employment involuntarily reduced.

High taxes can also undermine entrepreneurial behaviour. Donald Bruce and Tami Gurley have undertaken an extensive study on taxes and entrepreneurship.[18] They consider panel survey data over the period from 1979 to 1990 and investigate the impact taxes have on the decision to go into business, remain in that business, and ultimately exit. They find 'convincing evidence that tax rates have important effects on entrepreneurial entry and survival'. Decreasing marginal tax rates increase the probability of entry into a new business, and the longevity of existing businesses.

In a series of papers, Robert Carroll, Douglas Holtz-Eakin, Mark Rider and Harvey Rosen investigate the relationship between taxation and various aspects of entrepreneurial behaviour among sole traders. They find that a five percentage point increase in marginal tax rates led to a 9.9% decrease in these traders' investment spending.[19] Further, as the entrepreneur's tax rate increases, so their probability of employing workers declines and, to the extent they do employ additional labour, decreases the growth rate in wages. High rates of taxation on 'the rich' can therefore lead to less employment and lower wages over time for 'the poor' who then become relatively even poorer. In short, small business responds to tax rates in ways that common sense should lead us to expect.

Summarising all this evidence, we can say that labour supply curves may well bend backwards at some level of after-tax income for some individuals.

But this does not mean individuals do not respond to changes in tax rates. In particular, self-employed entrepreneurs and workers with control over their working hours do respond to tax changes.

Do tax cuts necessarily reduce government revenue? The Laffer curve

We turn now to the second core question to be addressed in this chapter: whether tax cuts necessarily result in reduced government revenues.

Arthur B. Laffer famously drew his 'Laffer curve' on a napkin on 4 December 1974. This curve plots the hypothetical relationship between tax revenue and tax rates. When tax rates are zero, no revenue is raised, and when tax rates are 100 percent, no revenue is raised either (because nobody will work for nothing). In between those two extremes there are two tax rates associated with every level of tax revenue—a high tax rate and a low tax rate. At some point there is a tax rate that maximises tax revenue. If the actual marginal tax rate is above that level, then a decrease in tax rates will lead to an increase in tax revenue, while an increase in tax rates will lead to a decrease in tax revenue. Conversely, if the actual marginal tax rate were below the revenue maximising rate, an increase in tax rates would lead to an increase in tax revenue and a decrease in tax rates would lead to a decrease in tax revenue.

The Laffer curve is nothing new. Max Moser describes it as a theoretical framework derived from 'an accepted, orthodox application of economic theory'.[20] All first year microeconomics students learn the relationship between price, demand elasticity and total revenue while studying the theory of the firm. In public finance theory that same relationship is the Laffer curve.

Nor does Laffer claim originality. He quotes Ibn Khaldun (1332–1406) who in his 1375 masterpiece *al-Mugaddimah* wrote: 'At the beginning of the dynasty, taxation yields a large revenue from small assessments. At the end of the dynasty, taxation yields a small revenue from large assessments.'[21] Adam Smith, JB Say and John Maynard Keynes have all written similar comments. John F. Kennedy famously said, 'It is a paradoxical truth that tax rates are too high today and tax revenues are too low and the soundest way to raise the revenues in the long run is to cut the rates now.'[22] Critics who dismiss the Laffer curve as belonging to some fringe element of 'voodoo economics' forget that it has a long and distinguished ancestry.[23]

Evidence for, and against, the Laffer curve tax predictions

There are two classic papers that 'estimate' Laffer curves. One relates to the US experience, the other to Sweden.

The US study, by Don Fullerton, makes use of a general equilibrium tax model and 1973 data to trace out Laffer curves with given tax elasticity.[24] Fullerton reports nine potential Laffer curves. The lower the tax elasticity, the higher the revenue maximising tax rate. Fullerton then surveys the literature and suggests a low tax responsiveness figure, which in turn indicates a high revenue maximising tax rate for the US. Based on this result, he concludes, 'Broad-based cuts in labor tax rates would not increase revenues'.[25] But this conclusion critically depended on tax elasticity being low. Seven of the nine estimated Laffer curves showed revenue maximising tax rates below the 1980 level of taxation. If any of these were the 'correct' tax elasticity, then a decrease in tax rates would lead to an increase in revenue.

By contrast, Charles Stuart argues Sweden was above its revenue maximising tax rate in the 1970s and 1980s.[26] Under various assumptions he is able to estimate the revenue maximising tax rate to be in the range of 69–73 percent. He settles on a total tax rate of 70% and argues that the Swedish tax rates (80% at that time) placed Sweden on the 'wrong' side of the Laffer curve.

Laffer himself identifies three major income tax events in US economic history. In the 1920s personal income taxes were dramatically reduced (from 58% in 1922 to 26% in 1926). In the 1960s, the top marginal tax rate fell from 91% to 70 %. And in 1982, the highest marginal tax rate was reduced to 50 percent. Laffer compares the growth in real (inflation adjusted) Federal revenue, real (inflation adjusted) GDP and unemployment before and after each of these events.[27] The before and after data are averaged for the four year period before any tax reform, and the four year period following the tax reform. Summarised results are shown in Table 3.2.

In each instance a rapid change in real federal revenue occurred. In 1925 and 1982 declines in real federal revenue were reversed, and real economic growth was higher after the tax change. Unemployment decreased after the 1925 and 1964 tax reforms, but not after 1982. Based on evidence such as this, Laffer concludes, 'Seldom in economics does real life conform so conveniently to theory.'[28]

Laffer argues that, 'Lower tax rates change people's economic behavior and stimulate economic growth, which can create more—not less—tax revenues.'[29] Precisely because workers and entrepreneurs typically work

Table 3.2: Consequences of US tax reform.

Year	Real Federal Revenue Growth %		Real GDP Growth %		Unemployment Rate %	
	Before	After	Before	After	Before	After
1925	-9.2	0.1	2.0	3.4	6.5	3.1
1964	2.1	8.6	4.6	5.1	5.8	3.9
1982	-2.8	2.7	0.9	4.8	7.6	7.8

Source: Data summarised from Laffer, 'The Laffer curve: Past, present, and future' tables 1, 4 and 7. These figures refer to the 'real' changes; that is, are inflation adjusted.

harder in response to reduced taxation, more wealth is created when tax rates that are too high are reduced, and government revenues go up accordingly: 'If the existing tax rate is too high … then a tax cut would result in increased tax revenues.'[30] This, however, begs the crucial question: When is a tax rate too high?[31]

Laffer's three US historical examples illustrate his theory, but there are other tax 'reforms' in US history that he does not investigate and which do not seem to support him. In 1993, for example, the top marginal tax rate in the US increased for the top 1% of taxpayers from 28 to 40%, and this does not seem to have generated adverse results.[32] A naïve application of the Laffer curve would suggest tax revenues should have fallen, but what actually happened was tax revenue from the high-earning taxpayers affected by the change increased dramatically.

By the late 1990s, the US budget was (briefly) in surplus, although it is not clear that this was due to higher taxes. I calculate that Total Tax Receipts grew on average by 7.2% between 1992 and 1999 (the Clinton presidency).[33] Over the same period GDP grew, on average, by 5.5%, but Total Government Expenditure only grew, on average, by 3.8%. The 'secret' behind the US budget surplus was not just higher taxes, but restrained government expenditure.[34]

I have also investigated 23 OECD economies, comparing their change in top personal income tax rates for the period 1980–2001[35] and their budget balance for 2001.[36] The average decline in top personal tax rate was 22.3%, while the average budget balance was 0.91%. The correlation between the two series of numbers was a statistically insignificant –0.012. The average decline in personal tax rates for the thirteen OECD economies in budget surplus was 21%, while the ten that were in deficit had an average decline in top personal tax rates of 23%.[37] This suggests it is not tax cuts that produce budget deficits so much as high government spending.

The latest evidence in support of the Laffer curve can demonstrate this point. In 2003, the US cut tax rates on dividend income and capital gains. According to Stephen Moore, writing in the *Asian Wall Street Journal*, tax receipts went up 30% in the two years since the tax cut: 'Federal expenditures are up $110 billion, or 7.2%, so far this year as the congressional Republican spending spree rolls on'.[38]

Cut taxes to get the rich to pay more

In the US literature, 'the rich' are usually defined as being the top 1% of taxpayers. According to the US Internal Revenue Service this group of taxpayers, in 2002, had an income above US$285,424. They earned 16% of all Adjusted Gross Income, but paid 34% of US income tax, paying an average tax rate of 27.25%.[39]

This group of taxpayers is most likely to be highly sensitive to high tax rates. They can afford the best tax planning advice, they may receive a large proportion of their total income in forms other than wages and salary, and they have the ability to shift assets and income into tax-advantaged (or at least, less tax-disadvantaged) forms, or to alter the timing of taxable income.

Martin Feldstein, chairman of the Council of Economic Advisors to Ronald Reagan, investigated the impact of the 1986 US tax reform by tracking 4,000 high-income taxpayers before and after the reform. The 1986 Tax Reform Act reduced the top marginal tax rate from 50% to 28%; it also redefined taxable income and broadened the tax base by closing a number of loopholes used to facilitate tax avoidance. Feldstein found a huge response to the lower taxation. Lower rates of taxation had a large positive impact on taxable income, and substantially reduced the deadweight loss associated with taxation. Table 3.3 shows (in inflation-adjusted dollars) that the US tax changes of the 1980s were very progressive in their impact.[40] As tax rates fell, so tax revenue collected from the top end of the income spectrum grew dramatically. The average revenue per return fell, but the number of returns grew. Revenue from the top 1% of taxpayers increased by 51%, after inflation. This is convincing evidence.

Ross Gittins thinks that, 'The notion that people require higher monetary rewards to induce them to work harder is likely to be truer for jobs at the bottom of the tree than those at the top,'[41] and many analysts have agreed with him that tax changes for the rich are unlikely to change their behaviour much. However, Jon Gruber and Emmanuel Saez investigated a panel of US tax returns over the decade of the 1980s, and they found that the biggest impacts of the tax reforms were at the top of the income

Table 3.3: Percentage change in US Tax Revenue 1980–1990.

Income Group	Group %	Per Return %
Top 10 %	28.8	5.6
Top 1 %	51.4	24.1
Top 5 %	35.9	11.4
Next 40 %	1.1	-17.1
Bottom 50 %	-8.5	-25.0
Total	14.1	-6.5

Source: Gwartney and Stroup, 129. Data are percentage changes calculated in inflation-adjusted dollars. Number of returns increased by 21% over the period.

distribution rather than the bottom.[42] The greatest tax disincentive applies to high-income earners, mainly because it is this group that is best able to organise its affairs in response to changes in the tax system.

Could tax cuts increase total revenue in Australia?

The question for Australia, of course, is whether our tax rates are too high—would a reduction in tax rates lead to an increase in tax revenue? To the best of my knowledge, no definitive Australian study into this question has been undertaken. In a 1991 paper, Gerald Scully estimated governments would maximise revenue when the income tax rate was 22.5%.[43] He used IMF data for 103 countries over the period 1960–1980 for his analysis. During that period Australia's marginal income tax rate was far higher than 22.5%.

In order to provide some guidance as to where Australia might be on the Laffer curve, I have calculated summary statistics for the OECD. I first calculated the median tax rates and the median Total Tax to GDP, Total Revenue to GDP and Total Expenditure to GDP ratios. The data are segmented into above and below median size. I calculate the averages for above median and below median data and report the results in Table 3.4. The median economy is identified in the table but is excluded from the analysis.

Laffer predicts that for every level of government revenue there are two tax rates, one high and one low. Bearing this in mind table 3.4 tells a startling story. When we look at the government size ratios (Total Tax to GDP, Total Revenue to GDP and Total Expenditure to GDP) it is clear Australia has a small government (the Australian measures for these variables are below

Table 3.4: Tax Rates and Government Size.

		Personal Tax Rate	Corporate Tax Rate	Total Tax/GDP	Total Revenue/ GDP	Total Expenditure/ GDP
Australia		47.0	30.0	30.1	36.8	37.9
Total Tax/GDP	Low	43.0	33.5	32.1	38.9	40.2
Median = Greece 36.9	High	46.5	31.8	43.4	49.5	50.0
Total Revenue/GDP	Low	40.7	32.0	32.8	38.2	40.0
Median = Iceland 44.9	High	48.7	33.8	42.7	50.2	50.2
Total Expenditure/GDP	Low	42.6	33.4	32.8	38.6	39.0
Median = Greece 46.8	High	46.9	31.8	42.7	49.8	51.1

Source: Data from *OECD in Figures*, 2004 Edition. Data are unweighted.

the 'low' OECD average statistics). But when we look at the personal tax rate, we see that Australia ranks 'high' (corporate tax rates are indeterminate—by some measures they appear high and others they appear low). Overall, bigger governments tend to have higher personal tax rates, but Australia has a small government, yet has high personal income tax rates. *This is exactly what we would expect to see for an economy on the 'wrong' side of the Laffer curve.*

A possible criticism of the view that Australia is on the 'wrong' side of the Laffer curve is that it implies that politicians and tax officials are irrational. Surely a rational politician, knowing higher revenue could be raised with lower marginal tax rates, would advocate lower taxes. But this overlooks the time dimension. It is well known in microeconomic theory that elasticities are lower in the short run than they are in the long run. James Buchanan and Dwight Lee have argued that a mismatch between short run and long run objectives can lead to a rational decision being on the 'wrong' side of the Laffer curve.[44] While government lives forever, the individuals who make up government have short time horizons. In their planning, they are sensitive to short run fluctuations in tax revenue. Taxpayers, however, have long run planning horizons. They respond to shortrun tax changes with a lag. In his analysis of the Swedish Laffer curve, Stuart suggested this lag might be as long as 10 years.[45] In other words, with a longrun perspective, tax rates could be lower and tax revenues higher, but with a shortrun perspective the political costs of lowering tax rates are too high. Consequently, it is politically rational to make inefficient decisions.

Conclusion

In this chapter we have seen that cuts in marginal tax rates induce people to work harder in situations where they have an effective choice as between work and leisure hours. High marginal tax rates lead to fewer hours worked and less productive behaviour in the economy. This effect is most noticeable for high-income earners. Furthermore, high tax rates inhibit small business formation and give rise to labour market discrimination against less-skilled workers.

Lower marginal tax rates can raise more government revenue and stimulate growth at the same time. Of course, if government wished to maximise the economic growth rate they would have to lower tax rates and decrease government revenue too. Big government inhibits growth. While the Australian government is small by OECD standards, nonetheless it is probably bigger than the growth maximisation size.

At the 2005 federal budget, tax relief was given to higher rate taxpayers by raising the thresholds at which the two top marginal rates cut in. But the economic literature is quite clear: High tax *rates* cause the damage. The 2005 budget did not modify tax rates; except for the very bottom, it increased income thresholds instead. The government put money back in people's pockets, but in the least efficient manner possible. Having incurred the political costs of tax relief, few of the economic benefits of tax reform will have been realised.[46] Inflation, economic growth and time will conspire to undo the 2005 tax relief, sooner rather than later.

Chapter 4

Who's Not Paying Their Fair Share Of Income Tax?[1]

Sinclair Davidson

There is a widespread belief in Australia that the 'rich' have benefited from income tax cuts since John Howard came to power, while the 'battlers' and middle-Australia have suffered under an increasingly heavy tax burden. The implication is that ordinary workers and their families are being 'unfairly' taxed while high-income earners do not pay their 'fair' share of tax. But when rhetoric is put to one side and taxation data are examined carefully, the evidence shows that it is the higher income earners who are paying the lion's share of personal income tax, and that if anyone is being taxed unfairly, it is them.

Who pays personal income tax in Australia?

The 1986 Nobel laureate in economics, James Buchanan, posed the question, 'Who finally pays for the public expenditures that are financed through the income tax?'[2] On the face of it this is a very simple question. Answers to this question tend to be 'fudged'. Wayne Swan, for example, has written, 'Australians on low and middle incomes are shouldering more of the tax burden than those at the top.'[3] Similarly, Stephen Harrison, chief executive of The Institute of Chartered Accountants of Australia, has stated: 'Australia has one of the highest levels of reliance on personal income taxes in the OECD with a disproportionate tax burden falling on the middle-income earner'.[4] And at the 2004 federal election, the Greens stated: 'At present, Pay As You Go (PAYG) taxpayers on low to middle incomes pay more tax in proportion to their income than people on high incomes'.[5]

These views are commonly held, but are not supported by any evidence. While Harrison is right that we rely more on personal income tax revenues than other countries do (see Peter Burn's discussion in chapter 1), it is not true that workers on low and middle incomes are paying proportionately more than those on higher incomes. Quite the reverse is the case.

To evaluate Wayne Swan's claim I investigated the Australian Tax Office *Taxation Statistics.*[6] Table 4.1 classifies individual tax returns into 20 quantiles ranked from the lowest to the highest income groups.[7] It then shows the percentage share of net tax[8] paid by each of these groups (i.e. the tax they pay is expressed relative to the total net tax paid by all individuals). Tax shares are reported for each year from 1996–7 to 2002–3. It is clear from Table 4.1 that the share of tax paid increases monotonically, and dramatically, as income increases. There is also a trend, albeit slight, for tax shares to fall across time except for the highest quantile.

Swan does not state what 'low', 'middle' or 'top' incomes are in his view, so I have classified the bottom five quantiles (that is, the lowest quarter of income earners) as 'low income earners' (they had an average income of in 2003 of $14,964); the middle ten quantiles as 'middle income earners' (average income of $35,083) and the top five quantiles (the top quarter) as 'high income earners' (average income of $83,784). The final three rows at the bottom of Table 4.1 indicate the tax shares of each of these three groups. It is clear that the tax burden has increased for high-income earners and fallen for middle- and low-income earners since 1996. Low earners have reduced their share of total income tax from 3.4% to 3.2%, while high earners have seen their share rise from 60.8% to 63.8%. Furthermore, the ATO calculations of 'net tax' do not appear to include the Superannuation Surcharge Tax, which was levied on higher rate taxpayers until it was scrapped in 2005. Including this means the contribution of 'high' income earners is even higher.[9]

The data in Table 4.1 help explain why tax cuts tend to benefit higher earners more than low earners. Challenged on the ABC's *7.30 Report* to justify his 2004 budget decision to limit tax relief to individuals earning more than $52,000, Peter Costello said it was difficult to provide large tax cuts to those earning less than $52,000 since they pay comparatively little in tax in the first place.[10] Given that low earners between them contribute only 3% of all the income tax paid in Australia, it is difficult to see how tax cuts could make much of an impact on them. In a progressive tax system, where low- and middle-income earners pay progressively less in tax, so they will receive progressively less when taxes are cut.

The figures in Table 4.1 do not include the impact of the Goods and Services Tax (GST) introduced in the 2000-1 financial year. When it was introduced, reductions in personal income tax were made to compensate people for the higher indirect taxes they would have to pay. This can be seen in the reductions to tax share for the bottom 75% of taxpayers in that year. It is possible to 'guesstimate' the impact of the GST of the relative tax shares. A problem arises in allocating the GST share to the various income groups. Using the 2000–01 financial year and the net GST revenue for that year I make two allocation assumptions. First, I assumed the GST could be allocated by income share (that is, the GST allocation is income weighted for each income group). This would have the effect of overestimating the impact of the GST on higher-income groups. The second assumption I made is in simply equally-weighting the GST allocation. This would have the effect of overestimating the impact of the GST on low-income groups. Overall, the GST had little impact on the distribution of tax share. The top 25% of income earners still pay the lion's share of net income tax, while the bottom 25% still pay a very small proportion of net income tax.

Table 4.1: Net Tax per income quantile as a percentage of Total Net Tax.

Quantile	1996-97	1997-98	1998-99	1999-00	2000-01	2001-02	2002-03
5	0.2	0.2	0.2	0.2	0.2	0.2	0.2
10	0.4	0.4	0.4	0.4	0.4	0.4	0.4
15	0.6	0.6	0.6	0.6	0.6	0.6	0.6
20	0.9	0.9	0.9	0.9	0.9	0.9	0.9
25	1.3	1.2	1.2	1.2	1.1	1.1	1.1
30	1.6	1.5	1.5	1.4	1.4	1.4	1.4
35	1.9	1.8	1.8	1.8	1.8	1.9	1.9
40	2.3	2.3	2.3	2.3	2.2	2.3	2.3
45	2.8	2.8	2.8	2.7	2.6	2.7	2.7
50	3.3	3.2	3.2	3.1	3.0	3.1	3.1
55	3.7	3.7	3.7	3.6	3.4	3.5	3.5
60	4.2	4.2	4.1	4.1	3.8	3.9	3.9
65	4.8	4.7	4.7	4.5	4.3	4.4	4.3
70	5.4	5.3	5.2	5.1	4.8	4.9	4.8
75	6.0	5.9	5.9	5.8	5.4	5.5	5.4
80	6.9	6.8	6.8	6.7	6.1	6.2	6.1
85	8.0	7.9	7.9	7.8	7.0	7.1	7.2
90	9.4	9.4	9.4	9.3	8.4	8.6	8.7
95	12.0	12.1	12.1	11.9	11.3	11.6	11.6
100	24.5	25.0	25.4	26.8	31.3	29.9	30.2
Bottom 25%	3.4	3.4	3.4	3.2	3.1	3.2	3.2
Middle 50%	36.0	35.4	35.1	34.3	32.8	33.6	33.3
Top 25%	60.8	61.2	61.5	62.4	64.1	63.4	63.8

Source: ATO, *Taxation Statistics*, see www.ato.gov.au

Five weak justifications for progressive taxation

How is it possible to justify a 'progressive' tax system, which results in one quarter of the population paying nearly two-thirds of all the income tax? Economists and philosophers have advanced many arguments, yet none are convincing.[11]

One argument that is often heard is that 'the rich' should pay more than their share because they have not earned their wealth, or they have acquired it illegitimately, or have been the recipients of good fortune. Wayne Swan appeals to this sort of argument when he claims that progressive taxation, where those on higher incomes pay an increasingly large proportion of their earnings in tax, delivers 'fairness rather than reward for inherited wealth'.[12] But this argument begs the question of why people who earn their own money through their own efforts should be penalised.

A second common argument is that income inequality is undesirable and that the tax system should therefore operate to equalise after-tax incomes.[13] This has been called the 'Total Confiscation' principle.[14] The Australian Council of Trade Unions (ACTU) lists this redistributive function as a primary objective of a fair tax system, but few economists (or voters) subscribe to such a policy.

A more subtle version of this idea is the 'ability to pay' principle. This is a price discrimination argument that states that 'the rich' can afford to pay a bigger proportion of their income in tax than 'the poor'. But even if this were true, it logically does not justify progressive taxation. After all, the 'rich' are not required to pay more for their groceries than 'the poor' although they could easily afford to do so. Ludwig Von Mises has argued that taken to its logical conclusion the ability to pay principle collapses into the 'Total Confiscation' argument (that is, we end up with a tax system that leaves everyone with the same net income, no matter how much they earn gross).[15]

A third, and much more sophisticated argument for progressive tax is the 'Equality of Sacrifice' principle. According to Hayek, this was the argument used to justify progressive tax rates when they were first introduced at the turn of the 20th century.[16]

The idea of equality of sacrifice is based on the economic theory of 'diminishing marginal utility'. This theory holds that individuals value any given commodity less, the more they have of it. Applied to money and wealth, this suggests that 'the rich' value their last dollar of income less than 'the poor' value their last dollar. This being the case, it is fair to tax the rich at a higher rate because their higher income is of less value to them. The pain of the tax burden is therefore equalised across rich and poor alike.

This may sound plausible, but economists have savaged this line of reasoning. Hayek himself believed that our improved understanding of utility theory has 'completely destroyed the foundations of this argument'.[17] And Paul Samuelson (who is certainly no anti-tax conservative) similarly acknowledges that progressive income tax is not necessarily consistent with diminishing marginal utility: 'Equality of sacrifice would imply proportional rather than progressive taxation'.[18]

The 'Equality of Sacrifice' theory relies on some strong and easily violated assumptions. For example, the theory assumes that individuals can be divided into income groups that are homogenous within themselves, who derive the same satisfaction from income and consume the same bundle of goods and services. It further assumes that this satisfaction is measurable, comparable and known to the tax authority, yet as John Stuart Mill reasoned, decision makers will never have this type of information 'with the degree of certainty on which a legislator or a financier ought to act'.[19] The application of diminishing marginal utility to income is also inconsistent with observable economic behaviour. Why would individuals make great sacrifices to increase their wealth if they did not highly value the marginal increase in wealth that their sacrifices generate?

The only way unequal rates of tax can generate equal rates of sacrifice is if money is worth less to the rich than it is to the poor, which it clearly is not. And even if this proposition were true, the Dutch economist Arnold Jacob Cohen-Stuart demonstrated as long ago as 1889 that, 'Progression does not follow from the general law of decreasing utility'.[20] Clearly Hayek is correct to refer to the whole idea as being a 'regrettable mistake'.[21]

A fourth argument for progressive taxation is that the rich should shoulder a bigger share of taxation because they benefit more from government services like policing and national defence. John Quiggin, for example, has written that, '(w)hile taxation payments are roughly proportional to income, the benefits of public expenditure are about the same for all members of the community'.[22] He thinks that while low-income earners receive higher welfare benefits, 'middle and upper income earners receive a greater economic benefit from services such as police and national defence, since they have more to lose'.[23]

But this argument not only slurs the morality and patriotism of low-income earners by assuming they have little or no interest in the survival of their country; it also stands reality on its head. Some 150 years ago, John Stuart Mill asked 'Who would suffer most if (government) protection were withdrawn?' and answered: 'It must be, that those would suffer most who were weakest in mind or body, either by nature or by position'.[24] In his *Utilitarianism*, Mill was explicit that, 'The rich would be far better able to protect themselves, in the absence of law or government, than the poor, and indeed would probably be successful in converting the poor into their slaves.'[25] Government and the rule of law protect the weak from the strong—without the forces of law, the people with least would suffer the most. The British Labour MP Frank Field has recently demonstrated the truth of this with his harrowing account of the fear and abuse that poorer city dwellers in Britain are now experiencing as a result of the weakening of traditional authority structures.[26] The Marxist belief that government and law are simply instruments of the rich ignores how much the poor depend upon them.

A fifth argument that attempts to establish the 'fairness' of progressive income tax rates refers to the totality of the tax system (that is, the incidence of indirect as well as direct taxes). John Quiggin cites research at the National Centre for Social and Economic Modelling (NATSEM)[27] estimating that in 1996–97, the total tax burden for low-income households (the bottom 20%) amounted to 36% of their gross income, as compared with 51% of gross income paid in taxes by high-income households (the top 20%).[28] Quiggin argues that these two numbers (36% and 51%) are 'roughly proportional', implying that those on lower incomes end up paying just as much proportionately as those on higher incomes.[29]

But the evidence simply does not support this interpretation. The NATSEM study clearly demonstrates that the Australian tax system is progressive, and remains progressive even after indirect taxation is taken into account:

> The overall impact of the tax system appears to be progressive, as the progressive impact of income taxes is not fully offset by the regressive impact of indirect taxes. This conclusion appears to hold irrespective of whether the measure of the economic resources of households is gross income, equivalent gross income, current weekly expenditure or equivalent current weekly income.[30]

Another tax incidence analysis conducted by the ABS confirms this.[31] And we should remember that the most strongly 'regressive' element in indirect taxation is accounted for by so-called 'sin taxes', such as duty on tobacco, alcohol and gambling.[32] Take these out of the calculation, and the total tax system looks very strongly progressive. Quiggin's argument is simply not supported by the data.

So while economists generally assume progressive taxation is fair, this assumption cannot be derived from any economic theory.[33] More importantly, economists have known this to be the case for over 100 years.[34]

Despite the weaknesses of the various arguments used to justify progressive taxation, however, progressive rates are now the norm in most economies. Hayek believes this is because tax authorities know more revenue can be raised with a progressive tax.[35] It has nothing to do with spurious arguments about fairness and equality of sacrifice.

Proportional taxation is fair

Under a progressive tax system, 'fairness' can only ever be arbitrarily defined according to whatever the current tax rates happen to be. As long as individuals pay the amount specified by the parliament, and not a dollar less, they have paid their 'fair share'. But under this definition, *any* share of tax paid could be considered 'fair'. Because 'fairness' in a progressive system of taxation will always be a matter for arbitrary judgement, it will always be contested.

This is not the case in a proportional tax system, where everyone pays the same percentage of their income in tax. Political economists and philosophers have argued for several centuries that fairness lies in proportionality. In the 18th century, Adam Smith supported proportional taxation because it rests on a commonly understood criterion of fairness as equal treatment.[36] Writing in the 19th century, John Stuart Mill agreed: 'I can see no fairer standard of real equality than to take from all persons, whatever may be their amount of fortune, the same arithmetical proportion of their superfluities.'[37] Scottish journalist John Ramsay McCulloch wrote:

> The moment you abandon the cardinal principle of extracting from all individuals the same proportion of their income or of their property, you are at sea without rudder or compass, and there is no amount of injustice and folly you may not commit.[38]

And in the 20th century, Hayek argued that proportional taxation is intuitively fair, while progressive taxation is arbitrary and unjust.[39] This long tradition of reasoning rests on the intuitive sense of 'fairness' as proportionality. This is completely absent in progressive taxation systems.

If 'fair' taxation is proportional taxation, then we have already seen in Table 4.1 that many individuals in Australia are *not* paying their fair share. This is made even clearer in Table 4.2 that shows the percentage ratio of tax share to income share for each of the income quantiles. If the individuals in any quantile were on average paying their fair (that is, proportional) share, their entry in Table 4.2 would equal 100. If individuals are paying less than their fair share, their cell value will be less than 100, and if they are paying more than their fair share it will be more than 100.

There are a number of features in Table 4.2 worth discussing. First, note that the overwhelming majority of taxpayers pay less than their share of income as tax. Before the 2000–01 tax year, 70% of all taxpayers had a greater income share than tax share and in 2000–01 this increased to 80%. There are, however, some anomalies in the data. Taxpayers in some quantiles, while still paying far less than their fair share, have experienced

Table 4.2: Net tax share as a percentage of total income share, 1996–97 to 2000–01.

Quantile	1996-97	1997-98	1998-99	1999-00	2000-01	2001-02	2002-03
5	16.7	17.0	17.3	17.7	14.4	15.7	15.4
10	25.0	26.9	27.7	27.2	24.0	24.6	24.7
15	31.6	33.2	33.5	33.2	34.3	34.1	34.0
20	40.9	41.6	42.2	41.3	41.7	41.7	41.2
25	52.0	48.6	47.4	47.1	45.0	45.1	44.3
30	55.2	53.5	52.1	51.6	49.6	50.9	51.7
35	59.4	58.5	58.3	58.2	58.8	60.2	60.9
40	65.7	66.4	67.5	67.7	66.5	67.5	67.7
45	73.7	74.5	74.9	74.7	72.1	73.1	73.2
50	80.5	80.4	80.3	79.7	76.9	77.8	77.7
55	84.1	85.3	85.2	84.5	81.2	81.8	81.5
60	89.4	89.7	89.0	88.4	84.8	85.5	85.1
65	94.1	93.7	92.8	91.9	88.1	88.8	88.2
70	98.2	97.2	95.9	95.1	91.5	91.8	91.1
75	101.7	100.7	101.0	100.9	94.2	94.8	93.9
80	107.8	107.2	107.2	106.7	97.3	97.7	97.3
85	114.3	113.5	113.0	112.3	102.2	103.6	104.0
90	120.5	119.9	120.5	119.7	110.2	111.7	112.1
95	129.0	129.7	129.9	128.7	123.0	124.6	124.8
100	141.6	141.0	140.7	138.2	158.1	156.4	155.3

Source: ATO, see www.ato.gov.au

an increase in net tax share as a percentage of total income. Overall, however, the data in Table 4.2 indicate that the overwhelming majority of taxpayers pay less than their fair share of tax.

There have, of course, been further changes since 2000–01. The rather derisory 'milkshake and sandwich' tax cuts in 2003 accentuated the unfairness of the existing taxation arrangements, for even fewer taxpayers would have been paying their 'fair share' after this budget. The 2004/5 budget made more substantial changes, increasing payments for families with children on household incomes less than $52,000 (meaning they ended up paying less in net tax) and raising tax thresholds for individual taxpayers with incomes above $52,000.[40] The raising of the top two tax brackets was widely presented as a 'regressive' policy for it reduced the amount of tax paid by higher rate taxpayers. But they will actually have had the effect of further reducing the proportion of Australians who pay a fair share of their income as tax. The tax reforms in the last two years will thus have the effect of increasing the relative tax burden on those Australians with the highest incomes and further reducing the tax burden for Australians with low and middle incomes.

Conclusion

When politicians and commentators claim that 'battlers' pay more than their share of tax, or that income tax cuts benefit the rich at the expense of the poor and are therefore 'unfair', they pander to ignorance and prejudice. And there is a lot of ignorance among voters about how our tax system works.

According to the 2004 Australian Election Survey,[41] only 43% of respondents know that low-income earners pay a smaller proportion of their income in income tax than higher earners do. Thirty percent of voters think, falsely, that low-income earners pay a greater proportion of their income in income tax than higher earners do. This level of ignorance is fed by politicians and commentators who make erroneous claims about the incidence of taxation and who thereby encourage a deeply damaging and unedifying 'politics' of envy among voters who all too eagerly believe they are paying too much, and that an ill-defined group of richer people should be paying more. As Cathy Buchanan and Peter Hartley suggest, proponents of progressive taxes over proportional taxes are ultimately 'motivated by envy and not by compassion'.[42]

In his January 2004 article in *The Australian*, Wayne Swan argued that Australian families are paying punitive rates of tax while some 'chief executives on multi-million dollar base salaries' are getting away with paying far too little. This sort of rhetoric is misleading and unhelpful. By concentrating on effective marginal tax rates, Swan confuses the tax system with the welfare system (as they earn their next dollar, many families lose means tested benefits at the same time as they pay tax, and therefore face high 'effective marginal tax rates', but in net terms they may still end up paying virtually no tax at all). More important, Swan gives the impression that individuals with multi-million dollar base salaries are common, yet in the 1998–9 financial year, the ATO reported only 431 individuals who earned more than $1 million. In its vagueness in defining who the 'rich' are,[43] and by citing extremely high-income individuals as examples, the revenue lobby sows confusion and reinforces ignorance.

Income tax is an emotive issue, and facts have often been early casualities in political debates on this issue. So let there be no more doubt. The income tax burden is not falling on middle-income earners and the poor. Evidence clearly shows that the bulk of the tax burden is falling on higher earners, that their share of tax paid has actually increased over time, and that they, and they alone, pay more than their proportionate share. Australia is a democracy, and to paraphrase Daniel Patrick Moynihan, everyone is entitled to their own opinions; they are not, however, entitled to their own facts.

Chapter 5

The Moral Case For A Flat Tax

Lauchlan Chipman

> If we consider the waste of energy and effort which progressive taxation in so many ways leads to, it should not be impossible to convince reasonable people of its undesirability. Yet experience in this field shows how rapidly habit blunts the sense of justice and even elevates into a principle what in fact has no better basis than envy.
>
> F. A. Hayek, *The Constitution of Liberty* (London: Routledge and Kegan Paul, 1960), 322.

Arguments about the desirability of different tax policies invariably involve assertions about their effects on human behaviour. Some claims are empirical (for example, the claim that lower taxes will encourage people to work harder). Other claims are more philosophical (for example, the idea that it is desirable that taxes should be reduced in order to encourage people to work rather than rely on state welfare).

The empirical claims are often very difficult to evaluate because they rest on assumptions about human psychology, about which we just do not know enough. This vacuum in our knowledge is often filled by intuitively grounded conjecture which equally frequently turns out to be wrong. We are on more secure ground when we analyse past changes—we observe that the introduction of such and such an incentive in the past resulted in a particular set of changes in people's behaviour—but because most debate about taxation policy is focused on the future, there are limits to how far past experience can guide our future actions. In sum, the limitations of the current state of the sciences of human behaviour mean that judgements about the probable effects of this or that change in taxation policy must be made under conditions of considerable uncertainty.

As for the philosophical questions, they can only be answered in relation to whatever is postulated as a preferred set of desirable outcomes, and this is an essentially contestable judgement. Arguments about what is desirable and what is not cannot be resolved by appeal to evidence. Instead, these arguments rest on ethical judgements regarding value-laden terms like equity, equality, justice, fairness, and moral obligation. Questions about what socio-economic objectives taxation policies ought to achieve are dependent ultimately on our vision for society.

For example, there is a widely-held belief that material equality is a desirable social goal. As will become clear in the course of this chapter, this is a philosophically contentious position, but, *ceteris paribus*, those who believe in the pursuit of greater equality tend to favour taxation policies that can be expected to lead to a 'more equal' distribution of wealth. In their view, whatever else may be usefully accomplished by a particular taxation policy, it ought to contribute substantially to progressing society towards material equality. State-mandated redistribution is therefore seen as justified even if it is not necessary to raise more revenue to enable the other purposes of government to be fulfilled—narrowing in the distribution of wealth is sufficient purpose in itself.

Those who think this way are generally attracted to a so-called 'progressive' income tax, for this is one key mechanism for preventing uneven accumulation of wealth. But not all political philosophies accept that progress towards material equality should be seen as an end in itself. Many, indeed, are perfectly consistent with increasing material inequality.

A minimalist or 'night watchman' philosophy of the state, for example, holds that the role of government should be limited to providing for the security of its citizens against external or internal assault, and the enforcement of private law between them. This perspective has no implications for a preferred pattern of the distribution of material wealth. Even a philosophy which places a strong emphasis on human welfare and the maximising of opportunities for individual advancement need not require taxation policies which result in a 'more equal' society, for it is perfectly possible for the rich to grow richer without disadvantaging those who are less affluent. The claim that progressive taxation is a 'good thing' because it compresses wealth and income inequalities is therefore far from being self-evident.

The morality of forcibly confiscating property justly acquired

This chapter is concerned with only one form of taxation, namely personal income taxation. For the sake of argument, it will be assumed that taxation of personal income is in principle a morally legitimate way for governments to raise revenue. But we should never forget the very strong onus on those who believe that any given tax is morally legitimate to demonstrate why this is so.

All taxation involves the forcible removable of the private property of another—a removal that, were it performed by another individual without the sanction of law, would be a felony. With the exception of the taxation of the proceeds of crime or civil fraud, taxation involves the confiscation of property rightfully acquired, and therefore rightfully owned, by the taxpayer. This is not to deny that taxation may be morally legitimate. But it is to say that all taxation, insofar as it necessarily involves the forcible transfer of rightful ownership to another, requires a morally compelling justification.

Whatever else a tax cheat may be, he or she is not a thief. The crime lies in not surrendering that to which the law has given an overriding entitlement to the state. Unlike the thief, it does not lie in securing and attempting to retain possession of something to which the perpetrator was never entitled.

No doubt some will dismiss this as a distinction without a difference, but I mention it to underline the point that taxation always involves the imposition of a law which overrides the prior legal rights of the taxpayer. While one can understand the emotional appeal of rhetoric accusing tax cheats of 'stealing from the revenue', this is not literally correct. The otherwise honest tax cheat's wrong consists in wilfully failing to surrender to the state that to which the lawmaker has given the state an entitlement which trumps the tax cheat's own. By contrast, someone who 'steals from the revenue', for example a welfare cheat or a taxpayer who claims a bogus rebate, takes something to which the thief has no prior right, but to which the state does have (relative to the thief) a prior legally justified entitlement.

The question of whether state taxation of personal income is morally legitimate is rarely raised today. This is because we have grown accustomed to having our incomes taxed. But while income tax is pervasive now, it only became commonplace in the developed world in the late 19th and early 20th centuries.

It is also commonly assumed that, unless one is an anarchist, one must accept the necessity of some form of taxation, be it an income tax, wealth tax, consumption tax, poll tax (standard lump sum per person), or some other tax or combination of taxes. This is incorrect. A state could be funded through monopoly possession of a valuable resource, such as oil or gold, through a portfolio of foreign commercial investments, or through revenue raised from voluntary activities, such as lotteries. Modern states commonly use some of these strategies to augment their revenue, but not to substitute for taxation.

As already indicated, taxation of anything, because it is a legally sanctioned confiscation of some part of the property to which the law abiding taxpayer has a prior legal entitlement, always requires a morally compelling justification. Moreover, a further specific justification is required for making *income* subject to taxation. Hall and Rabushka remind us that Adam Smith, for example, expressed dismay at the prospect of income tax:

> (He) strongly opposed direct assessment of income through an income tax, because it entailed an inquisition of each taxpayer. He felt that an income tax was too heinous a yoke to be imposed on any man because it would expose his finances to the scrutiny of the treasurer, who might then drag him through public disgrace. Smith viewed an income tax as especially harmful to the commercial classes, since it would likely have an adverse effect on capital formation.[1]

Even if we assume that an ethically convincing justification for taxation of income has been made out, the question remains of what proportion of state revenue should be derived from taxation of income as opposed to other sources. Plainly, one's view about the rate of income tax that is reasonable is not independent of one's views about what the total state revenue should be (in turn dependent on one's views about what functions the state should perform) and how much of it should be derived from other forms of taxation, and other state activities that earn revenue. All of these are debatable. For these reasons, I am concerned about principles only in this chapter, and not about what the particular rates of income tax should be. I will also be concerned only with personal income taxation, and not with the taxation of the income of corporations or other entities, although some of the same principles will apply, *mutatis mutandis*.

Flat, Proportional, and Progressive Taxes

Most income tax systems are steeply 'progressive' in structure. This means that the higher one's income, *the higher the proportion* of one's income is lost to income tax. This is achieved by graduating the tax scale into several brackets, so that as one's income rises into another bracket, the dollars which fall within that bracket are taxed at a higher rate per dollar (commonly referred to as a higher marginal rate) than obtained in the bracket below, which in turn were taxed at a higher rate ... and so on down, until one reaches a floor of zero income, or zero taxable income, should the scale recognise a threshold below which income is not taxable.

By and large, opponents of progressive taxation do not object to high income earners paying more income tax than low income earners. Few tax critics advocate a poll tax, or uniform lump sum tax on incomes, for most believe that it would be extremely unfair to require every earner to pay the same as every other, irrespective of the size of their income. What they do object to, however, is the principle that higher earners should pay a bigger proportion of their income in tax than lower earners. They argue instead that there should be a constant proportional rate of income taxation—a 'flat rate'.

Supporters of so-called 'flat tax' therefore accept that high income earners should pay more of their income in taxation than low income earners, but they do not accept that high income earners should pay a higher proportion of their income in taxation. What is 'flat' is not the amount of tax paid, but the proportion.

Plainly, a single proportionate rate has practical advantages over a progressive rate. The most obvious of these (discussed by Geoffrey Walker in chapter 6) is simplicity. A single flat rate should reduce costs to both tax payer and tax collector in the administration of the system. Depending on what scope there is for deductions, rebates, offsets and credits, completing and assessing tax returns is easier and so less demanding in terms of time. A related advantage is transparency—simple systems are easier to understand, and the impact of changes to them (for example, a proposed change in the rate) is easier to assess. And a flat tax should reduce the incentive to create or embrace schemes, often on the edge of legality, to conceal or massage part of one's income to avoid the higher marginal rates. This would indicate compliance advantages associated with a single proportionate rate.

These various practical advantages are relatively uncontroversial, and are generally accepted, even by those most strongly committed to progressive rates of income taxation. But they are not seen as compelling reasons for moving to a flat tax, and from here on in, the arguments are vigorously disputed.

How progressive income tax hurts those on lower incomes

As we have seen in earlier chapters, one argument commonly given for a single proportionate rate is that higher marginal rates are a disincentive to effort. As high income earners are often highly talented and productive people, or possess especially valuable and/or rare skills (as their ability to earn a high income commonly testifies) anything that leads them to reduce their effort represents a loss to the economy of a valuable resource. When the economy loses, we all lose.

But we saw in chapter 3 that it is also commonly argued that high marginal rates are an incentive to even greater effort by the highly talented and productive, for they have to work harder to secure a real rise in take-home pay. High marginal tax rates thus enable the economy to 'squeeze more pips from the juiciest lemons'.

Who is right? The answer is surely, neither and both. There is evidence some people respond by curtailing their effort, others by redoubling it. A perfect illustration is the different attitudes employees of the same firm may have to the offer of voluntary overtime. Some say it is not worth the effort, should it take them into a higher marginal tax bracket; others, on the same base income, actively seek it out at every opportunity. This clearly illustrates how difficult it is to give anything like precise weight to arguments about incentives. Different people in the same circumstances respond differently.[2]

A second practical argument against progressive income tax rates is that they are 'washed out' by the remuneration system. When employers and employees negotiate agreements on wages and salaries, they do so conscious of the progressive income tax scale. Boards of directors commonly defend the high salaries paid to senior executives on the ground that they are not really so high when you take into account the loss through high marginal income tax rates. Unions justify their wage demands for skilled workers in terms of the take-home amount; the amount left after taxation and other mandatory deductions are taken out of consideration. Thus bargaining and negotiating practice suggest that the gross wages and salaries paid to highly skilled, highly remunerated employees are higher than they would otherwise be, if these employees were not subject to higher marginal taxation rates.

Who pays these taxes? Although on paper they come from the employee, the employee's payment is largely compensated through the wage or salary level set. But the employer incurs the cost of a salary and wages bill higher than it would have been had the tax rate not been as high. The cost of payroll can be a significant business cost, and it is reflected in the final price charged for the goods or services the business produces. This means it is the consumers—those who purchase the goods or services delivered by the business—who end up paying the taxes. And since the price paid by the consumer does not vary according to the consumer's income, the progressive rates of income tax imposed on the employees of the business become a flat price component imposed on the consumers of its outputs. The progressiveness washes out through employee compensation and the pricing mechanism. A progressive income tax on higher earners morphs imperceptibly into what is in effect a flat consumption tax paid equally by all consumers.[3]

Of course, just as a disincentive to one person may be an incentive to another in comparable circumstances, so too, some income earners may be in a position to negotiate a higher wage or salary to compensate for higher rates of income tax while others may not. Furthermore, the argument about 'washing out' assumes that the total payroll for a firm whose employees are paying a flat proportion of their income in taxation will be lower than it would be if the employees were subject to progressive rates of income taxation, but this will in practice depend on the mix of salary levels within the organisation and on the income tax rate(s) set. But the key point about this argument is that it undermines the effectiveness of progressive rates of income taxation as a means for making the society 'more equal.' The intended equalising effects of progressive rates of income tax are defeated through the combined mechanism of compensatory salary setting and the fact that rich and poor consumers pay the same for most goods and services.[4]

A flat tax can be progressive

In the discussion so far it has been assumed that a flat tax cannot be progressive. However if the income tax system has a tax-free threshold, so that what is sometimes called a 'personal allowance' or 'subsistence allowance' is exempt from income taxation, the application of a flat tax to all taxable income above the threshold will necessarily be progressive in its impact, relative to total income.

If the rate is set at a flat proportion of taxable income, say 30%, then the proportion of each person's total income lost in tax will increase, the higher it is above the tax-free threshold. It will never reach 30% of total income, but will move closer and closer to that limit as total income rises. Low income earners whose total income is not far above the tax free threshold will lose a lot less than 30% in income tax. Thus in a flat tax system such as that proposed by John Humphreys (in chapter 9), where there is a 30% flat rate coupled with a $30,000 tax-free threshold, the resulting pattern of tax paid will be quite strongly progressive, for the higher one's total income, the greater the proportion lost in tax. While it is true that the first dollar over the tax free threshold is taxed at 30%, and that the last dollar over is also taxed at that rate, the proportion of total income lost in tax rises automatically with distance above the threshold. This rise is much smoother than that associated with familiar bracketed progressive tax, for every successive dollar earned above the threshold is taxed at a marginally higher rate than the previous dollar earned.

Flat tax purists argue that this smooth and shallow raked inclination of progressiveness (once the threshold is crossed) is objectionable, because it imposes a proportionately greater burden on higher income earners. Moreover because it is progressive the incentive for high income earners to conceal or disguise income remains, in order to reduce the proportion of total income lost in tax. The only way to avoid this is to abolish the tax-free threshold.

Abolition of the tax-free threshold carries the additional advantage that it allows the tax rate to fall. To achieve a given revenue target, the rate required will have to be higher if part of everyone's income is exempted from tax.[5] Taxpayers at-large pay a high price for a tax-free threshold. While it may well be politically difficult to abolish it, one can understand the reluctance of politicians to raise it to something credibly approximating the original idea of a bare individual subsistence allowance (see chapter 7 for further discussion of this issue).

Flat tax and vertical equity

It is generally agreed that justice and fairness require that an income tax system should embody horizontal and vertical equity. Expressed crudely, horizontal equity requires that taxpayers in comparable income circumstances be taxed comparably. Exceptions should only be of general application, that is, apply equally to all and only those who meet the conditions on which the exception is based, and be ethically fair in substance, as opposed to merely opportunistic or pragmatic. While not denying that comparability of circumstances requires judgement, and reasonable people can disagree in their judgements about whether particular circumstances are comparable, the jurisprudential principle behind it is straightforward. In its rejection of arbitrariness or capriciousness in the administration of the tax law it simply reflects the ancient doctrine of the rule of law, while its emphasis on comparability and the generality of exceptions reflects a key component of procedural justice—that like cases should be treated alike.

By contrast, vertical equity is equity not across the breadth of taxpayers, but through the range, low to high, of taxpayer incomes. While it is taxpayers who *pay* the tax, it is their *incomes* that are being taxed, and incomes are very different from one another. The corollary of the procedural justice principle requiring that like cases be treated alike is usually expressed, 'and unlike cases unlike, each in a way that is proportionate to its relevant difference(s)'. A high income is unlike a low income in size. Is this a relevant difference from the point of view of equitable taxation treatment? If it is, how does one reflect this difference in the way they are treated for taxation purposes, to ensure that the difference is treated proportionately? To answer these questions is to put forward a theory of vertical equity in the treatment of income tax.

Stated like that it seems obvious that the just way to tax incomes of different sizes would be through a flat proportional rate. Indeed, it would seem to be the arithmetically perfect mechanism for achieving vertical equity in a way that is procedurally just. However, there are three main arguments against this. For simplicity, they are treated here as discrete arguments, although in practice they are often bundled (critics would say muddled) together. None, in the end, is convincing.

Argument 1: Flat tax is unethical because it entails inequality of sacrifice

The first (considered by Davidson in chapter 4 in his discussion of the 'Equality of Sacrifice' principle) is that the value of each dollar in the hands of the earner is not equal. If this is correct, then—contrary to appearances—a flat proportionate tax is not procedurally just, and thus fails the test of vertical equity.

The assumption in this argument is that a low-income earner would miss the last dollar he or she earns more than would a high-income earner. But if we accept the logic of this argument, the only way of ensuring that the value of the last after tax dollar of the low-income earner is the same as that of the high-income earner would be through a tax regime that ensures absolute equality of net income. This may appeal to fanatical egalitarians, but would such a regime really implement equality of sacrifice? To claim that it did would be to insist that the person with the multi-million dollar annual income was being required to make precisely the same sacrifice as the person who was earning, say, $100 more than the uniform net income level. This is manifestly implausible.

In reality, how much a person misses the lost part of his or her income is not a function of the size of the loss, but depends upon the person's desires, tastes, ambitions and goals, their legal and personal commitments, and their social circumstances. Even if it were possible to measure the intensity of all of these variables on a common scale, the best we could get would be a highly individualised and subjective measure of felt loss. Income tax scales predicated on the need to achieve equality of felt loss would be unlikely to result in any two individuals with identical incomes being subject to the same income tax rates. And people with a large appetite for money would presumably cultivate a deep sense of loss at any deprivation, thus minimising their tax liability! If this is what is required to achieve vertical equity, then it could only be achieved by abandoning horizontal equity. Fortunately, such a world is not a practical possibility.

It seems that the only way of achieving an *objectively measurable* form of equality of sacrifice is through a flat proportionate tax rate without a tax-free threshold. No two taxpayers on different incomes sacrifice the same amount in tax, but every taxpayer sacrifices exactly the same proportion of his or her income as every other. If equality of sacrifice is one of the *desiderata* for an ethically sound income tax system, then a flat proportionate rate would appear to achieve it better than any of its rivals.

Argument 2: Flat tax is unethical because it harms those with least

The second argument against flat tax as the most ethical means for taxing incomes is that disparities in income are a bad thing, and progressive income tax rates represent an efficient mechanism for reducing such disparities. It is suggested, for example, that the 'income gap' between rich and poor means that those on the lowest incomes do not have enough to live a life of reasonable sufficiency and dignity. But while this may sometimes be true, it is not *necessarily* true, and it is not always *in fact* true. What is needed is to ensure that the lowest incomes are always, in real terms, above some agreed minimum threshold for reasonable sufficiency and dignity. Almost certainly, this will require tax transfers to those who would otherwise fall below the threshold, but this has no implication for *movements* in the size of the income gap, or the direction of its subsequent movements. Disparities of income do not necessarily imply that the lowest incomes will be inadequate by any reasonable standard, nor do they imply, if the lowest are in fact inadequate, that this can only be addressed by measures which reduce the income gap *over the medium to long term.*

Some advocates of strongly progressive taxation argue that a widening income gap is a bad thing, *even if it does not result in the lowest incomes falling below the threshold of reasonable adequacy.* The gap itself is bad. But why? Consider two different hypothetical societies A and B. In both these hypothetical societies, nobody's income is below whatever is taken as the base level of reasonable sufficiency. In Society A incomes range from a minimum of $50,000 per annum to a maximum of $70,000—a gap of $20,000. In Society B incomes range from a minimum of $50,000 to a maximum of $80,000—a gap of $30,000. Nobody in Society B is worse off than the worst off in Society A. But some people in Society B are markedly better off than anyone in Society A. Assuming both societies have the same number of people and all other morally significant factors are equal as between A and B, which is the better society? Society A has the narrowest income gap. But Society B has the greatest total wealth.

Now consider both societies in one year's time. Both make real material progress from which every income earner benefits (assume internal income relativities are evenly distributed and remain constant throughout). In Society A in one year's time (Society A+1) incomes now range from a lowest of $60,000 to a highest of $75,000. The income gap has been narrowed to $15,000 while its income floor has been raised by $10,000 and its ceiling by $5000. In Society B+1 incomes have also grown, now ranging from a minimum of $65,000 to a maximum of $110,000. But the income gap has widened, from $30,000 to $45,000. A year ago the income gap between lowest and highest in Society B was 50% greater than it was in Society A—now it is three times as much.

Consider the price the egalitarian is now paying. To prefer A+1 over B+1 is to say that reducing the income gap is to be preferred, even when it means not only the highest incomes but also the lowest incomes are lower than they are under an alternative scenario. Given a choice, the egalitarian not only prefers A to B, but prefers a transition from A to A+1, over a transition from B to B+1. Indeed, in terms of maximising social improvement, the egalitarian's preferred task would be to engineer a transition from Society B to Society A+1; this involves the maximum reduction in the income gap. It is doubtful whether anyone who experienced the transition from Society B to B+1 from within would agree.

In response, the egalitarian might argue that, although a society in which the gap between higher- and lower-income earners is increasing need not make low earners materially worse off, they nonetheless suffer a hurt of a non-economic kind, even if their material circumstances are improving. It could be contended that lower income earners *feel* they are making no progress, even if their material circumstances are improving (or even, if the gap between their income and that of higher earners is growing, that they *feel* that they are *going backwards*). The fact that their material circumstances are improving does not alter this feeling, for it is based on their perception of their relative income standing which is declining relative to the position of the highest earners. Objectively, they are better off in their materially absolute position, but worse off in their socially relative position.

How widespread are such feelings? For the sake of argument, let us assume that they are extremely common. The question then becomes, do they represent a compelling consideration in favour of a progressive income tax designed to do what a flat proportionate tax rate cannot do; namely narrow the net income gap between high and low earners, in such a way that low earners improve their relative position?

Sometimes we consider it appropriate to protect people's feelings by passing laws intended to reduce the chances of their feelings being hurt. Laws against offensive language recognise that in certain circumstances the hurt that people feel when demeaned by the words of others is something they should not have to suffer; so much so that it is worth imposing an appropriate legal restriction on the principle of freedom of expression. (Such laws also support a public good, namely civility of discourse.) In other cases we consider it less appropriate to 'pander' to people's hurt feelings. For example, policies that prevent the performance of school pupils being graded in terms of pass and fail, or ranked in order relative to one another, because this could damage the 'self esteem' of those who are failed or ranked near the bottom, are widely condemned by those outside the school systems. To critics, minimising hurt feelings in these circumstances is far less important than enabling parents, communities, and the children themselves to have maximum information about their performance relative to published standards and each other. In other words, we have to be satisfied that the price paid for preventing or reducing the incidence of hurt feelings in a particular context is worth it.

If we are to justify taxing high incomes in such a way that the relative position of those on lower incomes improves, it has to be because we consider that their feelings of treading water or being left behind—even when there is an absolute improvement in their material circumstances—are so bad that higher earners should pay the price for ensuring that these feelings do not occur. At the other extreme we might respond by saying, 'Just get over it.' After all, the mere existence of a feeling does not mean that the attitude or judgement grounded on it is justified. And Hayek suggests that the hurt feelings of low-income earners to which a progressive rate of income tax responds are really just feelings of envy:

> In the last resort the problem of progressive taxation is, of course, an ethical problem, and in a democracy the real problem is whether the support that the principle now receives would continue if the people fully understood how it operates. …That a majority should be free to impose a discriminatory tax burden on a minority; that, in consequence, equal services should be remunerated differently; and that for a whole class, merely because its incomes are not in line with the rest, the normal incentives should be practically made ineffective—all these are principles which cannot be defended on grounds of justice. If, in addition, we consider the waste of energy and effort which progressive taxation in so many ways leads to, it should not be impossible to convince reasonable people of its undesirability. Yet experience in this field shows how rapidly habit blunts the sense of justice and even elevates into a principle what in fact has no better basis than envy.[6]

Envy has been described as the most destructive of all of the seven deadly sins because it derives its satisfaction from seeing the object of envy stripped of the attribute which is the source of envy, even if nobody else, including the envious themselves, benefits as a result. John Stuart Mill called envy 'the most anti-social and evil of all passions'.[7] But it is envy that makes it attractive for politicians to promise to 'soak the rich' in order to finance their policies. Envy makes a progressive income tax system politically attractive because it guarantees that, however much a taxpayer is forfeiting, he or she can be consoled with the thought that there are others who are forfeiting proportionately more.[8]

If it is true that progressive rates of income tax defer to feelings of envy, then we can only conclude that respecting and reinforcing such feelings, far from overriding considerations of procedural justice, represents an ethically unacceptable basis for such a policy. To have one's envy triggered is not to suffer a non-economic hurt that must be ameliorated or as far as possible prevented. On the contrary envy is an all too common defect of character that we should do our very best to overcome.

There is another feeling easily confused with envy, namely resentment. It is manifest that people on modest incomes commonly resent the fact that there are others with incomes not only many times greater than theirs, but many times greater than anything within their prospects, no matter how long and hard they work. But this resentment-fuelled anger is directed selectively. When the very high earner is a sporting hero, rock star, novelist, or Hollywood celebrity, the resentment often disappears. But if that very high income is a salary paid to a chief executive officer of a major corporation or a senior government bureaucrat, then words like 'obscene' are hissed with undiluted venom.

Why do attitudes to high-income earners vary so dramatically? It seems that where the income is a reward for a personal performance the fruits of which are obvious to all, resentment diminishes or disappears. But where the high earner's personal contribution is a contribution to the work of an organisation, possibly through the discharge of onerous leadership responsibilities, resentment levels rise. Most consumers have no idea who company executives are, what they do, or what the relationship is between their contribution and the goods or services the consumers eventually buy. If an entertainer's earnings are not 'obscene', while those of senior corporate executives are, this has little to do with the quantum of the income, but rather reflects our understanding and knowledge of the way very high incomes are earned.

Resentment is not the same as envy, and I would suggest that resentment, more than envy, is the attitude to which politicians pander when they defend high marginal tax rates on higher earners. To feel resentment is to feel hurt or offended by the apparently more favourable treatment of someone with whom one regards oneself as comparable. It often takes the form of a felt sense of injustice or unfairness. This explains why the rock star's high income is not a source of resentment (except possibly among other rock wannabes), while the corporate executive's high income often is (because many people in positions lower down the hierarchy feel that their contribution is almost as vital).

Unlike envy, resentment is grounded in a sense that someone else has been awarded an advantage on a basis that is unfair or unjust, relative to one's own position. Accordingly, the feeling of resentment is based in the judgement that the advantage enjoyed by the other is unethical—not in the sense that the beneficiary has behaved unethically, but because the person, or the system, that has conferred that advantage is ethically defective. Given that felt resentment, unlike envy, has an apparently ethical source, does this mean that it is something that should be addressed through a progressive tax scale?

The answer, once again, is no. First of all, the fact that someone's advantage seems to arise from conduct which *appears* unethical does not mean that it is unethical. Moreover, the enterprise of trying to establish what has been called comparative wage justice on an objective basis, or equal pay for work of equal value, is one that has repeatedly failed. For all its imperfections, we really have nothing more robust for the pricing of work than an open and well-informed market, and it is inevitable that such a market will price some tasks at levels that surprise. Third, even if some of these surprises are deemed unacceptable, they cannot be addressed by progressivism in the income tax scale, for this relates only to the quantum of the income and cannot discriminate between two incomes of identical amounts, even if it is agreed that one is justly based and the other not. The only way of avoiding such an outcome is through a centralised wages and salaries system under which all wages and salaries are set according to a non-market judgement as to the value of the work performed. History shows conclusively that such a system is simply unworkable.

The upshot is that feelings of resentment based on disparities of income, even when it is thought that such felt hurts do merit being addressed, provide no basis for introducing progressivism into rates of income tax.

Argument 3: Flat tax is unethical because it violates 'social justice'

Nobody would seriously argue for or defend a *maldistribution* of material wealth—that is, a distribution which is the traceable consequence of wrongdoing in the acquisition and/or transfer of material wealth. To the extent that it is practically possible to track and allocate responsibility for such wrongdoing, justice demands restitution and/or compensation, together with retributive punishment where appropriate.

But some people argue there can be a distribution of material wealth which is socially unjust, even though this distribution is in no significant way the result of wrongdoing. They claim that large and growing inequalities in the distribution of material wealth violate any reasonable standard of distributive justice even if they are not a consequence of wrongdoing.[9] Is this argument sustainable?

Take a simple hypothetical example. Imagine there is perfect equality in the distribution of wealth, including equality of incomes, and that nobody steals, cheats, deceives or knowingly hurts or disadvantages their fellows. How long would it be before inequalities in material wealth emerged? One act of generosity, or one act of love expressed through material benefaction, would be enough to reintroduce inequality. Moreover, some people like, and therefore value, some things more than others. Through barter and trade, based on their subjective valuations, further inequalities in wealth would emerge. Clearly, even in a society of perfectly virtuous equals, material inequality will swiftly arise and grow.

As Robert Nozick points out, controlling the growth in inequality would therefore require perpetual state intervention to cancel out all new disparities as quickly as possible. The level of intervention required to contain inequalities, *whatever* the breadth of the proposed tolerance range, must be comprehensive, wide ranging and incessant. Starting with an initial distribution of wealth which is perfectly equal and more than adequate for anyone's needs, we will progress inexorably, solely by conduct that is ethically impeccable, to a distributive outcome which those who believe in 'distributive justice' will condemn.

In the real world it is true that much inequality results from wrongdoing, but much does not. It arises from differences in personal taste, frugality, affections and the way we choose to express them, propensity to illness, luck, and our differing subjective valuations of all that life has to offer, material and immaterial. It is to counteract these, and not just wrongdoing, that the forces of the state animated by the ideal of minimising distributive inequality must be directed. Is it really worth it? And is it really 'just'?

Consider an analogy discussed by Nozick.[10] Suppose that advances in organ transplant technology continue rapidly so that rejection is no longer a problem. The marginal loss of one kidney suffered by a person with two perfectly healthy ones would then clearly be very much smaller than the marginal gain to someone with two failed kidneys, of receiving one healthy one. Does this mean that the healthiest and fittest people should be required, in the name of 'distributive justice,' to contribute their 'surplus organs' to a central organ bank so that those most in need can benefit?

No doubt some utilitarians would say they should, but this is just another example of utilitarianism (or 'moral rationalism') yielding counter-intuitive results. Most of us probably feel revulsion at this idea. Is this based simply on the fact that we feel more 'attached' to our organs and bodily parts than we do to our money? One dollar is as good as any other, but my kidneys are special because they are parts *of me*. This feeling of personal integrity may well be part of the explanation, but it is not the whole of it.

In addition, there is a sense that the healthy and fit are *no more responsible* for the plight of those in medical need than are those of good or average health. Indeed, this is not an issue of responsibility at all.

Moral responsibility may be either historic or assumed. You are historically responsible for something only if you *caused* it, whether by act or omission, and you are morally responsible, in this historic sense, only if you caused it voluntarily and with an understanding of the likely consequences. You are responsible for something in the assumed sense if you are obliged to deal with it (for example, by maintaining it or correcting it, as appropriate), although you were not historically responsible for it. Where this obligation is a moral obligation (as opposed to, for example, a legal duty, a duty of your office, or a regulatory requirement) then you are morally responsible for dealing with it.

An assumed responsibility for something does not presuppose a historic responsibility for it; indeed it typically assumes its absence. Contrary to some of the rhetoric, those who are well-to-do in an open market economy are not (with some spectacular individual exceptions) historically responsible for the plight of the poor. Likewise the very healthy have no historic responsibility for the plight of those with organs or bodily parts in need of replacement unless they deliberately or with culpable negligence caused them injury. Our moral obligation to assist the poor to achieve an income of sufficient adequacy and dignity is an assumed responsibility. It derives fundamentally from our status as fellow citizens of the same community who together have the capacity to lift them over the line.

Assumed responsibilities have nothing whatsoever to do with distributive justice, or indeed justice in any form at all. Recognition that another has a fundamental need that is beyond their power to meet naturally begets sympathy or compassion. And sympathy in turn prompts acts of generosity to assist in meeting that need. It is this natural sympathy generalised that ultimately drives the emergence, and eventual acceptance, of the idea of a shared willingness of those above the threshold to *assume* responsibility for those below. But we must be clear that the proposition that the position of those below the threshold is *unjust,* or that their being permitted to remain in that position is an *injustice*, forms no part of the argument, and adds nothing of substance to it. The moral obligation to assist those in need derives *from* the assumption of responsibility, not the reverse, and the ultimate foundation of this assumption is sympathy. It is our heart that rules our head.

When it comes to those whose needs can only be met by the supply of vital or very important bodily organs or parts from among the living, our sympathy is just as real, but insofar as there is an assumption of responsibility it expresses itself only in terms of financial support–the supply of the organs and parts themselves is seen as wholly within the realm of private generosity of a highly commendable sort. Once again, it is simply wrong to suggest that whatever we may do to support those with a desperate need for bodily parts and organs is founded on justice. Their suffering is not an injustice, and its correction or amelioration is not the remedying of an injustice. Exceptional circumstances aside, the person in need—whatever that need may be for, and whatever may be necessary to address it—is not therefore the victim of some form of *distributive injustice*. It follows that there can be no claim founded on justice for access to the ethically acquired resources of those who have the capacity to assist in meeting it. That claim is justified only if the person to whom it is directed is *responsible* for the need (whether the responsibility be historical or assumed) and therefore has a moral obligation to address it. All else is generosity and charity.

Conclusion

Those who advocate a flat tax as understood in this paper are commonly ridiculed as advocating the economic equivalent of 'flat Earth science', or for lacking compassion and betraying callous indifference to social justice. But the upshot of the arguments reviewed in this chapter—many of which have bounced around the literature in various forms for much of the last century—is that it is *progressivism* in rates of income tax that cannot be squared with the demands of justice.

We have seen that, on the face of it, a flat proportionate rate of income tax meets the requirements of procedural justice with text book arithmetical perfection. It involves treating like cases alike, and unlike cases differently, each in proportion to their relevant difference(s). It is commonly claimed that a flat tax is unacceptable because it is regressive, but this is a misunderstanding. Prior to his re-election in October 2004, for example, Prime Minister John Howard conceded that the highest marginal rate of personal income tax was 'too high', but said he would stop short of supporting a flat tax 'because it is regressive'. But the Prime Minister was wrong. Regression is the contrary, not the contradictory, of progression. A flat proportionate tax rate is neither progressive nor regressive. That is precisely why it is just.

In this chapter we have reviewed (and dismissed) arguments designed to show that a single proportionate rate violates the requirement of procedural justice (for example, by violating the ethical requirement for equality of sacrifice), and we have seen that income disparities do not harm lower income recipients, either absolutely or relatively, in any way that warrants introduction of progressivism into the income tax scale. Nor is there a credible case for maintaining that the requirements of procedural justice should be displaced by a prior requirement of 'social justice'. If these arguments are sound, there is no strong logical or moral case for progressive taxation. The problems are more political.

In the revolutionary situation that followed the collapse of the Soviet Union, a number of the former constituent republics opted for a flat rate of personal income tax. Russia (for most categories of income) has a flat rate of 13%, Latvia 25% with no tax-free threshold, and Estonia 26% with a small tax-free threshold.[11] But in Australia, the political obstacles in the path of the introduction of a flat tax remain formidable.

Politicians worry that switching to a flat tax would involve increasing taxes to the lowest earners while slashing them for the highest. They have a point; as it involves replacing a progressive rate, the savings to very high earners would be spectacularly greater than the income forgone by the lowest earners, and it is understandable that rational politicians might be loathe to try persuading the electorate that this is acceptable. If everything else was left as it is, including the tax-free threshold[12] and the current income tax revenue target, we would have to set a flat rate at a level which would involve a big jump in the tax rate for low- to middle-income earners (this is hardly surprising, given Sinclair Davidson's estimate in chapter 4 that more than 64% of income tax revenue comes from just 25% of taxpayers). Even those who embrace the logic of the case for a flat tax argue that the pain to the lowest earners involved in making this transition is so great that it outweighs the advantages of changing to a just system. Nor is there any great clamour for change. Even those who currently pay the highest marginal rates do not seem to grumble very audibly, and some think, wrongly, that the disproportionate burden placed upon their income is 'only fair'. No wonder the political instinct is to leave well enough alone.

The only politically conceivable way of making the change from a progressive to a flat income tax rate in Australia is in the context of a comprehensive review of all taxation. The history of the Australian Goods and Services Tax (GST) shows how quickly a tax option can change from a dead duck never to be revisited, to a credible political option, to something that is accepted and unchallenged by all major political parties. The fact that a flat rate of personal income tax, for all its jurisprudential merits in terms of justice, now seems to reside in a political no-go zone, should not blind us to the possibility that these perceptions could shift relatively quickly.

But if a practicable case for changing to a flat tax is to be developed, it is imperative that a number of other issues be considered at the same time. There must, for example, be a hard look at all of the deductions, rebates, credits and offsets that so complicate the income tax system. While there is a strong case for retention of deductions relating to costs reasonably incurred in order to generate the income in question, the case is not nearly as powerful in relation to those tax concessions which are intended to achieve specific socio-political objectives. We must also question the repeated assumption that personal income tax reform should be 'revenue neutral' (meaning that the total revenue available to government as a result of reform should be neither greater nor less than it is now).

Even if we accept that the total revenue collection should not go up or down as a result of reform, it does not follow that the share of it derived from personal income tax must remain constant. To take just one option, it is worth recalling that the GST as originally canvassed was proposed at 15%, not the current 10%, and the concessions and exemptions originally proposed, and compromised out as a condition of Senate acceptance, were far more limited. Removing exemptions and concessions would increase the share of total revenue derived from a much fairer GST with lower compliance costs. Increasing the rate from 10 to 12.5%, with the additional 2.5% retained by the Commonwealth, would also take some pressure off the share of government revenue derived from personal income tax.

Ultimately however the challenge is to reduce the total government revenue target. This means raising the justificatory bar for every area of government spending, including a more full blooded approach to privatisation, with government funding focused much more sharply on supporting those in need to have affordable access to quality services, rather than government providing these services itself.

We shall see in chapter 6 that the integrity of the tax system is essential to the maintenance of a regime of predominantly voluntary compliance. Integrity applies not only to its day-to-day administration, but to the ethical principles governing the elements and instruments with which compliance is required. Progressivism in the rate of income tax demonstrably violates the requirement of vertical equity which is founded on the jurisprudential principle of procedural justice. A flat proportionate rate—uniquely—does not, and that is the fundamental reason why it is worth all the trouble of pursuing it.

Chapter 6

Tax Complexity And The Rule Of Law[1]

Geoffrey de Q. Walker

The importance for national prosperity of sound institutions of government, and especially of the rule of law, is well understood today. *The Australian Law Journal* notes that 'Institutional economics has established a high correlation between economic growth and the rule of law'.[2] Research indicates that most of the international variation in income per capita—perhaps as much as 85%—can be explained by the institutions and policies countries adopt.[3]

Equally well appreciated is the quasi-constitutional nature of tax law. It is the primary link between a nation's citizens and their government, a window into the nation's views about justice and civic society.[4] The Nobel laureate James Buchanan points out that part of its quasi-constitutional character comes from the fact that it remains in force, with minor variations, over a sequence of budgetary periods,[5] as well as electoral cycles. But it goes beyond that. Revenue law and policy played a central role in the evolution of Western constitutional democracy, not least because it triggered the three great constitutional revolutions—the English, the American and the French. Australia's only popular uprising, the 1854 Eureka rebellion, is generally regarded as a tax revolt. The United States experience with the income tax levied to finance the war of independence—which Jefferson attacked on the ground that it required the government to wage a war against the people to collect it—led the constitutional framers to deny Congress the power to impose an income tax, a power it did not receive until the 16th Amendment was passed in 1913.[6]

Economist Joseph Schumpeter once said that a people's spirit is written in its fiscal history, 'stripped of all phrases'. In like vein, the historian Charles Adams views the whole history of organised society as a series of events in which government increases its tax burden beyond what taxpayers are willing to stand. That then leads to taxpayer revolt, violence and drastic changes in the structure of society.[7] On that view, the state of a nation's tax system is a good pointer to its social and political future.

The Australian tax system displays a range of symptoms suggesting a virtual collapse of the rule of law. Those symptoms include the flourishing cash economy which, at an estimated 15% of GDP, is one of the developed world's largest and equivalent to New Zealand's entire economy.[8] An underground economy of that magnitude requires the involvement not only of many businesses, but also of millions of consumers, who apparently believe that the greater spending power they can achieve through cash discounts is worth more than the duty to comply with a law they obviously consider unworthy of respect.

Another symptom is the growing irrelevance of the law and its institutions. Tax advisers display increasing signs of disorientation in trying to cope with a body of law that the late Federal Court Justice Graham Hill, then a leading tax barrister, in 1987 described as 'unintelligible'.[9] Normal legal advice is problematic because otherwise lawful arrangements can be overridden through the semi-subjective appraisals of purpose creeping into the application of Part IVA of the Commonwealth Income Tax Assessment Act 1936. The High Court now seldom grants leave to appeal in federal tax cases, as if it had given up hope of keeping the tax system subject to legal principle and normal adjudication methods, despite revenue law's constitutional importance.

The present state of the rule of law in the federal tax arena stems from a number of immediate causes. These causes can also be viewed as symptoms because, as general systems theory tells us, effects have a tendency to feed back into the causation process.[10]

The volume and uncertainty of tax legislation

The sheer quantity and ever-changing content of tax legislation is undermining its ability to command general obedience. That is partly because of the practical difficulty of knowing what the law is and what it means. Before the High Court in the *First Uniform Tax Case*[11] needlessly gave the Commonwealth a monopoly (at first *de jure,* later *de facto*) of income taxation, the relevant federal legislation occupied 81 pages in the statute book. Now it has exploded to 8,500 pages, or 13,500 pages if one includes fringe benefits, capital gains and superannuation provisions. It has been estimated that if tax legislation were to keep growing at the present rate, it would cover 830 billion pages by the end of the century and would take three million years to read.

The sheer mass and continual amendment of this legislation, coupled with the hazardous interplay of lengthy and widely scattered definitions and deeming provisions, make predictable interpretation and reliable advice next to impossible. The Australian Tax Office (ATO) assessors themselves can understand only a small part of it. Even in 1987, Justice Hill, having described much of the legislation as 'unintelligible', went on to say that 'Many provisions in the legislation are not applied for the simple reason that no one is able to comprehend them'.[12] While the rule of law does not require that all laws be applied all the time,[13] beyond a certain point non-application creates a risk that normally unused provisions will be enforced for discriminatory or arbitrary purposes. That kind of uncertainty is inimical to productive investment and growth.

Behind the vast volume of actual legislation looms an equally massive bulk of ATO public determinations, public rulings, bulletins, interpretative decisions, policy papers, circulars, administrative guidelines and practice statements. Some of these are expressed to be binding on ATO officers, and, in general, staff (no doubt prudently) rely on these sources rather than on the legislation, thereby giving them in practice something close to the force of law. In perhaps 90% of cases these materials are consistent with the enacted law, but in the remainder, the ATO is effectively making its own rules. In generating this mountain of administrative norms the ATO may be doing little more than trying to make an unworkable law work. But the net result is to add to the system's unfathomable obscurity.

Uncertainty in the law is a major factor in undermining the rule of law, and tax is riddled with it. That stems in part from the legislation's sheer volume and detail,[14] for which the Treasury is usually blamed, and in part from such inherently indeterminate provisions as the general anti-avoidance rule (GAAR) in Part IVA.[15] Even the most punctilious compliance with all applicable specific provisions is liable to be second-guessed, and perhaps nullified, by the ATO or the courts under Part IVA. Purposive interpretation is thwarted when no clear principle underlies the law, as when the legislature uses tax incentives to promote objectives other than revenue raising.[16]

As Lord Oliver has pointed out, where there are legal rules in an area without a clear moral imperative, the rules must be clear.[17] On the question of tax law's moral content, Justice Learned Hand was blunter: '(N)obody owes any public duty to pay more than the law demands. Taxes are enforced exactions, not voluntary contributions. To demand more in the name of morals is mere cant'.[18] Whatever moral force the legislation may have is undermined when its complexity and ambiguity make outcomes depend, not on working out the right answer, but on inside knowledge, administrative concessions or luck.[19]

The attitude of many taxpayers (other than the wretched conscripts of the PAYG army) is increasingly to treat the law and the courts as irrelevant. Legal advice leaves them unmoved. All they really want is an ATO ruling that will protect them from penalties or prosecution. Many just surrender and let the government have its way. 'A common comment by corporates now', observes KPMG's Michael Evans, 'is, "I know I'm not getting it right but if the Tax Office wants to come out and go through everything and tell me where I've underpaid, I'll pay it because that is cheaper than putting a process in place to comply with it."'[20] We have come a long way—from John Hampden and 'the rights of Englishmen'[21] to Part IVA and hopeless resignation.

Taxpayers and their advisers repeatedly plead for tax law to be made shorter and clearer. Unfortunately, if other factors are held constant, it may be hard to have both. A tax act that is shorter and simpler may not be clearer or more certain—the legislation's stupefying detail is, after all, an attempt at certainty.[22] On the other hand, the revenue lobby (comprising the ATO, the Treasury and their allies in politics, academia, the media and the welfare industry) are less perturbed. They realise that the law's very uncertainty and incomprehensibility advances their agenda, because it enables the tax authorities to offer taxpayers the predictability they need for long-term planning and adjustment in exchange for somewhat heavier assessments. As Geoffrey Brennan and James Buchanan point out, 'If government can succeed in keeping taxpayers off balance in their planning, additional revenue potential may be available for exploitation.'[23] In other words, the government can run a kind of protection racket, offering immunity in exchange for larger tax payments than the law, properly construed, might require.

Others such as Payne, however, see a very different kind of advantage in the complexity of tax legislation: '(T)ax complexity has a positive role to play in our national evolution. It is history's way of telling us that we have the wrong system for raising funds for public purposes—and compelling us to find another'.[24]

Statutory Discretions: Wagging the dog?

A further symptom of the law's growing irrelevance in the tax field is the swelling number of wide statutory discretions granted to the commissioner.

Such discretions are not new. An early example from 1964 was s 99A of the Income Tax Assessment Act (ITAA), which left it to the commissioner to decide in certain circumstances whether a person should be required to pay tax on trust income at a higher or a lower rate. Over time such provisions have multiplied: in 1973 came s 80DA (prior year losses), in 1981 s 102AE(6) (non arm's-length transactions), and in 1984 the discretionary penalty remission provisions in s 222. By 1982 the trend was arousing concern, with Chief Justice Street of New South Wales pointing out the unequal bargaining positions of citizen and bureaucrat in litigation, with its tendency to enhance the power of the bureaucracy and make it more authoritarian in its dealings with the public.[25]

The ultimate grant of discretionary power is Part IVA, enacted in 1981, to which the rest of the Act is subject. Australia has placed more reliance on the GAAR than any other Western democracy,[26] and Part IVA's supporters argue that it may strengthen the rule of law by increasing compliance with tax legislation.[27] The problem, however, is that it seeks to encourage compliance by means that compromise the rule of law, for example by depending on discretion and opinion.[28]

Part IVA enables the ATO to alter the scope of the tax law, to impose what amounts to a tax by analogy where none was imposed by the statute. It can declare after the event how much tax is to be paid without saying it in advance.[29] There is also a problem in ensuring that in reaching these decisions the ATO applies only relevant criteria,[30] not least in view of the commissioner's policy of targeting taxpayers he considers to be 'aggressive' in their tax planning. Quite apart from that, Professor Jeffrey Waincymer argues, this approach 'offends against the separation of powers doctrine and the requirement that laws be made by parliament not bureaucrats'.[31]

The ATO's exercise of its discretions may be reviewable by a court but, quite apart from the difficulty of persuading a court to overrule a discretionary ATO decision when the burden of proof is reversed as in Part IVA appeals, vesting a wide discretion in a court is no great improvement on vesting it in an executive official. Professor Waincymer has warned that in Part IVA 'too many key policy questions have been left for judges to answer'.[32]

Judicial review serves the rule of law when courts apply known rules and principles, not when their decisions may turn on their opinion about someone's purposes[33] or on policy questions, and when the result may be to disapply explicit statutory provisions. Sir Harry Gibbs considered that Part IVA's discretionary power to override other provisions of the Act 'amount(s) to an abandonment of the rule of law'.[34] Neither Britain nor the United States has a GAAR, and practitioners from those countries aver that the rule of law has survived relatively well in their tax systems.

Another site of discretionary power is to be found in the commissioner's powers of settlement and compromise, which are described in the ATO's *Code of Settlement Practice* and in its *Receivables Policy*. Resting on the general provisions of s 8 of the ITAA 1936 and s 3A of the Taxation Administration Act 1953, these powers give effect to the 'good management rule', an accepted principle in revenue law that recognises the need to make efficient and sensible use of the ATO's resources. Particularly in relation to advance pricing agreements, the exercise of these powers carries the risk that the ATO may make arrangements with a taxpayer that operate outside the law, a possibility that became reality in the United Kingdom in the *Fayed* case.[35] In Australia, the settlement and compromise powers have so far worked reasonably well, but their existence adds to the growing irrelevancy of the law.

The grant of wide discretions on this scale has two main consequences for the rule of law. First, it conflicts with both the principle of legal certainty and the principle of equality before the law. It becomes harder for citizens to plan ahead if they have no sure way of ascertaining what their future tax liability will be (subject to the rulings system, of which more in a moment), while the discretions are so wide that there is no assurance that similar cases will be treated in a similar way. Secondly, broad discretions threaten the constitutional principle that no tax should ever be laid that has not been specifically authorised by parliament. That principle was established by John Hampden in his resistance to paying ship-money in 1637 and later reasserted, in different ways, in both the French and American revolutions. In Edmund Burke's words, 'Would twenty shillings have ruined Mr Hampden's fortune? No! But the payment of half twenty shillings, on the principle it was demanded, would have made him a slave'.[36] Thus A L Goodhart, writing in 1958, thought it self-evident that 'It would be a gross violation of a basic constitutional principle if Parliament were to give any Minister discretion in a matter relating to taxation'.[37]

The rise of the ATO as deciding authority

A third symptom of the growing irrelevance of the law is the growing ascendancy of the Australian Taxation Office as the final authority, combining aspects of the executive, judicial and even legislative roles. Only the largest corporations and wealthiest taxpayers can now afford to challenge an ATO decision in court or otherwise seek judicial review. The Administrative Appeals Tribunal operates a low-cost appeal system for assessments below $5000, but for larger amounts the cost of an AAT review can be as high as for a court hearing. For most citizens today, the best source of 'legal' certainty is an ATO ruling. The ATO knows this and encourages the attitude behind it by offering safe harbour to the taxpayer tempest-tossed on a sea of dubiety.

Under the system of self-assessment, itself made necessary by the inability of tax assessors to keep up with the flood of amendments and case-law, some form of binding ruling procedure was essential if any reliable predictions of tax liability were to be possible. Hence the introduction in 1992 of the present public and private rulings regime,[38] embodying dispensing powers of such scope as to make a James II sob with envy.

Useful though it is in present conditions, the rulings system has adverse consequences. One is that it weakens the separation of powers. A central tenet of that doctrine is that it must not be possible to change the law at the point of application. That ensures that the judicial function determines the citizen's rights by reference to previously enunciated legal rules and principles rather than by personal opinions or extraneous policy considerations.

The system of binding rulings puts the ATO in the position of giving effectively final determinations, thereby intruding into the judicial function and making the ATO judge in its own cause. At the same time it overlaps into the legislative role,[39] as in the system of internal directives described above, or when we see the ATO laying down what look very much like statutory rules, as in the case of limited recourse loans in *Firth*.[40] During the Boucher era the commissioner occasionally went so far as to announce that the ATO was proposing to 'amend the law' in some way.

Some tax commentators deprecate the role of the separation of powers in the revenue context and would prefer the roles of the three branches to be seen as a mere 'specialisation of functions', with the courts and the legislature 'simply play(ing) different roles in the policy-making process'.[41] 'The role of judges in tax cases should be to decide what result would reflect the most sensible tax policy'.[42] But there can never be that kind of collaboration or overlap among the three branches of government. The rule of law needs a degree of tension between them in order to ensure impartial enforcement and independent adjudication.

If those separation lines become blurred, as they have following the expansion of the ATO's role, other consequences will start to appear. Under such a system, Professor Waincymer points out, 'There is also no guarantee that the administrator will be impartial, fair or would appropriately balance the interests of taxpayers against the interests of revenue collection'.[43] On the contrary, there is good reason to fear that constant government pressure on the ATO to maximise collections will have the opposite effect. One sees this in emerging double standards, as when the ATO applies Part IVA when it considers an arrangement to be outside the 'spirit' of the legislation (as the ATO interprets that 'spirit'), but when the GAAR produces an unintended liability, commitment to the spirit of the law is discarded in favour of strictly literal interpretation. Again, while a concessional ruling is welcome to the parties, it can cause resentment in others who are not similarly favoured. Both these developments create a feeling that equality before the law is being compromised and strengthen perceptions of unfairness.

The advent of staff performance bonuses is unlikely to improve matters.[44] The practice of remunerating tax officers according to the amount of revenue they collect recalls the 18th century tax-farming abuses that helped to trigger the French Revolution. It may tend to weaken the principle of even-handed enforcement which, like equality before the law, is an important element of the rule of law.[45]

Heavy reliance on bureaucratic rulings has given rise to corruption in some Third World countries. And as we know from the allegations in a pending criminal case, that Third World phenomenon may have landed on our shores, an alarming development given the historical rarity of blatant bribery in Australian state and federal government.

The constitutional wilderness

The erosion over recent decades of vital constitutional and juristic principles has brought us to an anomic state in which the law has lost its intelligibility, certainty and predictability, where the executive government exercises legislative and quasi-judicial powers, the judiciary exercises policy-making powers, where rights effectively turn on opinions about a citizen's purposes, where the principles of impartial enforcement and equality before the law are undermined and where, in a variety of ways, the law is changed at the point of application. The notion that the courts should give effect to government policy, which was banished by *Entick v Carrington*[46] in 1765, is starting to return in areas such as GAAR, with the encouragement of some commentators.[47] The nation's highest court seems to have all but abandoned the federal tax field as doctrinally unrewarding[48] and scholarly writers have concluded that it is no longer possible to write a treatise identifying authoritative principles in Australia's federal tax law.[49]

The result is that the tax system can now scarcely be called 'law' at all rather than direct bureaucratic rule. While the law does retain vestiges of its role—judicial review would still prevent totally arbitrary treatment, such as a higher rate for blue-eyed taxpayers—for most citizens the judicial system and the traditional analysis of legal rights in the tax arena[50] are irrelevant. Some commentators take a relaxed view of that trend. Professor Graeme Cooper, for example, speculates:

> whether the rule of law is still important in the tax context. For example, the rule of law might be a value that should be given absolute primacy in cases where the curtailment of personal freedoms, or the expropriation of property without some attempt at lawful justification is threatened. But might it be appropriate to modify or circumscribe its application in a tax context . . . ?[51]

That would be a perilous step. The constitutional importance of tax law as a template for the relationship between government and citizen is widely recognised. Even Justice Lionel Murphy warned that vesting tax officials with more and more discretion 'may well lead to tax laws capable, if unchecked, of great oppression'.[52] Further, governments may use tax laws as the vehicle for the wider erosion of civil liberties. The Hawke government exploited an alleged 'crisis' of tax avoidance as a pretext for introducing compulsory ID cards, that recurring dream of elitists and authoritarians everywhere.[53] When the necessary implementing regulations were blocked by the Senate, the government dropped the idea and little more was heard of the tax avoidance 'crisis'.

Enforcement versus resistance

The Commonwealth's approach to avoidance and the underground economy has been to attack selected symptoms. The PAYG system and the GST have set off in pursuit of part of the cash services sector. Discretionary powers and Part IVA lie in wait for those who do not cleave to the spirit of the law, and Australia has placed more reliance on GAAR than any other Western democracy, to the detriment of more fundamental tax reform.[54] But for all that, the front-line has not moved far. Increasing the authorities' enforcement zeal, research into the psychology of taxation reveals, may be counterproductive if it fails simultaneously to deal with underlying causes. More effective policing may in fact cause more effective resistance by worsening attitudes,[55] and heavier penalties will only multiply the number of appeals.

Just as the symptoms approach to avoidance and evasion has produced disappointing gains and unintended consequences, merely targeting the specific anti-rule of law phenomena described above will not be enough to heal our institutions of government. Cutting back discretions, confining the ATO and the courts to their constitutional provinces and ending Part IVA's flirtation with imputed subjective purpose[56] will not reinstate the rule of law. The Taxpayer's Charter and the Inspector-General of Taxation will do little more than prevent or put out spot fires without mitigating the underlying problem. Simultaneously making the legislation substantially simpler, shorter and clearer—goals favoured on all sides—may be an unattainable objective.

The symptom-oriented approach will only ensure that the problems of evasion, avoidance and pathological administration will reappear in some other form, such as emigration, leisure substitution and the storming of the remaining shelters, such as negative gearing or the financing of ghastly motion pictures. That will follow inevitably if reform disregards the basic dynamic of federal taxation in Australia today. That dynamic is the irreconcilable confrontation between the two opposing forces of enforcement and resistance. Let us consider each in turn.

(a) Enforcement.

Economists and political scientists used to interpret the revenue-raising process through the 'benevolent despot' model, under which the institutions of power were assumed to act in the 'public interest'. Government was seen as raising revenue to the extent needed to pay for a suitable list of public goods. If citizens conscientiously paid their tax and a surplus resulted, government would reward them with a tax cut.

That perspective was associated with the public finance theories of such economists as Francis Edgeworth and A C Pigou. It was first questioned by the Norwegian scholar Knut Wicksell, who complained that it 'seem(ed) to have retained the assumptions of its infancy, in the 17th and 18th centuries, when absolute power ruled almost all Europe.' It was also criticised as being 'unmotivated', and thus unconvincing: it offered no reason why governments or rulers would be motivated to use their power to advance the public interest rather than their own.[57]

A model that would explain public finance in the context of a modern mass democracy was thus needed. It was supplied by public choice theory, which is essentially the application of economics to political science,[58] and which posits that politicians and bureaucrats act from the same motives of self-interest as everyone else. 'The State is not the agency that nobly and conveniently steps in to correct the supposed deficiencies of the free market', writes Professor Gary Anderson, 'but a giant rent-seeking machine that provides coercive wealth transfers to the highest bidder (albeit in a fairly efficient market)'.[59]

Public choice economics has replaced the benevolent despot theory with the model of government as a Leviathan that spends up to the limit of its revenue-raising capacity. This view, magisterially enunciated by Professor Geoffrey Brennan of ANU and the Nobel laureate James Buchanan, [60]offers a much better explanation of contemporary reality and has annihilated the old benevolent despot view among most economists.[61]

The public choice perspective points out that normal electoral processes are insufficient to restrain self-seeking governments and bureaucracies. The authors note that the tax revolt in the United States began in 1979 with Proposition 13, a California citizen-initiated referendum measure. It emerged from outside the normal parliamentary processes and inter-party competition, in the face of opposition from most of the political and media establishment.[62]

(b) Resistance.

There will always be some people who will break even the fairest tax laws. But today's trench warfare between non-compliance and government arbitrariness is a comparatively recent phenomenon that dates only from the 1970s.[63] The 1950s and 1960s, one perplexed commentator observes, were marked by an 'almost sheep-like taxpayer compliance' that mysteriously broke down in the next decade.[64] Apart from illustrating the academic tendency to portray the Australian people as somewhat less than human, this account overlooks the crucial development that transformed taxpayer attitudes. That was the ravaging inflation unleashed by Frank Crean's 1973 and 1974 federal budgets which distorted the established tax scales out of recognition and vastly increased the burden of government on the people. That may have been the intention,[65] though the government of the day tried to make it look like an accident. Those distorted scales remain substantially uncorrected to this day.

Until the massive bracket creep (or gallop) of the 1970s, most people complied with the tax laws, partly because they considered them reasonably fair, and partly because non-compliance did not pay—the relatively minor savings obtainable did not warrant the costs and risks involved. Thus, taxpayer compliance was rewarded with reasonable tax laws; or, more accurately, reasonable tax laws were rewarded with taxpayer compliance.

Unfairness in a tax system threatens compliance. Australians see the present federal tax system as unfair for two reasons. First, the rich are able to avoid tax in ways unavailable to earners whose tax is deducted from their wages. Secondly, income tax rates are too high. During the 1980s in Australia, the revenue lobby succeeded in diverting the political-media debate almost exclusively onto the first of these complaints, but it is the second (which was almost never mentioned) which directly affects and influences most people. That is still the case today.

The result of this neglect of the issue of high taxation was that the great tax revolt of the 1980s passed Australia by. While in Britain, the United States and New Zealand, income tax rates fell sharply, in Australia the abolition of the 60% rate was more than outweighed by the abolition of tax indexation[66] and the introduction of a raft of new taxes and restrictions, including capital gains tax, fringe benefits tax, heavy taxation of retirement benefits, the tax file number and later the goods and services tax. The income tax cuts accompanying the introduction of GST have also been swallowed by bracket creep, for Australia, unlike Britain, still has no tax indexation.

For Australians the only significant relief during the tax revolt era came at the State level, with the virtual abolition of death duties. That came about because the political establishment could not control Queensland's Bjelke-Petersen government, which was the first to do away with that unpopular impost. Interstate competition did the rest,[67] for unlike the Commonwealth, individual States lack monopoly power and cannot prevent people from voting with their feet. The establishment struck back, however, reintroducing death duties by stealth via Capital Gains Tax; and this time, the revenue flowed to Canberra rather than to the then hard-pressed States.

The result was that Australia ended the century with its tax take at an all-time high and the nation has moved significantly higher in the international tax burden league table. In 2000–2002 alone, Australian taxes on wages rose by 1.2 percent, while 19 OECD countries registered decreases in tax burdens, 15 of them reducing their top rate.[68] As Peter Burn demonstrated in chapter 1, Australian families now carry a heavier income and social security tax burden than average Britons or Americans. The OECD reports that a production worker's family in Australia loses 14.8% of gross earnings in income tax (after allowing for cash handouts), as against 11.5% in the USA, and 11.1% in Britain. Even France (14.5%) does better than we do.[69] The revenue lobby's promise that the new taxes and enforcement measures would lead to substantial rate cuts has been broken—another piece of evidence against the 'benevolent despot' theory and in favour of the government as Leviathan model.

The people have never voted for income taxes at the present rates and would have defeated any government that proposed them. The current situation is the result of bracket creep and failure to reform, and its results have been a decline in taxpayer morality: people do not regard working in the cash economy as cheating because they believe they are paying too much.[70] Government must increasingly rely on withholding or reporting at source.[71] While the cash economy has been called the tax avoidance of the masses, even the masses have been venturing into sophisticated forms of tax avoidance, with construction workers, Melbourne tram drivers and Sydney bicycle couriers being notionally employed by their own service companies and people of moderate means negatively gearing a second property.

Under our unreformed system, perverse incentives abound. At the lower levels, the growing tax burden is driving onto the welfare rolls people who could support themselves if taxes were lower.[72] The low tax-free threshold of $6,000 gives them every incentive to stay on welfare, as they face effective marginal rates of 70% or more if they resume work and thereupon lose welfare payments. At the higher levels, a tax-driven brain drain is developing. Professor Wolfgang Kasper warns: 'Young, mobile Australians know from a growing number of emigrated colleagues that, in most Asian countries, income taxes are much lower. This explains why Australia suffers from skill shortages and why occasional recruitment drives by short-staffed organisations so often fail'.[73] Robert Gottliebsen agrees: 'Many (expatriates) intend to return but discover the 48% tax rate cutting in at ridiculously low levels means they can't afford to move home until they've made their fortune offshore. It's then too late. ...(T)here is global competition for skilled migration, so if we wanted to increase total migration, we would have to lower our skills criteria'.[74] Australia's Diaspora now numbers over one million, a high proportion for a young country of 20 million which is in other respects regarded as a good place to live.

The disincentives are multiplied by large-scale distortions. The recent unprecedented housing bubble, for example, was fuelled by the tax treatment of negative gearing.[75] The resulting price inflation has propelled many ordinary family homes into the luxury land tax that most States levy on expensive real estate.[76] 'Parliaments and public commentators have lost sight of the fact that, beyond a certain point, government spending and taxation hamper economic growth', Professor Kasper points out. 'No country has ever achieved per-capita income growth of 4% on a sustained basis once general government spending exceeds 40% of the national product. Australia is now edging close to this mark…'[77] Others note that Ireland did not become the 'Celtic tiger' until it slashed its spending to GDP ratio, which in 1985 stood at 51%, but by 2000 was down to 29%.[78]

In a famous exchange of views in the 1940s, Lord Keynes agreed with the eminent Australian economist Colin Clark that if government spending and taxation exceeded 25% of GDP it would become counterproductive.[79] Ironically, Australia's underground economy, estimated at 15% of GDP, seems to bring Australia's spending and tax to GDP ratio back to the 25% level, via what law and economics doctrine calls 'a corrective transaction'. But it does so in a haphazard and lawless way.

The rule of law is thus being steadily undermined by increasing resistance by the population, which is met by ever-increasing arbitrariness by the authorities. The two sides are deadlocked in a downward spiral of dysfunctionality. The only possible outcomes are a collapse into total authoritarianism or a thorough reappraisal and reform of the tax system. Reform is obviously preferable.

Conclusion

In the realm of federal taxation the rule of law has all but been replaced by a system of direct bureaucratic rule. The separation of powers has broken down and key institutions have been compromised. The legislation has become unmanageable, unintelligible and unpredictable, the executive exercises legislative and quasi-judicial powers, the judiciary exercises policy-making powers and, in a variety of ways, the law is changed at the point of application. Major taxpayers increasingly treat the enacted law as irrelevant and acquiesce in the ATO's assumption of the role of supreme deciding authority. None of this was inevitable: in Britain and the United States the rule of law still largely applies to the tax system.

It is well understood today that the rule of law and healthy institutions of government are essential for long-term economic growth. Failure to uphold those ideals in the tax arena is producing major disincentives and distortions, including a massive and flourishing underground economy, a brain drain and a tax-driven property bubble that has given Australia the world's highest housing prices relative to income and is deterring overseas capital inflows.[80] Perverse incentives pervade the present system, which creates disincentives to work, learn, save, risk, innovate,[81] create wealth, support charity and even procreate.[82] It deters skilled people from moving to Australia and deters skilled Australians from staying here. It handicaps workers who have to compete internationally and rewards the devious and the indolent.

There is an old saying, and a true one, that people will work *not* to pay taxes but will not work to pay taxes. 'They no longer do what is useful to others and hence profitable to themselves,' writes Professor Kasper, 'but are instead guided by avoiding government-made obstacles, bending rules, seeking preferments, bribing officials and dissimulating their wealth'.[83] According to the OECD, Australia's tax system is the fourth worst in the developed world for rewarding effort.[84]

A vital part of any reform programme must be the immediate restoration of tax indexation, the lack of which is the main cause of our current misfortunes. [85] Even the present cumulative inflation rate of 3% while low by the standards of recent decades, is high by those of history and, if not compensated for in tax scale adjustments, will over time effect a substantial transfer of resources from the people to the government.[86] Leviathan must not be allowed to profit from his own wrong, silently debasing the currency so as to drive lower-paid workers into higher brackets.

Other measures which are necessary if taxpayer resistance is to be overcome, and the popular legitimacy of the tax system restored, include raising the value of the tax-free (zero-rate) threshold above the welfare minimum income level (so that people are allowed to earn a basic subsistence income before they are taxed); cutting the top marginal rate to 30% (so people are not deterred from working by confiscatory levels of tax on their incomes); and controlling the growth of public sector spending, especially welfare spending (to restore self-reliance).

Tinkering with tax legislation and procedures will not revive the rule of law or restore government institutions to their proper roles. Curtailing discretionary powers, rewriting the legislation or other symptom-oriented solutions that do not tackle the underlying enforcement versus resistance dynamic will only cause the confronting pressures to break out elsewhere in the system. True reform will need to be substantial enough to change the pattern of incentives so that, as in the 1950s and 1960s, most people will voluntarily meet their obligations and enforcement pressure is needed only to deal with the greedy few. The rule of law can operate only where most people are willing to obey the law voluntarily most of the time. That proposition has been promoted for decades by the political-intellectual elite in such contexts as drug law, pornography and abortion; it is time to recognise that it applies at least as well to revenue law.

Chapter 7

Tax Reform To Make Work Pay

Peter Saunders and Barry Maley

When assessing the amount of income people lose in tax, it is important to take into account how much money they get back from the government in the form of income support, family payments, and the like. A household's *gross* tax payments may look high, but if a lot of money is simultaneously flowing back into the household in government transfers, their *net* weekly payments to the government may turn out to be a lot lower than first appears.

Generally speaking, workers with no dependents pay a lot of tax and get very little or nothing back in transfer payments, but those with children are much more favoured. Childless workers are expected to look after themselves without cash top-ups from the government while shouldering a heavy tax burden to help pay for the benefits flowing to families with children. As some Labor politicians have pointed out, this means that single people and childless couples on low incomes are paying higher net taxes than workers with families on much higher incomes. In 2005–06, for example, a childless worker or couple earning $35,000 per annum paid $6,885 in net tax, which compares with just $6,330 net tax paid by a $60,000 per year family with two children under 13. Commenting on these figures, Labor's Craig Emerson warned: 'It's only a matter of time before taxpayers without children organise a tax revolt.'[1]

Yet OECD statistics reveal that Australia's childless taxpayers are being treated much the same as their counterparts in other western countries.[2] Once both tax and transfer payments are taken into account, a childless Australian worker on average weekly earnings loses almost a quarter of his or her gross income to the government, whereas an equivalent worker who has dependent children loses only about half this amount, for he or she claws back a considerable chunk of tax in the form of transfer payments. But this is common across the OECD. For nearly all types of households—single, childless couples and people with dependent children—the pattern of net tax paid by Australians (that is, after cash benefits are taken into account) is consistently around the middle of the OECD rankings. Redistribution from those without children to those with children happens in every country, and Australia looks no different from the international norm—with one significant exception.

One household type stands out as very favourably treated here compared with elsewhere, and that is low income single-parent households. They are much more generously treated in Australia than in most other countries. An Australian single parent with two children who earns two-thirds of the average wage pays a net tax of minus 10% on his or her earnings (that is, they receive a lot more in top-ups than they pay in income tax—effectively a Negative Income Tax[3]). Only five OECD countries (the Czech Republic, Iceland, Luxembourg, the UK and Ireland) treat a single parent bringing up two children on two-thirds of Average Weekly Earnings more generously than this. As we shall see, this generous treatment of low income single parent families is almost certainly contributing to their unusually high rates of welfare dependency in this country.

The tax-welfare squeeze and the problem of disincentives

Australia spends less on welfare transfers than most other OECD countries—18% of GDP against an unweighted OECD average of 21% (Table 7.1). Welfare groups like to claim this proves that Australia is less generous to those in need than other countries, and they argue taxes should therefore be increased to fund higher welfare payments. In reality, however, we run one of the world's most generous welfare systems. Even though we spend less in total on welfare than many other countries, more money is diverted to those on lower incomes in Australia than in any other OECD nation.

Table 7.1: Welfare spending as percentage of GDP in Australia and the OECD, 2001

	Australia	OECD 30 country average
Family	2.8	1.8
Age and survivors	4.9	8.5
Disability	2.3	2.6
Health	6.2	5.9
Unemployment	1.0	0.9
Other	0.6	1.5
Total	18.0	20.9

Source: Peter Whiteford, *'The welfare expenditure debate'*, Table 1. Totals do not sum due to rounding.

The explanation for this apparent paradox is that other countries channel more money to those on higher incomes than we do. This is because they have contributory, insurance-based, welfare systems whereas we have a non-contributory, means-tested system financed out of general taxation. Throughout Europe and North America, workers establish entitlements to welfare benefits through the payments they make to (real or notional) social security funds. When they are unemployed, sick or retired, they draw the benefits to which they have established entitlement, irrespective of their financial circumstances at the time. This means a lot of people get paid a lot of money, not because they 'need' it, but because they are entitled to it. The tax system then claws much of this money back, for welfare incomes are taxable. Extensive benefits necessitate high taxes, and high taxes enable extensive benefits.

This key difference between Australia's welfare system and those in Europe and North America shows up most clearly in their spending on age pensions. Table 7.1 shows Australia spends much less than other OECD countries on retirement and survivors' pensions (4.9% of GDP against an OECD average of 8.5%). This 3.6% gap more than covers the 2.9 percentage point difference in overall welfare spending, and it reflects the means testing of non-contributory pensions in Australia. It is not that elderly people are treated meanly in Australia. It is simply that retired people with private incomes or savings get paid a state pension in other countries and are then required to pay tax on it. In Australia, they don't get a full pension in the first place.

The reason Australia's welfare bills are relatively low compared with other advanced countries is, therefore, that welfare recipients are means-tested much more stringently here than in other countries. Fewer people end up receiving payments, but those 'in need' get as much or even more redistributed to them as in any other country. Indeed, Australia's welfare system turns out to be the most 'progressive' in the world. As Peter Whiteford explains:

> Even though Australia spends less than the OECD average on social security benefits, the formula for distributing benefits is so progressive—and the level of taxes paid by the poor is so low—that Australia redistributes more to the poor than any other OECD country (for which these calculations can be made).[4]

The Australian system is therefore very efficient at directing money only to those who need it. However, there is a heavy price to be paid for this efficiency, because strict means-testing creates huge disincentives to work or save. Because eligibility for government support is determined by 'need', rather than by past contributions, neediness is what gets rewarded while self-reliance is penalised.

For example, those who save for their old age are penalised because income from savings reduces the value of the age pension they can claim.

Not surprisingly, many people do not bother to save, or they blow their compulsory superannuation savings on houses, holidays or gifts to their children rather than forfeiting the means-tested government pension. Similarly, working-age adults who do not work are rewarded with means-tested welfare payments, but those who try to work harder in an attempt to increase their earnings are penalised, for they rapidly begin to lose their welfare payments as well as incurring higher tax liabilities. In some cases they end up little better off than before.

Progressive taxation + means-tested benefits = high Effective Marginal Tax Rates (EMTRs)

This problem of perverse disincentives affects many families, even when they are working. This is because most Australian families receive means-tested government payments.

We have already seen that low-income single parents are treated especially generously in Australia relative to other countries, but Table 7.1 shows we spend a lot more on family payments in general than most other OECD countries do. Gross spending on family benefits and services is 50% higher here than the OECD average. Although Australia is much more frugal (or less profligate) when it comes to government funding of things like childcare services and maternity and paternity leave, government spending on cash transfers to families with children is three times the OECD average.[5]

Most of these payments are means-tested, so when families start to increase their private incomes, they get penalised by a reduction in their welfare payments. The precise details of how benefits disappear as earnings rise are complex, but the problem can be illustrated by considering a single parent with two young children (one at school, the other under five). Assuming he or she has no private income (and with one child below eight years of age, there is no requirement that claimants should look for any paid employment), this parent will receive Parenting Payment (Single), or PPS, to provide for themselves, plus Family Tax Benefit (FTB), (Part A) and FTB, (Part B), to help with the cost of raising their children.

In early 2006,[6] this claimant was eligible to receive $488.90 per fortnight in PPS, plus $137.06 per child under 13 years in FTB (Part A), plus $117.60 (for the child under five) and $82.04 (for the older child) of FTB (Part B). They would also receive an annual FTB (Part A) supplement of $627.80 per child (this supplement was introduced by the government in the run-up to the 2004 federal election to placate voters who had over-claimed their FTB entitlements and were complaining about having to repay the excess). This generates a total welfare income (not counting rent assistance) of $25,726 per year.

Once this single parent starts to work, these benefits rapidly fall away. The PPS rules allow a claimant like this to earn $173.20 per fortnight ($4,516 per annum) before the benefit starts to reduce at the rate of 40 cents in every extra dollar earned. He or she would remain eligible for a part pension until fortnightly earnings exceeded $1,409.95 ($36,759 per annum), at which point no more PPS is payable. Any job paying between $4,516 and $36,759 per annum therefore incurs a reduction in PPS of 40 cents in every dollar earned.

The Family Tax Benefit also falls as earnings rise. The FTB (Part B) is not means tested for sole parents, but FTB (Part A) is means tested for all recipients. The maximum rate is paid until claimants exceed $33,361 per year, at which point it starts to taper off at 20 cents in every dollar earned until it reaches a 'base rate' of $44 per child per fortnight when family income reaches $57,600 pa. There it remains until family income rises to $89,644, when it again starts to taper off, this time at 30 cents in every extra dollar earned, until it eventually runs out at a family income of $101,495.

In addition to losing these means-tested payments, the single parent who decides to take paid employment must also begin to pay income tax. Currently, liability to tax starts as soon as earnings pass $6,000 per year (the zero-rate or tax-free threshold). Every dollar earned after that is taxed at 15% until earnings reach $21,600, when the marginal rate increases to 30%. To complicate matters, a 'low income tax offset' worth a maximum of $235 can be claimed against their tax bill by anyone earning less than $21,601, but this offset is then withdrawn at a rate of 4% until it disappears when income exceeds $27,475. This means that between $21,601 and $27,475, additional earnings are effectively taxed at 34%.

Now imagine the single parent in our example is offered a job at around the minimum wage (say, $25,000). He or she will face a marginal tax rate (that is, tax on the next dollar earned) of 34%, plus the Medicare Levy of 1.5%. Added to this, they will be losing PPSat a rate of 40% on every dollar earned above $4,516 per annum. At earnings of $25,000, therefore, they will find they are losing 75.5 cents of every additional dollar they earn.[7]

If this parent pushes his or her gross earnings up to around $35,000, his or her effective (or equivalent) marginal tax rate gets even worse.[8] At this level of income, each additional dollar earned attracts income tax at 30% (plus Medicare Levy of 1.5%), loses PPS at 40%, and loses FTB (Part A) at a rate of 20%—a total of 91.5 cents lost out of every dollar. With disincentives like this, it is little wonder that the labour force participation rate for single parents in Australia is so low—not only does the welfare system entitle them to stay out of paid employment for years on end, but if they decide to look for low-paid jobs, the interaction of the tax and benefits system ensures that they will end up little better off than before.[9]

Single parent families are not the only group caught in this pincer. The combination of a means-tested benefits system (the more you earn, the less you get) and a 'progressive' tax system (the more you earn, the more proportionately you pay) means that many Australians on low to middle incomes face dispiritingly high equivalent marginal tax rates caused by simultaneous loss of benefits and liability to tax. An unemployed single person claiming Newstart Allowance, for example, receives $202.25 per week (plus rent allowance). They can earn an additional $31 per week before they start to lose this benefit at a rate of 50 cents in the dollar, and once their earnings reach $71 per week the benefit taper increases to 70 cents in the dollar. The benefit disappears altogether at earnings of $331.35 per week ($17,278 per annum), but by that time they are also paying 15 cents in every dollar in income tax. Notwithstanding the low income tax offset of $235 they can claim against their total tax liability, they therefore face an equivalent marginal tax rate of 85% on every new dollar they earn between $6,000 and $17,278 per year.[10]

It is not only single parents on welfare or unemployed people who experience the frustrations of very high EMTRs. Ordinary working families can encounter them too. In 2004, it was calculated that almost one million people, or 8% of the working-age population, faced EMTRs of 60% or more, and three-quarters of them were living in families with children under the age of 16.[11] Only 3% of single people, and just 1% of those in couples without children, faced high EMTRs, but 15% of individuals in couples with children and nearly one-quarter of sole parents were caught by EMTRs of 60% or more. Only four other OECD countries had EMTRs this high.[12]

These figures were calculated before the 2005 federal budget cut the FTB taper rate from 30 to 20 cents in the dollar on family incomes under $57,600 (this was done precisely to reduce the daunting work disincentives that so many families face). But combined with a 30% income tax rate, even a 20% FTB taper still leaves families on average incomes exposed to a 50% EMTR on each additional dollar they earn (51.5% including the Medicare Levy). Furthermore, the 30% income tax rate rises to 42% once incomes hit $63,000 (or $70,000 after July 2006), and at this income level, FTB is withdrawn at 30% and a 1% surcharge is added to the Medicare Levy for those without private health insurance. A worker with children who is earning $70,000 thus sees 73.5 cents disappear from each extra dollar he or she earns.

For families, therefore, the problem of high EMTRs stretches way up the income scale. Nine out of ten Australian families receive some FTB payment, and every one of them is exposed to the double whammy of a progressive income tax rate coupled with a means-tested withdrawal of benefits.

The price we pay for means testing

The unique, targeted nature of our benefits system has one big advantage. It means we give much less welfare money to top income earners than is the case in most other OECD countries. The top one-fifth of income earners in Australia pay 60% of all income tax, but they receive only 5% of all welfare payments.[13] It is only because we withhold welfare from the very richest earners that we are able to keep the total cost of welfare payments below the OECD average.

The savings from this targeting are, however, modest, for below this top stratum of income earners, Australia hands out just as much welfare to middle income people (most of whom do not need it) as other countries do.[14] This is mainly because of the generosity of our family payments system. Despite our extensive reliance on means testing, we have not avoided funding 'middle class welfare', for families around the middle of the income distribution typically balance the large amounts of tax they pay with large amounts claimed back in FTB and other transfer payments.[15]

Our desire to limit welfare payments for the richest 10% or 20% of families means that most payments are subject to the operation of means test tapers. This creates high EMTRs through the broad sweep of the income range where households are eligible for payments. The result is that work incentives for millions of working-age people on both low and middle incomes are weakened. Combined with our steeply progressive income tax system, this means-tested transfer payments system leads to a much bigger problem of work disincentives than most other countries face.

The prospect of giving up half, two-thirds or even 90% of one's additional earnings inevitably leads some people to decide it is not worth their while increasing their work effort. The combination of high taxes and generous but tightly targeted welfare benefits also helps explain why one in six working-age adults still relies wholly on welfare at a time when the economy is booming, for the rewards from increased self-reliance can be quite thin. Erosion of the work ethic and the spread of a dependency culture represent a devastating indictment of our tax and welfare system, and it is a major reason why the system needs a fundamental overhaul.

Almost everyone agrees that high EMTRs are destructive of personal incentives and that we need to reduce them so that it pays people to work. There is, however, little agreement about how this might best be done. Logically, there are only three possible solutions:

- change the welfare rules so that people do not lose so much in benefits as their earnings rise. This implies reducing means-test taper rates;
- change the tax rules so low-income workers do not pay so much tax as their earnings rise. This could be done through various forms of refunds and credits; or
- change both the welfare and the tax rules so that workers do not pay tax until they have earned enough to look after themselves and their dependants, and benefits do not get paid to households that do not need them. This would require radical changes to the tax-free threshold and the system of family payments.

Changing the welfare rules by weakening the taper

The first possible solution is to reduce the rate at which welfare benefits are withdrawn as incomes rise. This could certainly help to increase work incentives, for quite small adjustments have in the past produced quite impressive consequences. When the government reduced the PPS taper from 50% to 40% in 2000, for example, work participation by single parent households rose by around 2.5%, and because more people were working, this halved the net cost to the government of making the concession in the first place. There was also a positive (though less dramatic) employment effect when the FTB taper was reduced from 50% to 30%.[16]

The problem, however, is that reducing the taper rate on welfare payments means increasing the income range over which the benefits are payable. Currently, for example, the welfare payment for single parents, PPS, is withdrawn at 40 cents in the dollar on earnings over $4,516 pa and it phases out altogether once people earn around $36,759. If the taper rate were reduced to 20 cents in the dollar, this would ease the problem of high EMTRs experienced by single parents, but it would mean the benefit would still be payable to those earning as much as $60,000 per year. Similarly, if the current 70% taper on NewStart allowance were reduced to 45%, it would mean having to pay an unemployment benefit to people working full time at the minimum wage.[17]

Reducing the taper rate on benefits is costly and inefficient, for it stretches eligibility for payments further up the income scale to encompass people who do not need help. This is precisely what has happened with family payments—reducing the rate at which FTB is withdrawn has necessitated extending the payment to include families earning over $100,000. Because these affluent households receive welfare payments they do not 'need', the tax and welfare bureaucracies have become increasingly entangled with each other as one pays people the benefits to which they are entitled while the other tries to claw them back again in increased taxes. This has increased administrative and deadweight costs, and it has also undermined work incentives as workers end up paying more tax at the same time as they become more reliant on hand-outs from the government. There must be a better solution.

Changing the tax rules by introducing an 'Earnings Credit'

The second possible solution to the problem of high EMTRs is to reduce the amount of tax lower income working households have to pay. This could be achieved by across-the-board tax cuts, but those who prefer to target low-to-middle income groups (who currently face the highest EMTRs and hence the greatest work disincentives)[18] have for some years been arguing instead for a new 'earnings credit' (EC) to be paid solely to low income working families.

In essence, an earnings credit would involve an additional cash transfer financed by the government but paid through the wage packet to lower income earners to compensate them for the increased taxes they pay and the reduced benefits they receive as their income rises. In other words, workers would continue to claim their benefits and pay their taxes, but a new payment would be laid on top of this existing system to reduce the net amount they end up losing.

The Americans have had a system like this (the 'Earned Income Tax Credit') in place for more than 30 years. Low income Americans complete a tax return at the end of the year and claim a lump sum reimbursement from the federal government. In the UK, too, the Blair government has introduced a series of tax credits aimed, not only at low-income families with children, but also at low-income workers without children, and at age pensioners with savings.

In Australia, a proposal to introduce an earnings credit (EC) was first outlined by five leading economists in an open letter to the Prime Minister in 1998.[19] In the latest version of this proposal,[20] the EC would be superimposed on the existing FTB (Part A) payment, tapering off until earnings hit the FTB base payment level when it would disappear. Those who developed this proposal estimate that it would reduce the EMTR faced by a jobless couple with two children who move into low-paid employment by four percentage points, and that it would encourage another 84,000 people into paid employment at a net cost to the Treasury of just over $2 billion per annum.[21]

This looks like a move in the right direction, but there are some serious drawbacks with this proposal. The main problem is that an earnings credit is just another means-tested government payment which would phase out as people's earnings rise. It would therefore create new or stronger work disincentives at the point in the income scale where it starts to fall away. The 'Five Economists' try to minimise this disincentive effect by linking the new EC to the existing FTB payment so that the taper is no sharper than it is currently, but while this would ensure there would be no increase in EMTRs faced by recipients, there would have to be an increase in the *number of people* affected by the taper (for payments would have to stretch across a broader band of incomes than before). As in the US and the UK, helping those on lower incomes would therefore inevitably create new problems of increased EMTRs higher up the income scale.[22]

Tackling tax and welfare together by raising the zero-rate threshold

Any means-tested payment aimed at working households will create work disincentives because it reduces as earnings rise. The only way of avoiding this is to move away from means tested in-work benefits altogether. This is the logic behind the third possible solution to high EMTRs, which is to disengage the tax and welfare systems so that (as far as possible) they no longer overlap. The key to achieving this is to raise the zero-rate (tax-free) threshold.

In 1980, a worker did not pay any tax until he or she earned $4,041 per year (one-third of average earnings). Wages have gone up by more than 350% since then, but the tax-free earnings threshold has risen by less than 50%, to just $6,000 (one-ninth of today's full-time average earnings). The result is that workers now pay tax on a much bigger proportion of their earnings than they used to. Had the 1980 personal threshold of $4,041 kept pace with earnings, it would now be over $14,000. There is a strong case for restoring the value of the tax-free threshold to something close to its 1980 level, and pegging it to rises in wages so that it cannot be eroded again. The argument for doing this is both principled and practical.

The principled case for raising the threshold is that workers should be allowed to earn and retain enough money to meet their own subsistence needs before any tax is taken away from them. At present, anybody who earns more than $6,000 per year pays income tax, but $6,000 is clearly not enough to keep body and soul together. This means the government is taking money away from people on low incomes who then have no choice but to request government welfare to meet their basic needs. Like feudal peasants tithing part of their incomes to the Church and then relying on church charity to survive, many workers who could get by without government assistance are being forced into welfare dependency by the high levels of taxation they have to pay. It would be far better to take low income workers out of the tax system so that they can spend their own money fulfilling their own needs without having to claim government payments. The way to do this is to raise the tax-free earnings threshold above the subsistence minimum income level.

We can define a 'subsistence income' as the minimum amount somebody would receive if they were unemployed and living wholly on welfare benefits. At the time of writing, a single person on the lowest level of welfare payments is entitled to receive $249.65 per week, or $12,965 per annum, from the State (see Table 7.2). If workers are to be left with enough of their own money to provide for their own bare subsistence, it follows that the tax-free threshold for single taxpayers should be raised beyond this minimum welfare level. This points to a tax-free threshold of around $13,000.

The practical argument for raising the threshold follows from this. Because the value of the personal tax-free threshold has slipped to less than half what the government itself defines as a minimum subsistence income, a lot of people on lower incomes find themselves paying tax and receiving welfare at the same time. This 'churning' creates the high EMTRs, for as they increase their earnings, they pay more tax at the same time as their means-tested benefits get reduced. The most effective way to overcome this problem is to allow workers to keep more of what they earn so they do not have to use the welfare transfer system in the first place.

If the threshold is raised above the welfare floor, nobody who pays tax would have an income so low that welfare assistance would need to be sought, and nobody receiving welfare would have an income high enough to create a tax liability. The tax-welfare pincer which generates the high EMTRs would therefore be broken, and this would significantly strengthen work incentives (raising the threshold by just $2,000 is estimated to raise labour force participation by around 50,000).[23]

Arguments against raising the tax-free threshold

The main argument against raising the zero-rate threshold is that it would be expensive, for it benefits all income tax payers, not just those on the lowest incomes.[24] One estimate claims that raising the tax-free threshold to $13,000 would reduce projected 2006-07 federal government revenues by $9.5 billion.[25] Critics say this sort of money could be better spent helping only low income workers, rather than spreading the money across all taxpayers. Peter Dawkins, for example, estimates that an Earnings Credit tailored to reduce the tax burden of low income workers would induce 50% more people into jobs than an increase in the tax-free threshold costing the same amount of revenue.[26]

But the fact that raising the tax-free threshold benefits all taxpayers is its strength, not its weakness.[27] Targeting always produces new disincentive effects somewhere in the system as the benefit gets withdrawn at higher levels of income. Raising the tax-free threshold, by contrast, benefits every level of income equally and therefore has no disincentive effect as people increase their earnings. Moreover, by disentangling the tax and welfare systems it would reduce churning and increase the number of households living self-reliantly from their own earnings without recourse to government assistance.

Sharing tax-free thresholds within families

Raising the zero-rate threshold above the welfare floor is an essential step in restoring incentives and self-reliance to the income tax system. However, a tax-free income of $13,000 is obviously only sufficient to maintain one person. Where a worker is earning a wage or salary which has to support a second, non-earning, adult, he or she clearly needs a more generous subsistence allowance if the couple is to achieve self-reliance. And if dependent children also have to be supported out of this income, the minimum subsistence level will be higher again.

The welfare system takes family circumstances into account when determining an applicant's minimum income needs. An unemployed couple with no children, for example, is currently guaranteed a total minimum weekly income of $406.50 ($20,196 per annum), which is 61% more than a single claimant receives (Table 7.2). The tax system, however, is blind to family circumstances. It treats individuals as distinct income units and taxes them separately on their own earnings, irrespective of how many other people might depend upon that income.

In chapter 8, Terry Dwyer argues that the tax system should be brought into line with the welfare system by taking account of the number of people who have to be supported from any one individual's earnings. This could be done by allowing a 'dependent' partner in a couple to transfer part of his/her zero-tax threshold to the principal earner (assuming this is what they both choose to do[29]). A couple should not be allowed to pool the

Table 7.2: Annual 'subsistence' income levels for different household types, based on welfare minimum payments[28]

Household type	Total welfare entitlement $	Implied $ subsistence cost for:			
		1st adult	2nd adult	1st child	2+ children
Single earner	$12,965	12,965	-	-	-
Single parent + 1 child	$21,130	12,965	-	7,165	-
Single parent + 2 children	$24,704	12,965	-	7,165	3,574
Couple	$21,196	12,965	8,231	-	-
Couple + 1 child	$26,745	12,965	8,231	5,569	-
Couple + 2 children	$30,318	12,965	8,231	5,569	3,573

whole of a second threshold because their joint living costs are reduced by economies of scale (two people can live cheaper than one). If one person needs, say, $13,000 for subsistence (the current welfare minimum), two people living together do not need $26,000 to achieve the equivalent standard of living. Most 'equivalence scales' suggest they need about 1.5 times what a single person needs (which would give them a joint threshold of $19,500), but the welfare system is rather more generous, giving them just over $21,000. This suggests that the shared zero-tax threshold for a couple who choose to pool their tax liability should be in the region of $21,000, which means the value of a partner's transferable threshold would be around $8,000 (Table 7.2).[30]

Dwyer recommends that family tax pooling could be extended to children as well as operating between partnered adults. This would mean dependent children would have their own thresholds (in recognition of the fact that they too must achieve a subsistence income in order to live). Part or all of these thresholds could then be transferred to one or both working parents to compensate them for that portion of their income that is consumed by their children. Referring again to Table 7.2, the welfare system seems to operate on the assumption that a first child has a subsistence need of anything between $5,500 and over $7,000, with second and subsequent children needing rather less (about $3,500 each). To simplify matters, let us assume that every dependent child could claim a transferable tax-free threshold of about $4,000 (we therefore put to one side the issue of whether child thresholds should be adjusted according to the age of the child, or the number of children in the family).

Allowing family members to pool their members' thresholds would substantially reduce (and in some cases eliminate altogether) the tax liabilities of most working families. The *quid pro quo* is that these families would then be expected to assume full responsibility for themselves without seeking government cash assistance, for their incomes would be above subsistence level and there should be no need for top-ups. In return for paying less or no tax, existing family payments could therefore be wound up.

Some very low income working families would, however, still need help. This would be the case wherever a family's combined tax-free threshold was higher than their actual earnings. For example, Table 7.2 indicates that a two-adult, two-child family with just one earner needs to earn over $30,000 in order to achieve basic subsistence (the principal earner in this family could claim a tax free threshold of $30,318 before having to pay any tax). But if this earner were on the federal minimum wage (worth $25,258 in 2005-06),[31] he or she would be earning $5,060 per year less than the family's pooled threshold. In this event, the family would fail to get the full benefit of their pooled allowance and would end up with an income below what the tax/welfare system defines as its subsistence level.

There are various ways this problem could be resolved. The simplest solution would be to top-up the family's income to its threshold level—to give them $5,060 in welfare payments. However, this would create a 100% EMTR, albeit across a compressed income range. It would also leave some low-wage, working families no better off than an equivalent non-employed family living wholly on welfare benefits. If we are trying to strengthen work incentives, this looks like a backward step.

A better solution would be to convert children's tax free threshold entitlements into non-means tested 'tax credits.'[32] For example, if we decided that each child requires an income of $4,000 per year to achieve subsistence, then working parents could be allowed to claim an annual reduction in their tax liability of $4,000 for each dependent child sharing their income. Those parents with a total tax liability less than this amount could then claim the shortfall as a cash transfer payment.

Why children should be allowed tax-free incomes of their own

Working out the operational details of a scheme like this is less important at this stage than establishing the validity of the principles behind it. Two key objections are likely to be raised:

- The first (the libertarian objection) asks why people who choose to have children should receive any special treatment in the tax/welfare system. Giving them child tax credits means that childless taxpayers are required to subsidise the cost of other people's children. Why should they?
- The second (the egalitarian objection) questions whether everyone who has children should be supported in this way. Given that child tax credits would not be means tested, wealthy parents as well as poor ones will benefit. But why should poor childless workers subsidise rich people with children?

These are important and serious objections. There are three main responses to them.

First, the principle of 'horizontal equity' (that is, people on similar earnings should end up with similar disposable incomes) requires that taxation take account of the number of people who are supported from any given income. Secondly, income should only be taxed once, and the person who pays it should be the ultimate beneficiary, not necessarily the one who initially earns it (Terry Dwyer elaborates on this in chapter 8). This means that children (the beneficiaries) should be recognised as income-receivers in the tax system. Thirdly, every individual needs a subsistence income, which means every citizen should be entitled to a tax-free income up to subsistence level. If we recognise children as income receivers for tax purposes, it follows that we should also give them their own tax-free income allowances or credits.

This third argument is the crucial one. All parents are obliged by law to maintain and care for their children. Children therefore have a legal claim on part of their parents' income. In effect, the law forces parents to transfer income-in-kind to their dependent children in order that they may subsist. Just as every adult, rich or poor, is entitled to earn their own subsistence before being taxed, so every child, rich and poor, should be entitled to a tax-free allowance on the (imputed) subsistence 'income' they receive from their parents. Like adults, therefore, the subsistence income of children should not be taxed (which means, in effect, that it should not be taxed in the hands of the parent-trustees of that income).

What of the argument that favouring children in this way creates inequity between taxpayers with children and those without? We saw at the start of this chapter that a number of federal Labor politicians have expressed concern about this inequity. But there is no inequity if policy is kept stable over the life-cycle, because every individual as a child would already have benefited from the taxation relief enjoyed by his or her parents. This would simply be an example of inter-generational tax equity, entailing no unfairness to any childless taxpayer.

There is also a strong case for arguing that children are to some extent a 'public good' from which we all benefit (for without them the society would disappear), and towards the cost of which we should all therefore contribute (though for an alternative view, see John Humphreys in chapter 9). A tax and welfare system which did not compensate parents for some of their lost income consequent upon transferring some of their earnings to the subsistence of their children would effectively allow those who remain childless to 'free-ride' on those who invest in producing the next generation of citizens and taxpayers.

Can the government afford to give up the revenue?

Raising zero-rate thresholds above the welfare subsistence floor and supplementing them with flat rate tax credits for dependent children would allow all families with at least one full-time worker to be taken out of the means-tested welfare system altogether. Working families would retain more of what they earn, would become more self-reliant, and would escape the 'poverty trap' produced by the interaction of the tax and welfare systems.

But is it financially possible to introduce a reform like this?

If our proposals were adopted, the existing battery of welfare payments propping up the incomes of people in employment who have dependent children would no longer be needed. Our proposal entails the complete elimination of FTB(Part A), FTB (Part B), Child Care Benefit, Child Care Allowance and Maternity Allowance. On 2004 estimates, this would generate savings of $13.2 billion per annum.[33]

Against these savings, our proposal incurs new 'costs' to the Treasury of nearly $9 billion, to cover the higher tax-free thresholds, plus nearly $16 billion for child tax credits worth $4,000 per child.[34] Setting these against the savings from eliminating existing welfare payments leaves a net shortfall of around $11.5 billion. If, in addition, the top rate taxes were cut to, say, 40% as a first step towards an eventual flat tax system, we could be looking at a shortfall closer to $17 billion. Does this mean our proposal is impractical?

The first point to make is that there would be efficiency gains. Modelling predicts that thousands of people currently claiming welfare payments would enter work and start to pay tax instead, and it is safe to assume that some people currently in work would also increase their effort and generate greater revenues. As Alex Robson and Sinclair Davidson point out elsewhere in this volume, tax cuts are not as 'expensive' as static Treasury models like to pretend, for they change economic behaviour.

The second, equally important, point is that government is currently collecting too much money in tax and its spending is too high. Tax reform proposals that start out by demanding 'revenue neutrality' take for granted levels of spending that can and should be questioned.

It was not very long ago that Australia enjoyed a system not unlike the one we have proposed here. As recently as 1980, the zero-rate tax threshold was worth around $14,000 in today's money (although tax rates were somewhat higher then), and there was a universal family allowance for families with children which was not means-tested or taxed. This means that 40 years ago, a single earner family with three dependent children living on an income one-and-a-half times average earnings (equivalent to about $70,000 today) paid no tax. Indeed, after receiving child allowances, this family's final disposable income was 3% *higher* than its earned income.[35]

Since then, the tax burden on middle- and upper-income families has grown much heavier as a result of ever-increasing government spending. We should not accept these trends as inevitable or irreversible. In the 1940s, Keynes famously held that it would be counterproductive if governments were ever allowed to absorb more than 25% of GDP in tax.[36] Australian governments are now absorbing well over 30%, and this has indeed proved counterproductive. It is time to require our politicians to trim their spending to a budget rather than budgeting according to their spending plans.

Would voters support the reforms?

Raising tax thresholds creates only winners. Nobody loses if the zero-rate threshold is raised from $6,000 to $13,000 (for singles) or $21,000 (for couples choosing joint taxation), and anybody earning more than $6,000 per annum obviously gains. In absolute terms, everybody makes the same money gain (at a 15% tax rate, this works out at $1,050 per annum for singles and $2,250 for couples opting for shared taxation), but in relative terms, lower-income earners gain a lot more, for an increase in the threshold lowers their average tax rate more than it does that of higher earners. A single person on the minimum wage ends up paying 44% less tax ($2,387 as against $3,437), compared with just a 3.5% tax savings for the equivalent person earning twice the average wage ($33,359 against $34,409).

It should prove a major political attraction of this proposal that every working family in the country will be allowed to keep $20 per week more of the money it earns, and research indicates that raising the tax-free threshold would indeed be popular. A poll carried out by ACNielsen on behalf of The Centre for Independent Studies asked at what level of earnings people thought income tax should begin. The results (Table 7.3) reveal strong support for raising the personal tax threshold above the minimum welfare floor. More than four out of every five respondents believed that there should be a zero rate on all earnings below the welfare subsistence level.

Table 7.3: Public opinion and the personal tax-free threshold

At what level of earnings do you believe people should start to pay income tax?	**Number**	**%**
On every dollar they earn right from the first dollar	217	4
On earnings above $6000 per year (as now)	764	13
Not until they earn above basic welfare benefits level	2445	43
Not until they earn above minimum award wage	2014	35
People should not have to pay income tax	230	4
Don't know/No opinion	51	1
Total	5721	100

Source: CIS ACNielsen survey [37]

Conclusion

Personal incomes are taxed too highly, and this is combined with one of the most targeted systems of means-tested income support in the Western world. This combination of high rates of progressive taxation and tightly means-tested benefits leads to two irrational and counter-productive outcomes:

- Working families which try to raise their earnings get hit by high tax levies at the same time as they lose eligibility for welfare benefits, with the result that they lose more than 50 cents (in some cases a lot more) from every additional dollar they earn. The system therefore creates huge work disincentives; and

- Families who earn enough to maintain themselves are nevertheless driven into dependency on government hand-outs because they lose so much of their earnings in tax. The system therefore generates unnecessarily high levels of welfare dependency and undermines self-reliance.

Tackling these problems with modest improvements like an earned income tax credit, a reduced taper on Family Tax Benefit withdrawal rates, or a more generous Low Income Tax Offset, offers no lasting solution, for measures like these inevitably create new disincentives elsewhere while leaving the core of the problem little changed. The answer lies in reducing the tax burden and thereby lowering people's need for government welfare payments. The best way to do this is to raise tax-free thresholds for single workers and for couples opting for joint taxation, and to replace means-tested child payments with a flat rate child tax credit. This would dramatically improve incentives and rewards from working, and it would reinforce self-reliance by reducing dependency on government hand-outs.

Chapter 8

The Taxation Of Shared Family Incomes [1]

Terry Dwyer

Economic theory assumes that in the absence of distortions, people will make choices which maximise their utility, that is their economic welfare. When a tax or transfer system is introduced it may well influence those economic choices. Sometimes this is deliberate, as in 'sin' taxes on gambling, smoking and drinking. However, tax theorists generally argue that a tax system should be as neutral as possible if economic welfare is to be maximised.

The meaning of economic neutrality is that a choice made after the introduction of a tax or transfer system should not be different from what it would have been before. Thus, if in the absence of a tax, a person would have preferred to work 40 hours a week, the tax is neutral if the person wishes to work the same number of hours after its introduction. The tax does not modify desired behaviour.

The principle of tax neutrality should apply to the way we tax (and pay benefits to) families (although because people have different preferences, design of a neutral tax system is not easy). Some women may prefer not to have children and pursue full-time careers; others may prefer to pursue a career raising children; and others again may, over their lifetimes, wish to pursue both. Some households may prefer to get by with two wage earners but no onerous overtime or promotion; others may prefer more specialisation, with one partner earning market income and the other partner caring for children at home. A neutral tax-transfer system should not interfere with the preferences of these households. The choices households wish to make after the imposition of the tax and transfer system should be the same as before. There should be no bias in favour of the choice of a one-earner household or the choice of a two-earner household. There should be no bias for or against raising children.

A second important principle of taxation (discussed by Lauchlan Chipman in chapter 5) is that people in similar circumstances should be liable to the same amount of tax (so-called 'horizontal equity'). Again, this principle is not easily translated into practical policies. What does treating equals equally mean? How, for example, does one achieve horizontal equity between one-income and two-income families earning the same total income? Because our tax system currently refuses to recognise income sharing within families, a single breadwinner family can pay more tax and be worse off than a two breadwinner family with the same (or even a much larger) total income, because the two income family obtains the advantage of two sets of thresholds and lower tax rates. This clearly violates the principle of horizontal equity.

Taxing individuals or taxing families?

When the United Kingdom introduced income tax in 1799, the incomes of husband and wife were added and taxed as one. Australia, however, has always taxed husband and wife separately ever since the introduction of federal income tax in 1915. This has also applied to children whose incomes have been taxed separately. But separate taxation of family members on their legal incomes ends up breaking both of our key principles of taxation—it distorts people's behavioural choices, and it treats people in similar situations unequally.

The Australian position has always been that income tax liability follows the ownership of income. Income is taxed in the hands of the beneficial owner. In the case of property income, it may be traced through trusts or partnerships to the ultimate beneficial owner. In the case of wage or salary income, however, the income is taxed in the hands of the person who earns it.

Even at the time income tax was introduced into Australia in 1915, it was quickly appreciated in *Purcell's Case* (1921) 29 CLR 464 that, with a graduated individual income tax scale, tax could be much reduced by splitting income between the family members who lived on it. In *Purcell's Case* a grazier executed a declaration of trust over his property which allowed the income to be split among family members. Although challenged by the then-Commissioner, Purcell was victorious in the High Court. The principle was firmly established that property income may be freely alienated among family members if ownership of the property is transferred to them.

For many years it was thought that while property income could be split for tax purposes among family members, this was not true of personal exertion income.[2] However, in *Everett's Case* (1980) 10 ATR 608 the High Court had to consider an assignment of a share of a partnership, where the partnership was engaged in rendering professional services. The High Court held that the alienation of income resulting from the assignment under the State *Partnership Act* was valid. The partner, if he transferred the right to income to his spouse, was no longer taxable on the income, even though it was largely attributable to his personal activities. The basis for the decision was that what was transferred was a property right, viz a share in the partnership, rather than personal exertion income itself.

Other methods have evolved over the years for transferring personal exertion income to other family members. For example, following *Phillip's Case* (1978) 8 ATR 783 professional partnerships could divert income through service companies to trusts for the benefit of other family members.

Other taxpayers have from time to time employed arrangements such as profit-sharing loans. Thus as far as the tax system is concerned, virtually all types of income can be shared among family members, except wage or salary income.[3]

The inequity of individual taxation

If one were to lay down a general principle for the allocation of income to taxpayers it would seem reasonable to insist that income should be taxed once, and once only, when in the hands of the ultimate beneficial recipient.

Naive individual taxation—taxing individuals solely with regard to the income they legally own or control—fails when tested against this principle because it ignores income transfers. For example, Australia does not tax trustees on the income they control. Instead it allocates the income to the beneficiaries selected by the trustees and the tax liability follows the income.[4] If one were to apply the same principle to the situation of a family breadwinner, the income which is earned by that breadwinner is to some extent transferred to other members of the family. Looked at from this point of view the question of family taxation is not a question of giving tax relief or a 'tax subsidy' to a breadwinner in respect of dependants. It is more basic—a question of asking who ultimately enjoys the income?

This logic has been accepted in some other countries. The Carter Commission in Canada took the view that the family and not the individual should be the unit of taxation.[5] Similarly, in the United States it has been taken for granted that the unit of taxation should be the household, that is, the couple or the sole-parent households or the individual. In the United Kingdom and many other countries, the married couple was traditionally the tax unit, and although it has moved away from aggregation as being inequitable, the UK continues to allow tax relief where a husband and wife are dependent upon one income.

In Australia in 1975, the Asprey Committee considered the question of family taxation. In regard to children it argued for replacement of tax deductions by child endowment.[6] But in regard to family taxation generally, and husband and wife in particular, the Committee argued against compulsory aggregation in favour of elective family taxation as a unit. It accepted the basic equity argument that two could not live as cheaply as one, having accepted the argument that a wife's income should not be added to and taxed as the husband's.

It is quite erroneous to assume that the only income transfers that are made in society are those which pass via the Treasury and emerge as income support payments. The greatest amount of redistribution of income clearly occurs within households. At an equity level, the argument that these intra-household income transfers should be recognised for income tax purposes simply amounts to an argument that an individual should not be taxed on income which is not enjoyed by him or her.[7]

The argument for family tax-splitting on equity grounds has been criticised, but the criticisms are rarely convincing. Some argue that where income transfers are voluntary they should not be recognised for tax purposes, but this logic is not compelling. If a husband takes his wife into a partnership in respect of business income, that is a voluntary act, but the income sharing which partnership law then creates is recognised by the tax law. Why should the obligation to share one's income with a marital partner be treated any less seriously by the tax system? Why should marriage be the only form of economic partnership not recognised by the income tax law?[8]

Another, and rather stronger, argument against the recognition of income transfers in family situations is that there is joint consumption. Two or more may not be able to live as cheaply as one, but there are economies of scale in living together—one electricity bill, one mortgage, one television. But this argument is really an argument for a partial rather than per capita recognition of income sharing within families for tax purposes. It is an argument for developing equivalence scales to determine how much income different households require in order to achieve the same material standard of living (we discuss the use of equivalence scales in more detail later in this chapter).

Tax and social security treatment of families

Not allowing family members to split tax liabilities on wage or salary income which they share is not only inequitable. It also leads to families on similar incomes being treated differently according to the way they come by their incomes, for the social security system takes family circumstances into account while the tax system does not. This violates the principle of tax neutrality, and its impact is felt directly in the decisions that people make about their level of participation in the workforce.

Over the post-war years the treatment of families under taxation and social security arrangements has diverged. Whereas the social security system has always adjusted its benefits scales according to the number of persons dependent upon a given income, tax allowances for dependants have gradually been removed altogether from the taxation system.

The social security system either pays a married (partnered) rate of pension larger than a single rate and splits it between the respective spouses; or pays an additional benefit in respect of a dependent spouse to the claimant; or adds additional payments in respect of children. Social security also adds disregards of income for each child in the administration of its income tests.

Between 1915 and 1976 the tax system allowed deductions for dependants on the grounds that a taxpayer's ability to pay was reduced by the amounts necessary for the subsistence of those dependants, but this changed over time. Dependants' tax allowances were never large in relation to the cost of children and were steadily eroded by inflation over the post-war years until finally replaced by Family Allowances in 1976. Among the reasons for shifting allowances for dependants out of the tax system into the Social Security system were:

- the fact that some families had incomes too low to be able to claim any benefit from tax allowances;
- a desire to direct the payment specifically to the person with the care and the custody of children (usually the mother); and
- a desire to bring together cash payments previously made as child endowment and tax rebates (formerly deductions) which recognised the extra costs incurred by taxpayers with dependent children.[9]

Whatever the merits of these arguments, the result of eliminating dependants' allowances from the tax system has been that many families now simultaneously pay tax and receive income-tested benefits from the social security system in respect of children. As Saunders and Maley show in chapter 7, the interaction of the tax system and income-tested benefits means that for many families additional income brings little or no net benefit, for every extra dollar earned attracts additional tax, additional Medicare levy, and loss of Family Tax Benefit or AUSTUDY. For some families on higher incomes, the net result has been they now get no support at all to offset the costs of dependent children.

The revamping of family payments as FTBs received either as cash payments through social security (the Family Assistance Office) or as tax refunds reflected a perfectly justified reaction against family payments being seen as welfare handouts, and it was a reaffirmation of the role of horizontal equity. However family tax benefits represent an amalgam of income-tested welfare transfers and (differently income-tested) income tax rebates. The attempt to combine poverty alleviation payments with tax credits has unfortunately resulted in a system of such baffling obscurity that many families have had trouble reconciling their entitlements and have ended up having to repay money. Further, the recognition of horizontal equity is far from complete as increasing numbers of families exceed income test limits.

If revenue were raised by the Treasury in a neutral or non-distorting way, it would not matter so much what the Treasury paid out as child payments. However, most of the revenue Treasury raises comes from the taxpayers themselves and the funding of income-tested Family Payments via income taxes (largely on labour income) creates a double barrelled disincentive effect. Wage earners may be discouraged from entering the workforce or doing additional work, not only by incremental tax, but also by the loss of income-tested family benefits. As Robson shows in chapter 2, the efficiency costs to the economy from churning this money is considerable.

Because social security and educational payments are income tested on family income, the more the father or mother earns at certain levels of family income, the less their entitlement to these benefits. Regardless of whether it is the first or second earner who earns the income, the income test tapers (shade-outs) for these benefits are based on total family income.[10] By increasing the income of the family on low earnings (the 'income effect') and imposing a penalty on extra earnings (the 'substitution effect'), these means-tested payments are a double disincentive to labour force participation by family income earners.

How many earners?

The first question a family has to decide is who is to be the first earner? Is it to be the husband, the wife or both of them? The taxation and social security systems are neutral with respect to whether it is the husband or the wife who becomes the primary income earner. Whoever enters the paid workforce will face the same pattern of equivalent marginal tax rates as tax is imposed and social security benefits are withdrawn.

But suppose a couple feel they need more income to support the family. They may then have the choice of either earning more income in the hands of the first earner, or adding a second earner to the family. The first earner could gain more income from extra overtime, promotion or a moonlighting job, or the spouse could boost family income by entering the labour market.[11] What then is the situation, assuming such a choice is available?

When one examines the pattern of EMTRs[12] faced by (a) the first earner and (b) the possible second earner, one sees a clear tax bias in favour of having a second earner. If the first earner seeks to earn more overtime he or she will be taxed at the higher marginal rates. But if the spouse enters the labour market as a second earner, he or she will gain the advantage of a new tax threshold and the lower marginal rates of taxation on additional income. Because the income tax is individual and graduated, there is a clear bias towards a family seeking to put a second income earner into the workforce.

Two qualifications are commonly made to this conclusion. First of all it is argued that the second earner is at a disadvantage because child care expenses are not deductible for income tax purposes. Secondly it is argued that the secondary earner is disadvantaged because of the family's loss of imputed income in having to surrender another forty hours, say, to the paid labour market.

The argument that the non-deductibility of child care is a disadvantage to the second earner had some acceptance in the United States with the introduction of a child care tax credit. It has also to some extent been accepted in Australia with the introduction of the child care allowance. But where there are no children, child care expenses are obviously irrelevant, yet the tax bias in favour of becoming a two-income couple still stands. Where there are children, however, the question of child care costs needs closer examination.

Child care costs are not unique to two-income families. Unless one is willing to make the sexist assumption that a spouse (typically a wife) is available as free labour to mind children, child care costs are equally incurred by one income families. The only difference is that the child carer happens to be the spouse of the income earner. If child care is accepted as a legitimate cost of earning an income, a child care deduction should therefore be available equally to one-income and two-income families. If, for example, a second earner in a two-income family is allowed a deduction for expenses paid to a crèche, family day care or a relative to look after that family's children, neutrality requires the same deduction be allowed to a breadwinner 'paying' a spouse to look after their children.

This kind of neutrality does not exist. The maximum rate of child care benefit as at 1 January 2006 was $144 per child per week. By contrast, FTB (Part B) was a maximum of $117.60 per fortnight ($56.80 per week) where any child was under five years, plus an end-of-year supplement of $306.60.[13] The two-earner family paying someone else to provide child care is therefore supported by the tax system much more generously than the one earner family which takes on this cost itself.[14]

Turning to the second argument, that there is a tax bias in favour of the one-income family because a two-income family has to supply 40 hours or so extra labour to the labour market, this confuses different concepts. Essentially it is an argument for an earned income deduction to recognise the disutility involved in earning income. Arguably, it is as disagreeable for a single taxpayer or a first earner to supply 40 hours of paid labour to the market as it is for a second earner to supply 40 hours. To even up the scales between market and non-market work, an earned income deduction seems an appropriate measure, but there is no reason to restrict it to second earners. Non-deductible costs such as journey to and from work, the extra cost of meals taken away from home are, like child care, equally examples of extra costs indirectly incurred in gaining an income.

Neutral tax treatment of voluntary redistribution

One of the major purposes of a modern tax-transfer system is to redirect income from those who earn it to those who have no incomes. It is, however, often forgotten that this is only one social mechanism by which income is redistributed. Historically, voluntary transfers between family members have been much more important. Even in the absence of tax-transfer systems, spouses tend to support each other and their children. Likewise, children often support their adult parents while parents bequeath assets to their children.

The question arises as to how the tax system should treat such transfers of income within families. One option is simply to ignore them—they are neither excised from the income of the person making the transfer nor included in the income of the recipient. Another possibility is to exclude an income transfer from the income of the person making the transfer and include it in the income of the recipient. The third possibility is to double count an income transfer—to count it as income of the transferor but also include it as income of the transferee.

The last option is clearly not neutral in regard to private income transfers.[15] The first is generally consistent with the existing Australian position. But it is the second option that is more neutral. If one looks to the *enjoyment of income* rather than its *earning* then the truly neutral approach is the one that takes full account of income transfers. It should not matter whether redistribution of income is achieved by private transfers (within families) or by government transfers (through the social security system). They should be treated in the same way, which means that the policies governing family taxation should be made consistent with government policies for distributing welfare to families.

Options for a neutral system

There are basically two ways of achieving a more neutral taxation arrangement for families.[16] The first rests on the argument that any decision to acquire or support dependants is voluntary. Expenditure in maintaining spouses or children is in this view treated as private consumption, which means no allowance should be made for it in either the tax or social security system, any more than these systems make allowances for the purchase of holidays.

The second position asserts that a neutral tax system should fully recognise the income sharing which naturally occurs within family units. This would mean the tax system should take account of family circumstances just as the social security system currently does.

The first option would bring the taxation and social security arrangements into logical consistency by ignoring family income transfers. However the cost would be a worsening in the per capita distribution of income as no account would be taken of dependants in the social security system, any more than in the tax system.[17] This option would produce capricious results. For example no payments or additional allowances would be made for children, but an unemployed spouse of a millionaire would be entitled to claim unemployment benefits in their own right as there would be no presumption of the income sharing associated with recognition of dependency. Such results are clearly undesirable and unacceptable.

The second option would accept that income sharing does occur between individuals, especially within families, and would therefore attempt to recognise it in the taxation system as well as in the social security system. There are various ways this could be done.

One possibility would be to allow taxpayers to transfer, by mutual agreement, any amount of income to a spouse and children who would then be taxed on it at their own individual marginal rates.[18] To the extent that a spouse or child received transferred income, their entitlement to social security benefits would be reduced to the same extent. While quite consistently logical, however, this proposal might be thought too generous to families because it takes no account of economies in consumption.[19]

An alternative strategy would recognise income sharing among individuals within a family but would adjust the taxation scales so that the benefits of full splitting were reduced. In France, for example, each child is regarded for tax purposes as the equivalent of half an adult. Adopting this principle, the total income of all family members could be added up and divided by a figure comprising the sum of all the adults in the family unit plus one half for each of the children. Tax would then be struck on the family income at the average rate applicable to the standardised income.[20] One problem with this sort of approach would be determining appropriate equivalence scales (for example, should a child count for half an adult? Should a second adult count the same as a first adult?). But notwithstanding these difficulties, an equivalence scale approach to family taxation is probably the most neutral that could be devised. As Keynes once remarked, it is better to be vaguely right than precisely wrong.

A different version of tax-splitting would allow income sharing between family members to be recognised, but only up to the level of an appropriate threshold. Just as the first $6,000 of income each year is currently exempted from tax in the case of an individual as a minimum subsistence income, so one could allow other family members to have their own subsistence thresholds which could then be pooled. This is basically what Saunders and Maley argue for in chapter 7. It is worth remembering that pensioner couples are currently allowed to pool their pensioner tax rebates, which is similar to allowing them to pool tax thresholds, so there can be no objection in principle to allowing similar treatment for working families.

Allowing income sharing to be recognised through pooled tax thresholds is decidedly less neutral than a system of equivalence scales. It would, however, be a considerable improvement in terms of recognition of ability to pay of families as compared with the present arrangements under which tax burdens are essentially unchanged regardless of the number of people being supported by a given income.

To the extent that income transfers are made within families, individuals' eligibility for direct government transfers through the social security system should be adjusted. If a person acknowledges an income transfer from another family member, then that income transfer obviously ought to be taken into account in determining any need for income support for the recipient from the social security budget. At the moment the system is biased: unemployed married women and young people at home are denied unemployment benefits on the basis that they are being supported by someone else's income, yet that other person is denied any tax recognition for providing that income support.

Advantages of recognising income sharing

All of the options involving some recognition of family income sharing share common advantages. They would all bring about greater equity as between one-income and two-income families; they would all ensure recognition of reduced ability to pay where one income supports more than one person; they would all create greater neutrality as between the decision to send one or two income earners into the paid labour market; and they would all help reduce EMTRs.

Any of these options could be implemented without making stereotyped gender assumptions of dependency. By allowing income transfers to be made *on a wholly elective basis* by consent between the spouses, any woman who wishes to be taxed as an independent income unit would remain free to do so, and many would continue to opt for individual assessment. Where husbands and wives both have separate incomes, whether from work or property, there would be little need to transfer income between spouses. This simply underpins the point that the tax system should recognise that different families have different financial arrangements.

At the same time, recognition of income sharing in each of the options outlined above could avoid one of the criticisms commonly levelled against 'family unit taxation', that is, the necessity for couples to file joint returns and thereby disclose to each other *all* their financial affairs. Income sharing can be recognised through income transfers but with each person continuing to file separate tax returns. The only knowledge required to pass between the two parties is the common acknowledgement of the transfer and the actual or constructive payment from one party to the other or into a joint account. If an income transfer were recognised for tax purposes only where there is an actual cash payment from one spouse to another (for example, into a joint account), the tax system could even achieve the same result for spouses as was claimed for the introduction of family payments, that is, an actual payment received by a spouse.[21]

Recognising income sharing between family members would considerably reduce pressure for tax minimisation. One of the most common and successful forms of tax minimisation is income splitting. Although income splitting has been argued by some academic theorists as being contrary to the interests of women it is notable that, wherever it is possible, married couples seem to participate happily in it. Of the partnerships and trusts registered with the Commissioner of Taxation, the vast majority are family affairs. As more and more wage and salary earners enter the top marginal bracket the attraction of diverting some income to a spouse in the lower brackets has increased.

A further advantage of recognition of income sharing is that it can be employed for social security purposes as well as tax purposes, thereby eliminating double dipping. When family allowances were introduced in 1976, income splitting households (where the children enjoyed income) lost nothing through the abolition of dependent rebates but were able to gain a windfall in eligibility for family allowances. The recognition of explicit income sharing could make possible the more logical adjustment of social security payments so that they were not paid to dependants to the extent that an explicit election to share in a family member's income was made by the recipient or, in the case of a minor, by both parents.

One of the greatest benefits of recognising family income sharing would be the contribution it would make to disentangling the overlap of the social security and the tax system. As Saunders and Maley argue in chapter 7, a major reason for the high EMTRs faced by many family taxpayers is that they are simultaneously paying tax and receiving income tested benefits. From a logical point of view this is absurd. If a family is earning enough that it can afford to pay tax, it should surely not be receiving income-tested welfare payments. Conversely a family poor enough to be receiving welfare assistance ought not to be paying tax. Recognising income transfers in the tax system would have the effect of delaying the point at which families start to pay tax. This would mean a reduced overlap of income tax, marginal tax rates, and social security income test tapers.

Disadvantages and objections to income sharing options

One criticism made of any form of recognition of family income sharing in the tax system is that it would create a disincentive to female labour force participation.[22] Thus Apps and Savage argue that, as the elasticity of married women's labour supply is lower than men's, they should ideally be taxed at a lower marginal rate to increase female labour supply. They argue that *any* system of taxation which takes account of spousal income would be a mistake because it would reduce the incentive for women to enter the paid workforce.

But a similar criticism could be levied at family allowances, whether in the tax or the social security systems. *Any* form of income transfer to a spouse who is not a member of the paid workforce is going to increase her ability to decide to stay where she is, whether that income transfer comes from her husband or from the government. If incentives to labour force participation by married women are so desirable as to override other considerations, we might just as well argue that a special head tax be imposed upon married women, for this would reduce the ability of their husbands to support them and thus force them to enter the paid workforce. Indeed if one were to pursue the workforce disincentive argument to its logical conclusion, one might even forbid bequests of wealth to married women on the grounds that it might discourage them from entering the paid workforce.

The key point, of course, is that the income sharing options would be made available to be adopted on an *elective* basis. The question of disincentives thus dissolves, for women who choose to go out to work will still be able to organise their tax affairs on an individual basis, just as they do now.

We should also remember that increased labour force participation is not the be-all and end-all of economic policy. As Catherine Hakim has demonstrated, different women and different families have different preferences. Some women opt for paid work, even to the total exclusion of family or children, while others see their work as raising well-adjusted children and do not feel they need to be fulfilled by paid work—if they do it, it is because they and their families need the money. Many women like a balance of both work and family life. However women perceive their role in raising children, there is a clear social interest in respecting their different preferences.

It is also important to counter the claim that any system of joint or family taxation is inconsistent with the legal emancipation of married women.[23] This argument might apply to the old UK system of *compulsory* aggregation of husbands' and wives' incomes, but it is not appropriate to an *elective* system of voluntary income sharing. Besides, it is a misconception to assert that husbands and wives are totally financial independent. One can hardly be a partner with someone, whether in marriage or commerce, without some financial interaction. No matter how independent their financial arrangements, the *Family Law Act* imposes upon husband and wife an obligation to maintain the other. In some States legal obligations of a similar nature are also now imposed in the case of de facto spouses. The law simply does not recognise the right of the married man or women to assert: 'This is my income and my income alone and I will refuse to allow you any subsistence out of it.' Indeed property proceedings on dissolution of marriage are designed to secure a liquidated sum in discharge of that obligation of maintenance.[24]

Another argument sometimes employed against any recognition of family income sharing in the tax system is that it would be regressive. However this argument confuses horizontal and vertical equity. Analysis of the distribution of incomes must necessarily proceed on the basis of equivalent family or household incomes. For example, a taxpayer on $80,000 a year supporting a family of six will be found to have a lower equivalent income than two single people, each earning $30,000 and living together. A tax increase on incomes of $80,000 to finance tax cuts for incomes of $30,000 will in this case be regressive, for it will transfer income from the less well off to the better off. This, incidentally, helps explain why two-income childless couples appear to have fared better over the post-war period than taxpayers supporting a family on one income.[25]

Another objection which is sometimes raised to any form of recognition of family income transfers in the tax system is that this would amount to yet another 'tax expenditure'. Much of the current discussion of tax reform seeks to reduce tax rates by reducing or eliminating special allowances and deductions, so extending tax exemptions by allowing family income sharing might look like a step in the wrong direction. Two points may be made about this.

Firstly, an adjustment of the tax system to recognise horizontal equity cannot really be described as a tax expenditure at all. No one describes the tracing of income through trusts to its ultimate beneficiary as a tax expenditure. Nor does anyone describe the splitting of income between partners in a partnership as a tax expenditure. In each case the object is to trace the income through to the person who ultimately beneficially enjoys it. The same objective is involved in recognising family income transfers.

Secondly, we should not in any case assume that all tax expenditures are bad. For example, tax concessions are allowed for superannuation arrangements on the basis that they provide a more efficient means of people providing for their retirement than leaving the burden wholly on the government and the old age pension. Similarly, tax expenditures may be involved in accelerated depreciation or investment allowances, but these are justified on the basis of the contribution they may make to increasing the nation's productive capital stock. Recognition of family income transfers to dependent children can be seen as simply the human equivalent of the depreciation recognised as normal and natural for income from capital.[26]

There are also various administrative objections that sometimes get raised against recognising family income transfers in the tax system. It is sometimes asserted, for example, that the rise of informal relationships means that marriage is not a sound basis upon which to found tax policy, but this problem is overstated given that so much legislation has now assimilated the status of legal and de facto relationships. From the administrative point of view, we simply need to enquire whether there is an obligation, either actual or implied by law, to share income with family dependents. In the case of a legal marriage (or a de facto relationship in some States) there is such a legal obligation imposed and all that is required is to obtain from the parties to the marriage a jointly signed statement of the transfer. Where a legal system does not recognise the status of de factos as implying obligations and mutual support, it should be possible to ask the parties to submit to the Tax Office a legally binding deed of covenant. As for keeping track of family transfers, this seems no more difficult than keeping track of the formation and dissolution of partnerships and annual income distributions from them.

In the past an objection raised against taxation allowances for dependants was that they were claimable by the breadwinner without any proof that the expenditure incurred actually went to the dependants. This objection can be answered by requiring that any form of income sharing with family members would be recognised only where there is consent by both spouses to the election, and where an actual income transfer is made into a bank account which can be operated by the spouse (this could be either a joint or an individual account). Any consent could also be revocable at any time. Where consent was withdrawn by a spouse to any recognition of income sharing (for example, on the break-up of a relationship) that spouse would become eligible for social security payments on the new basis.

Anticipated effects of income sharing

Recognising family income sharing in the tax system would increase the reservation wage (the lowest wage for which people are willing to work) demanded by married women (and, sometimes, men) before entering the paid workforce. The greater the after-tax income of the family subsisting on one income, the less need there would be for that family to put a second breadwinner into the paid workforce.

To the extent that families were more capable of surviving on one wage, there would also be a higher reservation wage for workers generally. This could offset any downward wage pressure from greater deregulation of the labour market such as changes to the minimum wage. Instead of being a matter of necessity, a second income would be more a matter of choice.

Recognition of income transfers between family members could also reduce the combined EMTRs of tax and social security income tests over large income ranges. As reduced EMTRs encourage less welfare dependency, one might also expect greater output and reduced Budgetary expenditure.[27]

Conclusion

As far as possible, a tax-transfer system should be neutral as between different methods of household organisation. There should be no discrimination for or against households with one or two earners, or with one full-time and one part-time earner.

Existing tax-transfer arrangements do not satisfy this objective. There are considerable public subsidies paid for child care for married women entering the paid workforce. Subsidies payable to mothers minding their own children are considerably less, notwithstanding the narrowing of the difference through increased FTB (Part B) being paid to single income families. At the same time, the tax system treats extra family income earned by a second earner more favourably than overtime or promotion by primary earner. Factors such as these may have contributed to a growth in labour force participation by second earners beyond their preferred level.

From time to time, arguments are made that the playing field should be levelled. Some would argue that equal subsidies should be paid to mothers at home as for child care for working women. This was the logic behind the introduction of FTB (Part B) as well as the so-called 'baby bonus' for mothers leaving the workforce to raise children. But another approach is to allow taxpayers recognition for the income transfers they themselves make to their family dependants. This general approach can be justified on both equity and efficiency grounds. No income tax system can be described as fair which fails to takes account of the number of people depending upon a given income, but this is essentially the system we have in Australia.

There will always be persons dependent upon the sharing of the incomes of those in the labour force. A failure by the tax system to recognise this massive family redistribution of income tends to force those who cannot be supported by the incomes of other family members to enter the paid work force on their own account, quite possibly against their inclinations and at the expense of other socially worthwhile activities.

Chapter 9

Rebuilding Australia's Tax And Welfare Systems[1]

John Humphreys

It seems that everybody these days has a suggestion on how the current tax and welfare system in Australia can be reformed. Some ideas include cutting the top marginal income tax rate, increasing the tax-free threshold, cutting middle-class welfare, broadening the income tax base and flattening the rates, slowing the phase-out of welfare benefits and reducing the endless array of tax concessions.

This chapter argues for a fundamental reform of our tax/welfare system that would include all of these elements. It also develops a total rethink of the way in which we help the poor. It therefore addresses the two pressing problems in Australian public policy today: our tax system and our welfare system.

Our income tax system is complex, arbitrary, inefficient, wasteful—and the level of taxation is too high. Our top marginal tax rate is higher than the rate in communist party-controlled China, our income tax burden is one of the highest in the developed world, and Australians are currently suffering from the highest level of tax in our history. In chapter 2, Alex Robson estimates that 80,000 people are employed to avoid or enforce taxes, and those taxes result in about $30 billion of lost efficiency every year.

The current system of welfare payments is complex, expensive, inefficient and ineffective. If we distributed the current federal welfare budget directly to the poorest 25% of Australians, each family of four would receive $72,000 per year.[2] And welfare spending continues to increase quickly. In three years, we will reach $100 billion of federal spending on welfare ($80,000 for each of our poorest 25% of families). Yet despite this massive level of expenditure, poverty remains entrenched. One reason is that our current approach to poverty prevents people from getting jobs, and then fails to reward people who do work.

The idea: 'Reform 30/30'

My proposal, which I call 'Reform 30/30', includes a tax-free threshold of $30,000 and a flat income tax of 30%, with no deductions. The Fringe Benefits Tax (FBT) would be reduced to 30% and the Medicare levy would be abolished.[3] In addition, all welfare payments would be replaced by a sliding scale of payments made only to people with an income below $30,000.[4] This sliding payments system, called a Negative Income Tax (NIT), would pay the recipient 30% of the difference between his or her income and the tax-free threshold ($30,000).

Rates of welfare payments are outlined in Table 9.1. As the NIT is paid to low-income earners, it would also replace the minimum wage.

No special treatment is given for parents, the disabled or the aged. This is not because these issues are unimportant, but because I do not want to link the Reform 30/30 to any particular agenda on child subsidies, disability support or retirement policies. Each of these issues deserves the attention of policy makers, but this does not have to be linked to the central elements of Reform 30/30. Additional welfare payments for these groups are considered in the Appendix to this chapter.

This reform will decrease welfare payments to the unemployed and increase the payment to the working poor. For every additional dollar earned, the NIT payment is reduced by $0.30, so work incentives are identical for all workers irrespective of whether they are above or below the tax-free threshold. For more details on the theory of the NIT see Friedman[5] or Humphreys.[6]

Table 9.1: Basic welfare payments under Reform 30/30

Wage	TFT	Shortfall	NIT	Final income	NIT rate of withdrawal
$0	$30,000	$30,000	$9000	$9000	n/a
$5000	$30,000	$25,000	$7500	$12,500	30%
$10,000	$30,000	$20,000	$6000	$16,000	30%
$15,000	$30,000	$15,000	$4500	$19,500	30%
$20,000	$30,000	$10,000	$3000	$23,000	30%
$25,000	$30,000	$5000	$1500	$26,500	30%
$30,000	$30,000	$0	$0	$30,000	30%

Replacing the minimum wage

One of the primary advantages of replacing the existing welfare system with a NIT is that directly helping low-income earners through the welfare system removes the need for the minimum wage. Instead of legislating for higher wages, the NIT allows wages to stay at their market rate and instead supplements low incomes with a NIT payment.

This proposal is an extension of the so-called 'Five Economists' Plan' first published in 1998. Their basic idea was to freeze minimum wage increases in nominal terms (allowing the minimum wage to decrease in real terms) and replace minimum wage increases with a tax credit.[7] Both the Five Economists' Plan and the 30/30 NIT directly confront the fact that the minimum wage causes unemployment and recognise that the minimum wage is a uniquely bad instrument for helping poor workers.

The minimum wage does not target poor households. Dawkins[8] cites evidence that only 10% of minimum wage earners are from families in the bottom 10% of disposable incomes, and 25% of minimum wage earners come from families in the top 30% of disposable incomes. More importantly, the minimum wage results in unemployment which is the main cause of poverty in Australia. This is because wages in the labour market approximate their level of marginal productivity. If the minimum wage is set above a person's level of marginal productivity, they will not be employed. For example, if I bring $7/hour of value to a business, but the business is forced to pay me $8/hour, it will simply not employ me or it will make a loss.

Dawkins claims that freezing nominal wage increases over four years could lead to a 1–1.5% reduction in the unemployment rate and he notes that this would specifically help unskilled workers and the long-term unemployed. There is an ongoing debate about the exact size of the relationship between wage rates and employment. One recent Australian estimate by Lewis and MacDonald suggests a wage elasticity of labour demand of -0.9 (for hours worked) and -0.8 (for employment).[9] That is, if average wages were increased by 10% then employment would decrease by 8%. Some economists have suggested a lower estimate of around -0.4.[10] Either estimate is plausible and consistent with previous studies both in Australia and internationally.[11]

How much employment would Reform 30/30 create? The original Five Economists' Plan suggested an increase of 2.5–3% (250,000–300,000). Dawkins later estimated an effect of 2–2.5% (200,000–250,000), though he added that it could be higher. Borland[12] has estimated a 2.1–7.2% (210,000–720,000) increase in employment from the Five Economists' Plan. Richardson[13] suggests 169,000 after ten years and Dixon and Rimmer[14] estimated 2% (200,000) after five years and 4% (400,000) after ten years. The impact of Reform 30/30 would be even greater, for it would enable the minimum wage to be abolished altogether (although as the minimum wage is lowered, the marginal benefits from further reductions are smaller as fewer people are on the minimum wage). A rough estimate of 400,000–600,000 (with a midpoint of 500,000) new jobs leading to a 2–3% reduction in the unemployment rate seems reasonable. And this gain could be even bigger if we combined scrapping the minimum wage with fixing the income disincentives in the tax and welfare systems.

Fixing incentives by reducing the effective marginal tax rate to 30%

The incentive to work is determined by the effective marginal tax rate (EMTR). This measures how much of an additional dollar earned has to be given to the government (either in tax or reduced welfare payments). If the EMTR is 100%, then an extra dollar earned must be given straight to the government and the worker is no better off.

In Australia, the EMTR is highest on low-income families because of the quick withdrawal of welfare payments when people start to earn income combined with income tax. For example, in late 2005 the Parenting Payment (Single) is withdrawn at a rate of 40% once one has an income over $4411 per year. The Newstart allowance is withdrawn at 50% or 70%, depending on income. The Family Tax Benefit (Part A) is withdrawn at 20% once one has an income over $31,755. In addition, 17% tax (soon to be 15%) is paid on incomes earned over $6000 and 30% tax on the income over $21,600. Also, the Medicare levy is phased in at $0.20 in the dollar for incomes between $26,834–29,010. Other welfare benefits are also removed as incomes increase, such as the low-income tax rebate and housing assistance.

The combination of these impacts can result in a low-income earner suffering from EMTRs approaching 100%. Almost one million people face EMTRs of 60% or more. The consequence of this is a significant incentive *not* to work, and the fact that this leads to a cycle of poverty is referred to as the *poverty trap*.

To reduce poverty, high EMTRs have to be addressed, and there are only three ways this can be done. First, welfare benefits for jobless people can be lowered in order to reduce the rate at which benefits get withdrawn when people start earning. Second, welfare top-ups for the working poor can be increased. Third, tax on the working poor can be decreased or removed. Reform 30/30 does all three. Unemployment benefits are reduced from over $10,000 per year (for a single person) to $9000 per year. Welfare top-ups for low-income earners are increased as the NIT payment is withdrawn at only 30%. Finally, no low-income person would pay income tax.

The key point is that by increasing the tax-free threshold to $30,000 and limiting welfare to people with incomes below $30,000, there is no overlap between taxpayers and welfare recipients. Not only does this remove the problem of overlapping work disincentives, but also it removes the pointless churning of money from taxpayers to bureaucrats back to the same taxpayers. The size of this churning has been estimated as high as $85 billion.[15]

The reform suggested in this chapter would ensure a constant EMTR of 30% for everybody, in all situations, with the welfare withdrawal rate mirroring the 30% marginal tax rate. The biggest winners are clearly the working poor who previously had the highest EMTRs and who now get to keep more of their welfare benefits and are exempt from income tax.[16]

Economic efficiency and growth

In the medium term, Reform 30/30 would impact on economic efficiency through lower efficiency costs of taxation, reduced unemployment/poverty, and less waste from a simpler system. These three benefits are estimated to save $20 billion, $60 billion and $10 billion respectively, resulting in total savings of about $90 billion, or $4500 per person per year. In the longer term, there will also likely be an impact on economic growth. This benefit is more difficult to estimate but even a small improvement in the growth rate will lead to substantial benefits.

There are two elements of Reform 30/30 that reduce the efficiency cost of taxation. The first is the reduction in tax, and the second is the switch from a multi-level income tax to a flat income tax, including the alignment of company tax, individual tax, CGT and FBT.

As Alex Robson shows in chapter 2, taxes involve a change in incentives and consequently a change in behaviour away from a person's first choice of actions. This results in a loss of welfare, referred to as the deadweight loss (DWL) of taxation.

Raising the tax-free threshold to $30,000 represents a tax cut of $26 billion. Removing the 42% and 47% brackets is a further $8 billion tax cut.[17] Abolishing the Medicare levy and bringing FBT into line with other income taxes would cut revenue by about $6 billion and $1 billion respectively. The total tax cut is about $41 billion. Such a tax cut would reduce DWL by between $8 and $24 billion per year.

In addition to a reduction in tax, Reform 30/30 replaces the current multi-stage income tax with a more efficient flat tax. A multi-stage tax creates disincentives against risk, by taxing the proceeds of high-risk, high-return investments at a higher rate than low-risk, low-return investments, even though both may have the same expected return. A flat tax is also more efficient because it does not discriminate against volatile annual incomes or different levels of income. In addition, by taxing all incomes (fringe benefits, capital gains, wages, dividends, interest) at the same level, businesses and individuals have the incentive to structure their finances in the most efficient way. Consequently, the DWL of the remaining income tax would be lower under Reform 30/30.

A total efficiency gain of about $20 billion from the tax changes is a reasonable estimate.

As discussed previously, these reforms would also generate more jobs and better incentives for poor Australians. About 500,000 new jobs could be created, cutting unemployment by 2–3%. Okun's law suggests that for every percent of unemployment, the national product is 2–4% lower than what it otherwise would be. Using this rule of thumb, a 2–3% reduction in unemployment would result in a 4–12% increase in GDP. Australian GDP for 2005–06 is estimated at $927.6 billion. Consequently, Okun's law predicts an economic benefit of $37.1–$111.3 billion. Given the uncertainty, a reasonable point estimate is $60 billion per year.

A simpler system will also result in less wasted spending on compliance, administration, rent-seeking and tax evasion. Robson estimates over 80,000 people are currently employed in avoiding and enforcing tax. Most of these jobs would be unnecessary under Reform 30/30. We can therefore estimate a reduction in waste of perhaps $8 billion per year. In addition, Leigh estimates that on average the compliance cost to each taxpayer is about $300, for a total annual impact of around $3 billion.[18]

Another benefit from a lower and simpler tax system is the reduced incentive and ability to avoid tax—leading to more reported income and a smaller black market. The size of the black market is difficult to estimate, but a total benefit from increased simplicity of around $10 billion seems reasonable.

More controversial, and much harder to measure, is the long-run impact of tax/welfare reform on economic growth, but there are good reasons for believing that a more efficient tax/welfare system will have a growth benefit. There is a growing body of evidence that suggests a link between competition and growth,[19] and tax and the minimum wage act as barriers to entry and therefore as restrictions on competition. By including an additional 500,000 minds to the workforce there are more opportunities for new ideas to be developed and tested. Some of the best minds of the country will switch their attentions from tax avoidance to innovation and wealth creation. Finally, income tax cuts increase the incentive to invest in income-generating activities like education and research—which are drivers of growth.[20]

A conservative estimate of a 0.1% increase in the rate of growth would increase the size of the economy by nearly $1 billion every year. Note that while the medium-term benefits do not grow over time, the growth benefit does—so that the annual benefit is $10 billion after 10 years or $20 billion after 20 years. As can be seen, it does not take long for reforms that increase economic growth to pay for themselves.

Equity

There are two ways of looking at the winners and losers from this reform. The first is to look only at the actual transfers—in which case welfare reform is largely a zero-sum game with some winners and some losers. The second, and by far the more useful way, is to consider the consequences of the reform. Unfortunately, while the latter approach is more appropriate, the former approach is more popular because it is easier.

Table 9.2: Static impact of Reform 30/30 on an individual (comparison with 2004)[21]

Income	Current Welfare	30/30 Welfare	Current Tax	30/30 Tax	Current Total	30/30 Total	Change
No income	$10,147	$9000	$0	$0	$10,147	$9000	-11%
Half minimum ($11,658)	$3512	$5504	$962	$0	$14,209	$17,162	+21%
Minimum ($23,316)	$0	$2005	$3166	$0	$20,150	$26,482	+31%
Average ($48,993)	$0	$0	$10,869	$5698	$38,124	$43,295	+14%
Double Average ($97,986)	$0	$0	$32,859	$20,396	$65,127	$77,590	+19%

The static consequences of Reform 30/30 on individual incomes for different wage categories are shown in Table 9.2. Such a table does not consider the primary benefits of reform: higher employment, better incentives, higher growth and less poverty. Still, the table provides some interesting starting information.

In static terms, the biggest winners are workers–especially low-income individuals. Those on half minimum wage see their disposable income increase by 21% while those on the minimum wage see their disposable income increase by 31%.

Note that the current system has people on half minimum wage both paying tax ($962) and receiving welfare ($3512) while the Reform 30/30 option has no such churning. In the current system, people moving from no income to half-minimum wage see their welfare payment decrease by 57% while they also pay an average of 8% income tax, giving them an EMTR of 65%. People currently on half minimum face an EMTR of 49%, those on the minimum wage face an EMTR of 30% and those on an average wage face an EMTR of 45%. Under Reform 30/30 they all face a constant EMTR of 30%.

Average and above-average wage earners also benefit by 14% and 19% respectively. The income tax paid by a worker on an average income almost halves from nearly $11,000 to $5700. In contrast, the unemployed see their disposable income reduced by 11%. Their welfare payments are cut from over $10,000 to $9000 per year. Some will argue that this is inequitable. However, this ignores the total impact on poor people and ignores the dynamic consequences of this policy. Indeed, the most important consequence from this policy is a reduction in unemployment and poverty.

Reform 30/30 continues to ensure that nobody need live in absolute poverty, but it also removes the poverty trap and allows the creation of hundreds of thousands of new jobs.

If we look at the total consequence of Reform 30/30 on people who are currently unemployed, the impact is positive with the creation of 500,000 new jobs. The average disposable income for people who are currently unemployed will increase despite the decrease in welfare payments, because of the increase in employment. If cutting the welfare benefits for the unemployed is considered inequitable, then how much more inequitable is it to continue with a policy that keeps people unemployed?

Some will also argue that Reform 30/30 is inequitable because it cuts income taxes for all earners, including high-income earners. Against this, we should remember that the reform ensures that high-income earners cannot access welfare (other than the tax-free threshold), and it removes the myriad tax concessions that tend to benefit high-income earners. Moreover, as Lauchlan Chipman reminds us in chapter 5, there is no reason to think that forcing high-income earners to pay exorbitant levels of income tax is inherently moral.

A perfectly flat tax would be proportional, with each person paying the same percentage of his or her income and the rich paying more than the poor. However, the 'flat tax' in Reform 30/30 is not proportional, it is progressive. It is progressive, both because it double taxes savings (and rich people have a higher marginal propensity to save),[22] and because the $30,000 tax free threshold (TFT) makes the average tax rate progressive. Thus, while a person with an income of $30,000 pays an average tax of 0%, a person with an income of $40,000 pays an average tax of 7.5%, a person with an income of $50,000 pays an average tax of 12%, and a person with an income of $100,000 pays an average tax of 21%. The higher the income, the higher the average tax paid. As Andrew Norton indicates in chapter 10, there is little evidence that Australians want high-income earners punished any more than the above tax scale would achieve.

Another equity consideration is the treatment of couples compared with singles. Here I would dispute Terry Dwyer's arguments in chapter 8. Noting that the tax system treats individuals separately while the welfare system takes account of their family circumstances, Dwyer argues that the tax system should be brought into line with the welfare system by allowing families to share their tax burden through a system of pooled thresholds. Saunders and Maley argue the same thing in chapter 7 where they echo the conventional view that families and household units enjoy the benefit of economies of scale, and should therefore receive less welfare and pay more tax.

However, economies of scale can be seen as an appropriate reward for people who make economising decisions. Punishing people for making low-cost decisions (sharing accommodation and living costs) makes no sense and offers a perverse set of anti-family, anti-shared house incentives. It punishes couples for being couples. There is no clear rationale for undermining family units and denying people the benefit from economies of scale. Indeed, not only is this inequitable, but it is also inefficient as it encourages people to make sub-optimal lifestyle choices.

The alternative way of bringing the tax and welfare systems into line is for the welfare system to treat people as individuals, just as the tax system does. NIT does this, and thereby avoids distorting people's incentives when determining family structures.

An additional, but often overlooked, equity consideration is inter-temporal equity, or equal treatment over time. One of the foundation principles of horizontal equity is that people in the same position should be treated the same. For example, if we both earn the same income, we both pay the same tax. However, once we introduce time into our consideration then a multi-level income tax system will discriminate against people with volatile incomes.

For example, under the current tax system a person on $50,000 will pay a top marginal tax rate of 30%. However, a person whose income fluctuates between $10,000 and $90,000 each year will occasionally fall into a higher tax bracket and will end up paying a higher average tax rate —even though total income over time is the same as the first person. Not only does this create an inefficient disincentive against pursuing risky jobs and businesses, but this violates the rules of horizontal equity.[23]

Simplicity

Another important benefit from Reform 30/30 is the simplicity of the system. Currently we have myriad programs, tax law that runs to about 10,000 pages, various tax rates and tax offsets and tax deductions and tax minimisation schemes, as well as a broad range of welfare payments and welfare supplements and withdrawal rates and top-up payments and penalties, and so on. Thousands of administrators are given the task of removing tax from workers, so that the same money can be paid back to the same workers. Taxpayers struggle with tax returns and wealthy Australians find tax loopholes.

By having a flat tax at the same level as company tax, and removing all tax expenditures[24] (that is, removing all tax offsets and deductions except those necessary to retain the integrity of the income tax system), there would be no need for tax returns for the majority of taxpayers. Compliance cost is removed. The dreaded 'Tax Pack' would become a thing of the past for most Australians, saving considerable time, money and headaches. [25]

There would be no question of tax avoidance and no need for complex accounting procedures. People would have a choice between paying a 30% fringe benefits tax, a 30% company tax, a 30% individual tax, a 30% capital gains tax or having their welfare reduced by 30%. No need for trusts or shell companies. Tens of thousands of tax lawyers and accountants would be out of a job. The biggest losers from Reform 30/30 would be tax accountants—which is surely a sign of good tax reform.

Further, lower tax rates, lower compliance costs, a more simple system and a perfectly flat incentive structure will reduce tax evasion.[26] Some people will continue to be employed in the black market and some businessmen will claim personal expenses as business expenses. However, these problems are unavoidable in any income tax system and Reform 30/30 would decrease the incentive for, and ability to achieve, tax evasion.

Every avenue of government activity opens up the cost of rent-seeking. Differential tax rates, tax expenditure and a complex range of welfare payments open up significant scope for interested parties to lobby the government for special favours. This lobbying behaviour is itself an economic waste as rent-seeking behaviour is not directed at creating extra production. A low, simple and flat tax offers fewer possibilities for special favour and, therefore, less scope for rent-seeking activities.

Public finance

One potential criticism of Reform 30/30 is that it is not affordable. However, rough estimates indicate that it would more than pay for itself.

There are eight ways that this reform impacts on the budget:

- A tax cut of about $40 billion per year (as estimated above).
- Replacement of all welfare with an NIT would save about $15 billion. Welfare payments to the unemployed are reduced to $9000 per year, and more jobs and better incentives will result in fewer unemployed

people claiming full benefits. These gains are partially offset by increased welfare payments to the working poor. The cost of the NIT payments would be about $70 billion per year.[27] As current welfare payments total $85 billion, this represents a cut in basic welfare payments of $15 billion.

- Additional spending on children, aged and disabled of about $25 billion per year (see Appendix).
- Abolish tax expenditures of about $30 billion per year. The Tax Expenditure Statement shows that current tax concessions sum to about $35 billion in 2005–06 and are increasing rapidly. While tax expenditures are nominally reductions in tax, for all intents and purposes they are spending proposals. For efficiency purposes, tax concessions do not reduce the DWL of tax (and may actually increase it by further changing incentives). For equity purposes they have the same impact as spending proposals, except that the primary beneficiaries of many tax expenditures are high-income earners. For simplicity purposes, tax expenditures distort our tax system, create tax avoidance opportunities, create considerable administration and compliance costs, and decrease public policy transparency. It is necessary to retain some tax deductions for companies and the self-employed to ensure that they are taxed only for their profit and not for their entire revenue. But allowing any tax concessions beyond this will open the door to another round of perverse modifications of the tax system, destroying the benefits of simplicity and undermining the efficiency of the system. While some tax concessions may have merit, they can be achieved through other means. The total savings from abolishing tax expenditures is estimated at $30 billion.
- Higher tax from a bigger economy of about $25 billion per year. The Laffer curve (discussed by Sinclair Davidson in chapter 3) suggests that tax cuts can increase tax revenues by encouraging greater work effort and a larger economy. While the strict interpretation of this for Australia's current position is controversial, the broad point that tax cuts are partially offsetting should not be in question. Using estimates outlined earlier, the DWL from tax are around $20 billion. With a government/GDP ratio of 30%, the Laffer offset is estimated at only $6 billion per year.[28] But in addition to tax cuts, the other factor contributing to a larger economy is the higher employment from welfare reform. Given the estimated benefit of about $60 billion to the economy, the government should gain an additional $18 billion from this, giving a total benefit to the government of about $24 billion (of this, perhaps

$8 billion will go to State and local governments, mostly through the GST).

- Administrative savings of about $5 billion per year. The simplicity of the tax system will lead to a number of budgetary savings. The ATO currently spends $2.6 billion per year and The Department of Family and Community Services spends $2.3 billion, which could be severely cut under Reform 30/30. Other areas of the government that also have to deal with the complex tax and welfare systems could be cut back—including Treasury and Finance. A total administrative saving of about $5 billion could be expected.
- Decreased tax avoidance and evasion of about $5 billion per year. A low and flat income tax with no deductions removes both the incentive and ability to pursue tax minimisation schemes, which will result in more tax revenue. In chapter 3, Davidson notes that income reported by high-income earners is likely to be more sensitive to changes in marginal tax rates. After Reagan's tax cuts, the share of income tax paid by the richest 5% of Americans grew from 35.3% to 38.9%. In the UK, the top marginal tax rate was cut from 83% to 40% by Thatcher and the top 10% of income earners saw their share of the total tax bill increase from 35% to 42%. The increased tax from high-income earners that follow tax cuts can be partly explained by increased work effort, but some of it also likely comes from less tax avoidance. In addition there is the issue of illegal tax evasion. High-income earners have access to tax schemes that approach or pass the fine legal line, but average taxpayers also have plenty of opportunities for (and incentive to commit) tax evasion under the current system. This would be reduced under Reform 30/30. It is difficult to put a value on this benefit, but an increase of several billion would not be unexpected.
- Potential future benefits of higher economic growth could be $3 billion after ten years even on conservative estimates. In the long term, the impact on the budget will be more positive.

While the above estimates indicate that Reform 30/30 will be good for the budget, a few caveats are important. First, these are rough costings and further investigation of the impacts of the reform is needed. In addition, the above estimates consider the impact of Reform 30/30 in the medium term. It may take several years for the full impact of the tax and welfare reforms to be felt in the economy and by the government. In the short term, the impact on the budget will be less positive.

However, if the benefits of Reform 30/30 are real, then this policy deserves to be pursued *even if* it costs the budget. There are plenty of government programs in need of removal, most specifically corporate welfare. The possibility of short-term deficits is a poor excuse to deny people the benefits of Reform 30/30.

Conclusion

The reforms suggested in this chapter are more radical than most other suggestions being considered today. This chapter calls for implementing a flat tax, cutting taxes significantly, aligning all income tax rates, removing all tax expenditure, abolishing the minimum wage and introducing a new and unique welfare system. It would be easy for a conservative mind to dismiss these ideas as too bold or too controversial.

Even strong supporters of tax/welfare reform and tax cuts shy away from proposing such fundamental reforms. Others refuse to consider any proposal that is not strictly budget neutral in the short term, or that could potentially lead to any loss in the static analysis. But the potential benefits from Reform 30/30 are difficult to ignore. In a perfect world, we may well combine high welfare payments with good incentives, or a range of tax expenditures with a simple and efficient tax system—but we do not live in such a world. In reality we must choose among competing priorities.

This chapter has outlined how a negative income tax can replace the minimum wage as an effective means of helping the working poor and how this will lead to 500,000 new jobs. The constant EMTR of 30% is a significant improvement on the current poverty trap that sees some people face an EMTR of around 100%. Combined, these two effects would help combat poverty and allow greater upward mobility for all Australians.

The impact on economic efficiency is unambiguously positive, with a benefit of perhaps $90 billion in the medium term and larger still in the longer term. Likewise, the impact on simplicity is unambiguously positive and leads to significant benefits through lower compliance costs, administration costs, and tax avoidance costs.

The impact on equity is more complex because the criteria for equity are so often subjective. However, as the biggest benefit of Reform 30/30 is the reduction in unemployment and poverty, it is hard to see how it could be called inequitable. Given the only consistent objective criteria of equity, a flat tax (and flat incentive structure) seems more equitable than any alternative. Further, Reform 30/30 ends the current inequitable discrimination against couples.

We have a choice between a high, distorting, complex and costly tax system, a failed and counter-productive minimum wage and a welfare system that creates poverty—or a simple system that keeps people out of poverty,

APPENDIX: CHILDREN, DISABLED AND AGED

This chapter has not considered the complicating factors of parents of children, the disabled and the aged. This is not because these areas are unimportant, but because they are not central to the functioning of the Reform 30/30 system. The basic ideas of Reform 30/30 hold whether you want to abolish, change, cut or increase child subsidies, disability payments or the aged pension.

Based on current welfare policies towards the aged, disability and children, an additional \$20–30 billion (with a midpoint of \$25 billion) could be spent on welfare supplements.

For each of these categories there are broadly five approaches that can be considered:

1) Increase the TFT for these groups, with the associated increase in the NIT payment. This is the same as introducing an additional non-means tested welfare payment.

2) Introduce an additional means-tested welfare payment. This approach would undermine many of the benefits of Reform 30/30.

3) Decentralise responsibility for these groups to State and/or local governments (note that Reform 30/30 would lead to more revenue to State and local governments).

4) Decentralise responsibility for these groups to civil society, potentially with government subsidies (Reform 30/30 would arguably lead to more philanthropy by cutting the tax burden)

5) Consider non-traditional government support, such as supporting disability-related services or adjusting other taxes.

The important thing to note with additional welfare payments is that they should seek not to undermine the efficiency and simplicity of the tax/welfare system by introducing tax expenditures or withdrawal rates. This can be done by adjusting the TFT if necessary, by decentralising responsibility to a more individual level (States and civil society), or by using non-traditional methods to help those in need.

Parents of children

While the decision to have children is made by parents and not the taxpayers, arguments that suggest parents be solely responsible for their children are unlikely to find political support.[29] Perhaps the best response to the demand that families be helped to meet the costs of raising children would be to adjust the tax-free threshold for parents, and consequently the size of the NIT payment.

If the tax-free threshold was raised by $6,000 per child this would cost an additional $7.2 billion in higher welfare payments and lost tax revenue. If the tax-free threshold were raised by $10,000 per child, this would cost an additional $12 billion (with a 30% tax rate, this second option is identical to offering a $3,000 non-means tested child subsidy). For comparison, the current approach of Family Tax Benefit (Parts A and B), Child Care Benefit and Maternity Allowance cost about $13.2 billion per year.

With a child TFT supplement of $6,000, a couple with two children would now have a combined TFT of $72,000 ($30,000 + $30,000 + $6,000 + $6,000). An unemployed couple with two children would receive $21,600 through the NIT.

Such a policy would not impact on the incentives or consequences of the basic reform plan except to increase its budgetary cost. One important point to note is that such a policy does not differentiate between working parents and stay-at-home parents and so does not discriminate for or against any particular lifestyle choice.

Table 9.3: Static impact of Reform 30/30 on a single-income family (2+2), 2004 comparison.

The first 30/30 figure represents a child TFT supplement of $10,000 and the bracketed figure represents a child TFT supplement of $6000 per child. [30]

Income	Current Welfare	30/30 Welfare	Current Tax	30/30 Tax	Current Total (EMTR)	30/30 Total	Change
No income	$27,148	$24,000 ($21,600)	$0	$0	$27,148	$24,000 ($21,600)	-12% (-20%)
Half minimum ($11,658)	$20,536	$20,503 ($18,103)	$962	$0	$31,232	$32,161 ($29,761)	+3% (-5%)
Minimum ($23,316)	$12,385	$17,005 ($14,605)	$3166	$0	$32,535	$40,321 ($37,921)	+24% (+17%)
Average ($48,993)	$3132	$9302 ($6902)	$10,869	$0	$41,256	$58,295 ($55,895)	+41% (+35%)
Double Average ($97,986)	$2037	$0 ($0)	$32,859	$5396 ($7796)	$67,164	$92,590 ($90,190)	+38% (+34%)

With even the lower child-TFT supplement, nearly all couples with children will still gain from the reforms, both in a static sense and more especially in a dynamic sense. In a static sense there are significant benefits to most workers, especially those on an average income, but also those on double the average wage and those on the minimum wage.

More importantly, in a dynamic sense the EMTR for families is dramatically reduced under Reform 30/30. Under the current system, people on no income have an EMTR of 65%, the EMTR for people on half minimum wage is 89%, the EMTR for people on the minimum wage is 66% and the EMTR for people on an average wage is 47%. In contrast, the Reform 30/30 system has a constant EMTR of 30%. The biggest winners in a dynamic sense are clearly the low-income workers.

In addition, note that the current system takes tax off all earnings categories and churns that money back in welfare to all earnings categories. In contrast, under the 30/30 system, people either receive welfare or pay tax; they don't do both.

However, with a low child subsidy, fewer unemployed single parents will gain as (1) they do not get the economies of scale of living with another adult; (2) the current system is particularly generous to this group; and (3) single parents are less able to take advantage of workplace opportunities because of domestic responsibilities. There are several options for dealing with unemployed single parents. One option is simply to pay a higher child subsidy. Perhaps a better option is to decentralise responsibility to State and local governments and civil society groups who are better able to deal with the day-to-day realities of single parents living in poverty. The situation of single parents is not something easily fixed by throwing money at it and is best addressed at a more personal level.

Irrespective of which approach is taken, it is unlikely that a budget for child subsidies would exceed $10–15 billion.

The disabled and aged

Another important issue for welfare is the protection of people who are particularly disadvantaged such as the disabled, and policies for retirement income. This paper does not aim to deal with these complex issues and Reform 30/30 is consistent with various approaches to disability and retirement policies.

Both disability payments and the aged pension could be paid as TFT supplements (as suggested for parents of children). However, there are potentially better alternatives.

With disability services there is an argument for decentralising responsibility to the State level and civil society. The needs of the disabled vary considerably and it makes little sense to bundle in the seriously disabled with those who are suffering in the recent epidemic of convenient bad backs and depression. These issues are best addressed at a more personal level.

With regards to the aged pension, there is an argument that the compulsory superannuation system removes the need for any additional welfare payments beyond the NIT. One approach would be to introduce a TFT supplement for current aged pension recipients and phase this out as the generation of compulsory superannuation savers reach retirement. Civil society would be more than strong enough to offer any additional help that would be necessary.

Using current disability pension and aged pension payments, the cost of additional disability and aged welfare supplements is likely to be about $10–15 billion.

Chapter 10

Why Politicians Aren't Rushing To Increase Taxes[1]

Andrew Norton

In 2003 we started to see opinion poll results we'd not seen for over 30 years. Surveys showed larger numbers of voters choosing more spending on social services than choosing less tax. Asked whether they would forgo tax cuts or pay higher tax to fund health and education services, majorities said they would. Anomalies exist—a belief that the top marginal tax rate is too high, for example[2]—but too many surveys from too many polling organisations say similar things to doubt the general trend. Tax is less unpopular than in the past.

Unsurprisingly, big government's supporters are keen to enlist these results in their cause. The ACTU highlighted its own poll showing that 'the community values public provision of health and education ahead of individual tax cuts'.[3] Shaun Wilson, a left-leaning academic and key public opinion researcher in this field, thinks, 'The public wants its government to follow enlightened social democracies elsewhere and invest in their future.'[4] John Quiggin, a prominent left-of-centre economist, hopes these polls mean 'that social democracy has won the public debate, at least for the moment'.[5]

Politicians seem less convinced, however. In both the 2004 and 2005 Budgets the Coalition government announced tax relief, with Labor disagreeing only on how much and who it should go to. Though policy is rarely perfectly responsive to public opinion, the parties' behaviour had pundits puzzled. Writing just before the 2004 Budget was delivered, political journalist Michelle Grattan suggested that either the Liberals' private polling showed something different to the pro-tax polls, 'or that the Liberals are not easily coming to terms with the way in which electoral thinking is moving'.[6] Writing after the Budget, when Labor had offered even more tax relief than the Coalition, Ross Gittins said that 'the ground has shifted under the politicians' feet, but they're having difficulty recognising the change'.[7]

This chapter looks at the polls from a politician's point-of-view. It finds that recent surveys do not provide a solid public opinion foundation for any large increase in taxation. Before exploring why not, we must first examine what the polls are saying, their meaning, and the driving forces behind them.

The polls

Since 1967, in a series of slightly varying questions, voters have been asked about their relative preference for reducing tax or spending more on social services. These surveys aren't in themselves good guides for politicians. They omit an option that is always popular if available, the status quo.

Figure 10.1: Long-term trends in taxing and spending opinion[8]

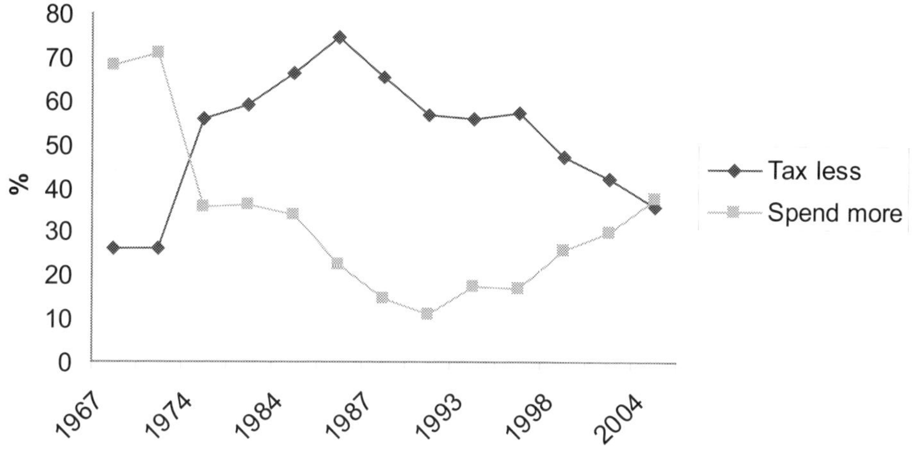

They leave implicit the higher tax corollary of more spending, and the lower spending corollary of less tax, creating an artificial choice between two positives. They ask about what the government should do, not whether the respondent personally wants less tax or more social services. As we will see, these issues are potentially significant. But these surveys do have value in allowing us to track broad tendencies in opinion over a long period of time.

Figure 10.1 shows the peak in pro-spending opinion occurred in the late 1960s. By 1974, support for more spending had halved and twice as many respondents as before wanted less tax. In the mid-1980s the lower tax option increased its popularity, with very few people wanting more social service spending.[9] Though the anti-tax view subsided from its 1980s peak in the first half of the 1990s, it was still a majority position, and support for more spending remained at low levels. In the second half of the 1990s, however, opinion began to change, with less tax trending down and more spending trending up. In the last poll, for the first time since 1969, increased spending was more popular than less tax, though still well short of a majority on 37%.[10]

Other surveys taken over the last two years confirm the impression given by the final poll in Figure 10.1. In 2003 ACNielsen conducted a survey after the May Budget which had offered a small tax cut, equivalent to $4 a week for middle-income earners. Twenty percent of those polled wanted the tax cut, but 77% preferred better health and education services.[11] Although the trivial size of the tax cut may have affected the trade-off, this was a strong pro-spending result for a survey that reminded its respondents that government expenditure was not costless.

Later in 2003, the Australian Survey of Social Attitudes (AuSSA) looked at spending priorities and personal willingness to pay tax, again prompting respondents to consider the potential personal financial consequences of their answers. It found 68% were willing to pay extra tax to spend more on health and Medicare, 64% for schools, 55% for defence and national security, and 54% for environmental protection. All up, 73% nominated at least one area in which they were prepared to pay more tax.[12]

Newspoll arrived at a similar result in January 2004. It asked 'If the Federal government has a large surplus, should this be spent all or mainly on health and education, on personal tax cuts, or spent on both equally?' 72% said it should be spent all or mainly on health and education, 9% supported tax cuts, and 14% wanted it spent on both equally.[13] All up, 88% favoured at least some additional spending.

In April 2005, ACNielsen again found services were a higher voter priority than tax cuts. When asked whether the surplus should be spent on tax cuts or services, 68% of its respondents preferred services, and 29% wanted a tax cut.

The questions asked influence the answers received

While all polls conducted on taxing and spending issues between 2003 and 2005 arrived at similar conclusions, there were anomalies. For example, the 2004 question about reducing tax or increasing spending on services (Figure 10.1) shows a much narrower gap between preferences for less tax and more spending than other polls conducted at around the same time.

Part of the explanation for this discrepancy is that voters have clear preferences about which parts of the Budget should receive more resources, and they answer general questions about spending differently from more specific ones. In the 2003 AuSSA, for example, respondents were asked to choose among spending on health and Medicare, primary and secondary schools, environmental protection, defence and national security, and welfare benefits. While 73% of respondents nominated at least one of these for additional taxing and spending, only 27% wanted more in all five areas. Welfare was the least popular spending option, with just 34% favouring more taxes to fund it.[14] Additional income support for able-bodied adults consistently registers low levels of support.[15]

Health, on the other hand, is a high priority. Over many years the Morgan Poll has asked its respondents which are the most important issues the Federal government should be doing something about (a national question), and what the Federal government could do that would be of most benefit to them personally. As Figure 10.2 shows, health has increased very significantly as a top issue since the early 1990s.[16]

Figure 10.2: The rise of health as an issue[17]

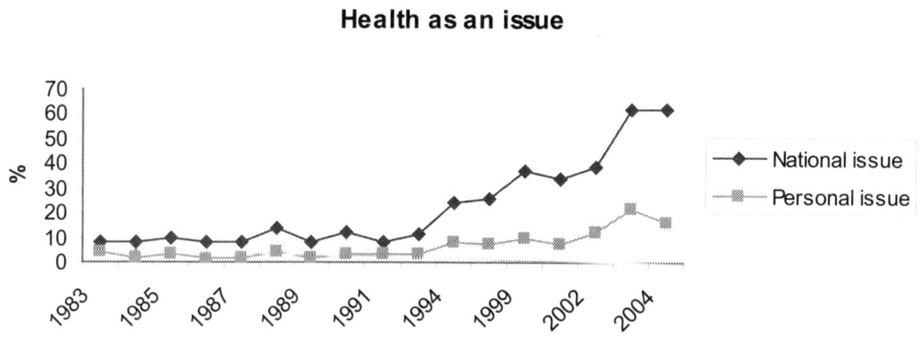

Questions which do not specify that the money is going to services that the respondent wants, or which raise the possibility that it might be spent on things that they do not want, receive more negative answers than tightly-worded questions focusing attention on services respondents do want. Voters do not trust politicians enough to given open-ended support for more spending.

Discrepancies between different polls also reflect the economic context in which surveys are conducted. Most Budgets in the Howard-Costello era delivered surpluses, collecting more in tax and other government revenue that they spent. This reversed the budgetary pattern of the preceding 25 to 30 years. This fiscal turnaround may have changed the way people think about taxing and spending issues, for spending can appear more attractive if it does not require any new taxes to fund it.

A forgone $20 a week tax cut out financed by a government surplus obviously has the same effect on personal finances as a $20 tax increase from a balanced budget. In both cases, the taxpayer is $20 a week worse off. However, psychologically the two are not the same, and rejecting a tax cut is easier than accepting a tax increase. The taxes that finance surpluses are already factored into taxpayers' financial calculations, so rejecting a tax cut will not interfere with their anticipated spending. A tax increase, by contrast, would reduce their forecast spending capacity. It hurts less to lose something you did not expect to have than to lose something you thought you had.

The psychology of the surplus helps explain differences between the 2003 AuSSA and the May 2003 ACNielsen poll. The 2003 AuSSA omitted mention of a budget surplus, and as noted, 57% of its respondents supported paying more tax for both health and education. The May 2003 ACNielsen poll, by contrast, found 77% of voters said they would prefer the $10.7 billion budgeted for tax cuts to be directed to health and education.[18] That's 20 percentage points higher support than for the same spending options when funded from increased personal taxation, consistent with the thesis that spending is considered less painful when it comes out of the surplus.[19]

The psychological literature on loss aversion finds that, in normal circumstances, losses loom larger than gains.[20] Most people are more upset about losing $100 than they are happy about gaining $100. When extra money is taken from voters in tax, it will be seen as a loss to the taxpayer. However, when the money is already held by the government, not spending the money on services becomes the 'loss' in people's minds, rather than paying tax. There are signs of this phenomenon in recent polls.

The May 2003 ACNielsen poll, taken after that year's Budget, is one example. The tax cut was only $4 a week for average earners, with which you would be lucky to buy 'a milkshake and a sandwich', as government minister Amanda Vanstone famously observed. In this context, it was easy to see the 'lost' health and education services as exceeding the small gain from lower income tax. Accordingly, 77% went for more health and education spending. Similarly, the January 2004 Newspoll question framed the issue as tax cuts or services financed from a surplus. Because the surplus was the status quo, the negative of a potential loss of health and education services outweighed the positive of a tax cut.

For people who are net beneficiaries of the tax and social service system, the 2004–05 Budget was easily framed as a 'loss'. They received negligible or no benefit from the tax cuts, and a Newspoll published in *The Australian* after the Budget shows how they came to consider themselves losers without incurring any losses. This Budget was unusually pain free for voters, yet 22% proclaimed themselves to be 'worse off' as a result.[21] Ignorance may partly explain these replies, but it is likely that some voters believed that with a large surplus they were entitled to a share of it, and failure to receive that share was a 'loss'. People earning less than $52,000 a year (the point at which tax relief started in that Budget) were nearly three times as likely to say that they were worse off as people on higher incomes.

Results from the one-off surveys suggest that opinion is acutely sensitive to context, including the way the question is asked and the concerns it makes salient. Question wording cannot, however, explain the long-term trends recorded in Figure 10.1, because the questions asked in these surveys were similar. Broader social, economic or political circumstances must therefore have been driving these changing responses over time.

Underlying causes

Shaun Wilson and Trevor Breusch argue that opinion has changed because voters want better health and education services (see Table 10.1). They find that, after controlling for other factors, voters who believe that health and Medicare have declined in the last two years support more spending by half a point more on a five point scale. Similarly, those who think public education has declined move toward more spending by a third of a point. Those who think both have declined move by three-quarters of a point.[22]

The difficulty with Wilson and Breusch's argument, however, is that it assumes that the perception that health and education standards are in decline is new (for if it is not new, their analysis would not explain why we see a trend towards increased support for higher taxes). Yet polling over the

Table 10.1: Perceptions of service standards

(a)

% of voters believing standard of health services has...[23]				
	1996 to 1998	**1998 to 2001**	**2001 to 2003**	**2001 to 2004**
Increased	12	13	15	12
Stayed the same	25	33	24	28
Fallen	63	54	59	60

(b)

% of voters believing quality of education has...[24]				
	1996 to 1998	**1998 to 2001**	**2001 to 2003**	**2001 to 2004**
Increased	11	12	15	12
Stayed the same	39	41	35	44
Fallen	50	47	42	43

Source: Australian Election Survey 1998, 2001, 2004; Australian Survey of Social Attitudes 2003.

last 20 years reveals there is nothing new about people thinking there are problems in health and wanting to see them fixed. Questions like this have always tended to draw negative answers.[25]

Back in 1984, when the polls were strongly for less tax, the National Social Science Survey (NSSS) nevertheless found that 57% of people believed that too little was spent on hospitals and medical care. The 1987-88 NSSS found 70% wanted more government spending on 'health, hospitals and Medicare'. In the 1989–90 NSSS, with a reminder that more spending might mean more tax, 67% went for more government spending on 'health, hospitals and medical care'. The 1993 NSSS found 86% wanted more spending to reduce waiting lists for surgery, 69% wanted spending to train more nurses, and 82% wanted new equipment for hospitals. Of all the polls in this anti-tax era, there was only one partial exception to this strong emphasis on health, the 1990 Australian Election Survey. While 89% classed health as an important issue, 51% disagreed with increasing tax to spend more. It took the direct threat of more tax to push health down the list of priorities.

People therefore emphasised the importance of spending more on health services long before the strong pro-tax and spend polls of the last few years. Right from the time Newspoll started measuring opinion on health and Medicare in July 1990 it has been an important issue, with a debut on 63%.[26] It reached the high 70s in the mid-1990s, and with a few ups and downs remained there until June 2003, when it moved into the 80s. It was at 85% in October 2003 when the 2003 AuSSA was conducted.

It is conceivable that dissatisfaction with the quality of health services is the dynamic influence on public preferences; that over the last few years we reached a tipping point that reversed opinion on taxing and spending. Perhaps the demographic and technological changes driving up health costs finally overwhelmed the system and the public's patience. But a more plausible interpretation is that health services have been a major concern for a long time without any dramatic effects on opinion about government spending. From 1986 to 1996, support for more spending overall was below 20%—a number that doesn't match with the concern shown in specific questions about health during this time. Voters undoubtedly want health services to improve, but this fact on its own does not fully explain the trends we see.

An alternative theory to explain these trends is that what varies is not the desire for better health and education services—this is an underlying constant—but the capacity to pay for them. In other words, prosperous people want to buy additional health and education services (along with other new or improved goods and services) which they forgo when they feel less well-off.

The last time we saw strong pro-spending opinion was in two surveys conducted in 1967 and 1969. This was a period of strong real wage growth.[27] Contemporary opinion polls suggest people felt prosperous (Table 10.2). Two Morgan polls conducted in 1966 and 1967 found that hospitals and medical services topped the list of most important election issues, with education second, just as they have again since 2001.[28] It is plausible that, in the late 1960s, Australians wanted to increase their overall consumption, and where government was the dominant financier of services (as in health and education), they accepted that the mechanism for doing so was more taxation.

By the time Australians were next asked about their preferences for taxing and spending, in 1974, opinion had changed markedly. What drove this shift? Perhaps the Whitlam government's spending spree satisfied some demand for more services.[29] A consequence of increased spending was that the tax burden rose from 22.5% of GDP in 1972 to 25.9% of GDP in 1974.[30] Though real wages were still growing, by the mid-1970s,

Table 10.2: Late 1960s feelings of prosperity

Question: Are you and your family better off now than you were three or four years ago, are you worse off, or have you stayed about the same?

Year	Better off	About the same	Worse off
1967	40	39	20
1969	43	42	14

Source: Australian National Political Attitudes Survey

the marginal tax rate on average weekly earnings exceeded 40%.[31] Added tax had a perceptible impact on many families' finances, and consistent with what we would expect if household finances were the main variable, support for less tax greatly increased.

At the time of the mid-1980s anti-tax peak in opinion, as seen in Figure 10.1, households' overall financial situation was worse than in the 1970s. Wage increases were not keeping pace with the cost of goods and services.[32] Average income tax rates trended up to a record peak in the late 1980s, and the marginal tax rate on average weekly earnings exceeded 40% for several years from 1985.[33] In 1983 the McNair polling organisation asked, 'During the last few years has your financial situation been getting better, getting worse, or has it stayed the same?', and 48% said they were worse off with only 14% believing they were better off.[34] In 1987, the Australian Election Survey found 43% thought that they were worse off and 19% better off. The public chose lower tax over more spending, needing financial relief more than additional services. Consistent with this, as can be seen in Figure 10.2, health was barely rating as one of the top three issues the Federal government should be doing something about, with economic issues dominating.

Real wages grew strongly from the mid-1990s, easing financial pressure on households. Between 1995–96 and 2002–03 real wages grew by 14.5%, compared to 6% in the previous eight years. After the Howard government's 2000 tax reforms the marginal tax rate on average weekly earnings was 30%, less than it had been through most of the 1970s and 1980s, though indirect taxes were higher because of the GST. Since 1994, the consumer confidence index has been in strongly positive territory, and above 120 since 2002.[35]

We are therefore back where we were in the late 1960s. With real wages increasing strongly, unemployment declining, interest rates low, and inflation under control, economic issues are less significant.[36] Voters feel more prosperous than they did in the 1970s and 1980s, and want to buy more goods and services, including those services primarily financed through government. Figure 10.3 shows that over a nearly 30 year period consumer confidence and support for spending on social services broadly track each other, as we would expect if financial circumstances are the key variables driving trends in tax and spending opinion.

Figure 10.3: Consumer confidence and preference for social service spending

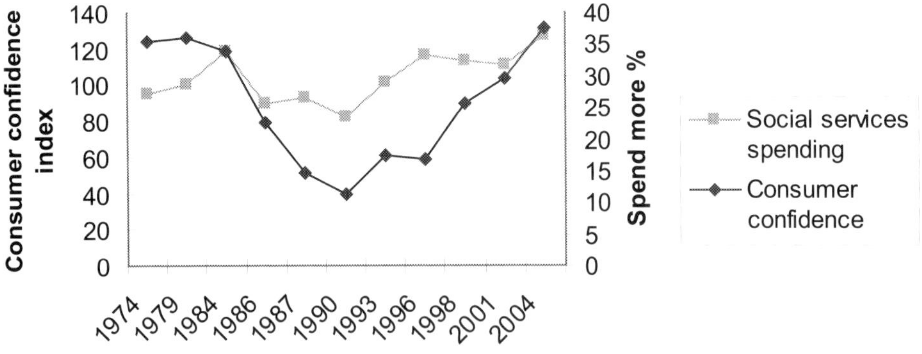

Sources: Consumer confidence data: Roy Morgan consumer confidence surveys. Spending data: As for Figure 10.1

The tax trap

There is a widespread perception that publicly provided health and education services are deteriorating, and polls suggest that concerns about health and education go back to the 1960s. But if these problems have continued for decades, and majorities still think the standards of health services are falling, shouldn't private sector alternatives look like better options than paying more tax into the public health and education services? People know that taxes have been going up since the mid-1990s (Table 10.3), but to little effect. So why support a remedy that has failed in the past?

Table 10.3: Perceptions of tax burden

Percent of voters believing taxes have...[37]				
	1996 to 1998	**1998 to 2001**	**2001 to 2003**	**2001 to 2004**
Increased	47	60	75	58
Stayed the same	48	20	15	28
Fallen	5	20	6	14

Source: Australian Election Survey 1998, 2001 2004; Australian Survey of Social Attitudes 2003.

The reason is probably that many Australians are in a tax trap. They pay so much in tax that they cannot easily afford to opt out of public sector provision. For example in 2001–02 couples with children aged between 5 and 24 on average paid between $390 and $475 and week in tax, and received between $500 and $565 in government benefits. [38] If they opt out of the public sector and go private they will end up paying twice, once for the public services they no longer use and once for the private services.

Given the large cost leap involved in moving use from government services to the private sector, there is logic to voters' willingness to pay more tax. It looks like a cheaper way of getting some improvement in health and education. But if taxes do increase, they have to hand even more money over to the government, leaving them even less able to afford private alternatives. They therefore become trapped in the government's churning of tax revenue, taking from and spending on the same people.

The view from Parliament House

If tax cuts are less popular than at any time since the late 1960s, and extra spending, especially on health, has high support when paid for from increased tax, and overwhelming support if financed from the surplus, why did the 2004–05 Budget not follow those preferences, and why did Labor go along with the tax cuts? And why did the Coalition again for the 2005–06 Budget not divert money for tax cuts into health expenditure, with Labor only arguing about how to cut taxes, rather than whether they should be cut? For politicians so often condemned as 'poll driven' there must be more going on. There are at least five reasons why tax cuts still make political sense, notwithstanding the polls discussed above.

The first reason is that tax cuts are short-term, but spending is long-term, and there is no evidence that voters' preferences are undergoing an enduring change. The dominant driving force behind fluctuating trends appears to be economic prosperity. If economic growth slows significantly (as almost inevitably it must at some time), consumer confidence will drop and surpluses will disappear. With these preconditions of pro-spending opinion gone, public preferences could quickly change. Since 1967 that has occurred twice over a five year period. Political leaders need to think of the longer-term consequences of anything they do now, and the options they will have if circumstances change.

While tax cuts and increased spending can have the same effect on the current year's fiscal outcome, they have different longer term dynamics. Tax cuts of the kind announced in the 2004–05 Budget do not disrupt the tax system's capacity to generate ever-increasing revenue from the same rates. In our progressive tax system, revenue can grow even in a stagnant economy, for nominal wage increases push workers into higher tax brackets ('bracket creep'). Aided by the fact that full-time job growth since 1989 has disproportionately been in the relatively well-paid occupations,[39] the proportion of taxpayers paying a top tax rate of 30% or less decreases each year by 1.5% to 2%, all without the government doing anything.[40] Despite the 2004 tax cuts, the Commonwealth predicted real tax revenue growth of 2.7% in 2004–05 and 2.3% in 2005–06, and it actually achieved far in excess of this.[41] Only serious recessions, such as those in the early 1980s and early 1990s, reduce tax revenues in real terms.

The expenditure side of the Budget lacks these self-correcting mechanisms. To the contrary, it has self-expanding tendencies. Demographic change means that spending on health and old age pensions cannot easily be controlled, and income support for disabled and single parent claimants has continued to expand.[42] Because spending programmes create their own clienteles, and because losses are felt more acutely than the gains from reducing or reallocating expenditure, spending cuts are very difficult to implement. Since 1970-71, only three budgets—two Labor, one Liberal—have reduced total spending in real terms.[43] Spending programmes are like marriages, not necessarily forever but requiring pain and misery to bring them to an end.

By contrast, through tax cuts politicians can flirt with the electorate, knowing—as in 2004-05—that they are reducing the rate of revenue growth rather than taking in less revenue than before. The tax cuts will slowly disappear of their own accord as inflation and real income increases push more taxpayers and a larger share of total taxable income into the higher tax brackets. For politicians trying to manage economic and electoral cycles, tax cuts are the safer option.

The second reason why tax cuts make more political sense than increased spending is that politicians don't get much credit when they increase expenditure. In his study of the relationship between increased Commonwealth government spending per person and subsequent election results, Michael Warby found a *negative* correlation.[44] Under John Howard, public spending on health and education increased more rapidly than under Paul Keating (Figure 10.4) but few voters know or believe this. Federal government policy has actually matched what the polls say people want, increasing tax to record levels and spending more on services, yet many people think services are getting worse.

One political problem is that spending increases do not directly improve services. Very rapid growth in spending on pharmaceuticals (averaging 14.3% annually in real terms between 1997–98 and 2001–02) improved health outcomes, but not more obvious aspects of the health system's performance, such as waiting lists for elective surgery or long delays in hospital emergency rooms.[45] Pay increases to staff working in health and education ease long-term recruitment and retention problems, but do little or nothing to improve services in the short term. It is possible to spend a lot more without making any or much progress on key problems.

The public's estimates of government spending are usually wildly inaccurate.[46] Add to this the confusions created by divided Commonwealth and state financing responsibilities, with each level of government blaming the other for shortfalls and shortcomings, and the electorate can be forgiven for being rather confused. The political danger is that voters will clearly see the tax increases, but will not accept that money is being spent where it should be, or being spent effectively.

Figure 10.4: Health and education spending as % of GDP

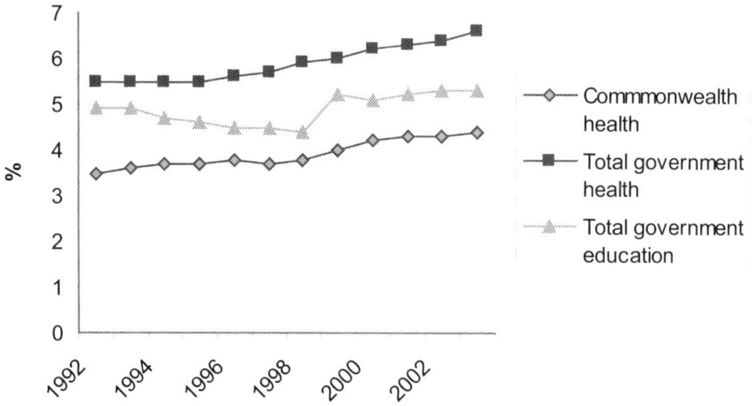

Sources: For health spending, Australian Institute of Health and Welfare, *Health Expenditure* Australia 2003–04 (Canberra, AIHW, 2005).
For education spending, Australian Bureau of Statistics, *Social Trends 2005*, (Canberra: ABS, 2005).
The AIHW Figures are financial year, and ABS calendar year.

This is particularly troublesome for the Liberal Party. There are long-standing political stereotypes of the Liberal Party as the lower tax party, and Labor as the stronger services party. Newspoll regularly asks which party would best handle various issues. In 41 surveys since July 1990, the Liberals have come out ahead of Labor on health and Medicare on only three occasions. By contrast, the Liberals have been ahead of Labor on tax on 42 of 46 occasions (despite their recent high tax record).[47]

This helps explain why the Howard government receives minimal public opinion credit for its spending programmes, and why in an election year it chose to cut tax. They did something that fitted with Liberal stereotypes, and which had easily verifiable consequences. Tax cuts can be seen on pay slips and in bank accounts. Spending increases can be, and have been, politically invisible. The 2004 Coalition election victory does not suggest their tax-cut strategy was a mistake.

The third reason why increased spending does not necessarily make political sense is that improving public services significantly would attract additional users from the private sector, thereby creating additional expense. Currently, just over 43% of the population is covered by private health insurance.[48] In 2003–04 private spending on hospital treatment was $4.8 billion, compared to $20.4 billion in public expenditure.[49] Any substantial cost transfer from the private to the public sector would put major new strains on the public system. As Ian Harper has argued, the steady decline in the proportion of Australians with private health insurance from the early 1980s coincided with steep increases in real public hospital expenditure, which eased off only since various measures were introduced to boost private health coverage in the late 1990s.[50]

In school education, too, there is a large private sector, especially in secondary schools. In 2004, 38% of secondary students were in independent or Catholic schools. These schools are subsidised to varying degrees by government, but also charge parents fees. Any large scale transfer of these students into the public system would impose enormous additional expense on governments and taxpayers. Parents sending their children to a Catholic rather than a government school saved taxpayers $4,200 per child per year (2001 figures), and parents sending their children to an independent school saved taxpayers $5,500 a child.[51] If 20% of current non-government school students shifted to the public sector it would cost taxpayers another $1 billion a year without improving the government school system at all.

Because the public and private health and education sectors interact, governments face a paradox: more spending in the public sector could make things worse, by making schools and hospitals more over-burdened than they were before. Demands would follow for still more spending to fix problems that would not have occurred were it not for the original spending increase. And by this time, tax increases may exceed political acceptability.[52]

A fourth factor weighing on politicians' minds when they consider the electoral wisdom of increasing taxes and spending is whether voters are telling pollsters the truth when they say they are prepared to pay more tax. With several well-publicised polls between 2003 and 2005 showing popular support for more spending, there is the possibility of a bandwagon effect. Bandwagon answers are not lies, but they are so superficial that a change in real-world events (such as taxes going up) could see these respondents switch sides very easily.

Another group of respondents may conceal their real preferences for reasons of social acceptability. With an apparent national consensus that public services should be a top priority, nominating something else, especially something self-enriching like tax cuts, looks selfish. In these circumstances, fewer people than in the past say they prefer tax cuts, even if privately they still want them. They give the answer they feel they should give, the socially or politically safe response, not what they genuinely believe.

The Morgan Poll surveys give some insight into differences between public and private opinion on political issues. By inquiring about what would benefit the respondent and his or her family, as well as what should be done for Australia, they minimise pressure to give the socially acceptable response. As Figure 10.5 indicates, tax is always more nominated as something that the Federal government could do for respondents and their families than it is nominated as a national issue.

The last two years are particularly interesting. While all other polling data suggests that tax is less of an issue than in the past, it has increased significantly as a personal and family issue. These figures look more like the 1980s and early 1990s era of strong opposition to increased tax than what we would expect from an electorate 'relaxed and comfortable' with its tax bill. Figure 10.5 warns politicians of a constituency still very concerned about how much tax they are paying, despite the pro-tax impression given by other polls.

The fifth reason why wise politicians hesitate about raising taxes and increasing spending is that some people who support higher tax may do so because they believe that they themselves will not have to pay. It is easy to say sincerely that *other* people should pay more tax, but another matter if you believe the burden will fall on you.

Sinclair Davidson shows in chapter 4 that the top 25% of earners pay 64% of the tax. Furthermore, research by UNSW's Social Policy Research Centre shows that many affluent Australians significantly underestimate their position in the nation's income distribution. When asked which income decile they were in, only 2% of those in the top 20% of earners located themselves correctly.[54] They could get a nasty surprise from the first Budget to increase taxes.

Another difficulty is that tax cannot be targeted on those willing to pay. Even for relatively popular spending priorities like health and education, between one-quarter and one-third of voters in the 2003 AuSSA say they are not willing to pay any more tax. Shaun Wilson and Trevor Breusch note that those without any political party identification tend to favour tax cuts more than other voters.[55] These are also the people whose votes are most likely to swing in an election campaign. Politicians may believe that these people are a key constituency, and structure their tax policies accordingly.

Figure 10.5: Tax as a national and personal/family issue[53]

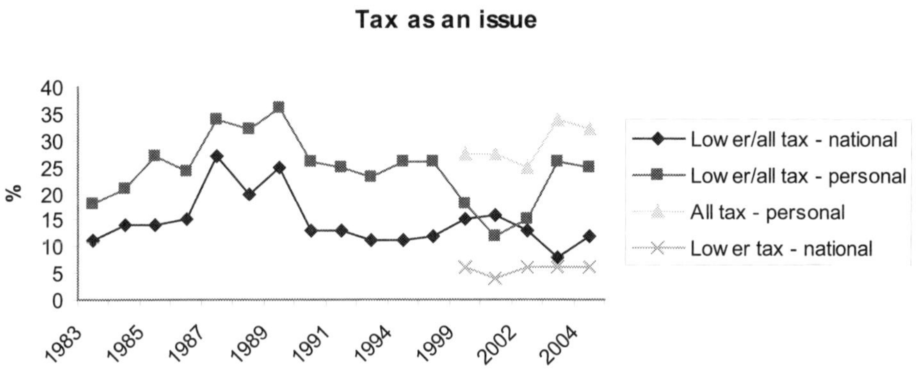

Source: Morgan Poll

Conclusion

Australia's politicians are prudently cautious about following the advice of poll-driven pundits, for there is no clear evidence of a stable constituency for significantly higher taxes. The strong support for more health and education spending seen in the last two years is a product of prosperity, not ideological change. An economic downturn would re-focus voters' attention on their household budgets, and wipe out the surpluses that made spending seem easy.

Even while the polls remain pro-spending, political caution is advisable. Support for higher taxes that is based on a bandwagon effect, or on public statements that belie private sentiments, or on the mistaken belief that others will pay, is unlikely to survive the transition to higher tax reality. Even those who genuinely support higher taxes may be disillusioned when they fail to deliver significantly better services (Table 10.1 suggests they are disappointed already, just not yet disillusioned). The Liberals in particular are unlikely to get political credit for high spending, and are politically better off working on their lower tax credibility.

We are accumulating a large population of long-term welfare dependants, each with a vested interest in taxing the economically active population. The demographic element of this—the elderly—cannot be substantially reduced in the short to medium terms.[56] In fact, they will grow considerably. Add them to those with an ideological preference for more spending, and we probably have a bigger constituency for taxation than we did before. But while widespread welfare dependence underpins support for more tax, it is also a complicating factor for those wanting higher taxation, for there is little evidence of altruism in recent tax-and-spend polls. Voters support more spending on services they or their families use or might use. If increased taxes disappear into transfer payments, rather than funding health and education services used by income tax payers, the demand for 'less tax' will reassert itself among those paying Australia's tax bills.

Opinion on taxing and spending contains ironies for both the free-market right and the high-tax left. The left supports higher taxation, not only because it wants more money spent on government services, but also because it wants to flatten out the distribution of final incomes. But dissatisfaction with public health and education services appears to be a necessary condition of public support for more tax. If and when satisfaction with government services rises, the left would therefore see support for its high tax agenda fall.

Conversely, the free-market right faces the problem that growing affluence is undermining popular support for lower taxes, for people become more willing to spend their money on more public sector services. As Australia becomes wealthier, it is unsurprising and unobjectionable that people want better health and education services. The political difficulty is that these services are traditionally provided or financed by government. The public already half-understands that government is a very clumsy intermediary between spending desires and service delivery. The figures in Table 10.1 suggest dissatisfaction with the state agencies' health and education performance, despite the ever-increasing sums spent on them. But because of the tax trap many taxpayers have a practical choice only between increased taxes and paying twice for health and education services. For them, increased tax is the cheaper of the available alternatives.

Very few polls ask their respondents to think outside the constraints of the current system. The 'less tax' option is usually just that; it is not less tax so that better health and education services can be purchased privately. A small poll carried out by ACNielsen for The Centre for Independent Studies in 2003 was a rare exception. It asked respondents about a hypothetical alternative to Medicare where taxes would be reduced so people could afford their own health insurance (government would help to pay the premiums of low income people). Opinion was fairly evenly divided, with 42% favouring the idea and 46% opposing it. That's a higher preference for tax cuts than in any other recent poll offering an explicit or implicit trade-off, but it is still minority support. These divided views on how to fund the health system are longstanding.[57]

Opinion on taxing and spending in Australia is linked closely to opinion on how health and education services should be delivered. Only minorities see taxation and government spending as inherently good or bad; everyone else sees both as means to ends. For as long as the electorate retains (despite experience) its belief that government should deliver these services, we have the necessary (though not sufficient) condition of support for higher taxation. Stinginess does not make sense if important services are inadequate as a result. Only with attractive alternative sources of health and education services can a low tax agenda have any serious chance of political success. The absence of these alternatives in the 1980s helps explain why the strongest anti-tax sentiment yet recorded in the polls did not translate into lower taxes, and why flaws in government services in the early 2000s are not triggering demands from taxpayers to get their money back, so they can spend it more effectively themselves.

Endnotes

Introduction. What We Need To Do And Why We Need To Do It.

1 Many journalists were sceptical when the inquiry was announced, believing it had more to do with political tactics than policy strategy. See, for example, George Megalogenis, 'Foregone conclusion of little relevance' and Matt Price, 'Treasurer quick to prejudge', both in *The Australian* (27 February 2006).

2 Quoted in David Uren, 'Howard rules out big tax reform' *The Australian* (1 March 2003). John Howard has been quite consistent and explicit in arguing that voters want tax cuts and that tax reform (which produces losers as well as winners) is of no interest to him (see Fleur Anderson, 'PM says voters want relief, not sham reforms' *Australian Financial Review* (10–11 December 2005)). On the government's recent and consistent history of resistance to tax reform, see: Brad Norrington, 'Howard rejects bid for top rate tax cuts' *The Australian* (28 December 2004); Steve Lewis & Patricia Karvelas, 'Minchin opposes push for tax cuts' *The Australian* (24 January 2005); David Uren and Elizabeth Coleman, 'Out on a limb' *The Australian* (19–20 March 2005); Samantha Maiden, 'Costello rips into tax plan' *The Australian* (11 October 2005); Laura Tingle, 'Costello ridicules 30pc flat tax option' *Australian Financial Review* (17 October 2005).

3 'Taxation' ABS, *Year Book* (Canberra: ABS, 2003), Table 27.19.

4 Sid Marris, 'Income tax up 36 pc in six years' *The Weekend Australian,* (16–17 April 2005), 3.

5 Tax Freedom Day is explained in J. Buckingham (ed), *State of the Nation* No 4, (Sydney: Centre for Independent Studies, 2004).

6 Michael Keating, 'The case for increased taxation', *Academy of the Social Sciences Policy Paper* 1 (2004), 6.

7 In 2003–04, the Commonwealth raised $209 billion in tax revenue, of which $99 billion was tax on individual incomes and $42 billion was tax on company incomes. See: Australian Bureau of Statistics, *Taxation Revenue, Australia* (Cat 5506.0, April 2005).

8 The latest evidence from the USA suggests that the big tax cuts introduced by President Bush in 2003 and 2004 actually reduced the budget deficit in 2005 as a result of the increase in employment, profits and output. Tax receipts rose in real terms by more than in any previous year in history (Editorial, *Wall Street Journal,* 8 December 2005).

9 Company tax receipts never exceeded 3.6% of GDP until 1999–2000 when the tax rate was cut. By 2004, company tax receipts had grown to 4.5%, which KPMG saw as vindication of US supply-side economic theory. See David Uren, 'Ralph rolls in tax barrel' *The Australian* (25 March 2004).

10 In addition, there is a Medicare Levy of 1.5% on all taxpayers, and higher rate taxpayers also pay a Medicare surcharge of 1% if they do not have private health insurance.

11 Elizabeth Coleman 'Howard rules out "unfair" flat tax' *The Australian* (30 September 2005).

12 See Peter Saunders, 'The $85 billion tax-welfare churn' CIS *Issue Analysis* No 57; and 'Six arguments in favour of self-funding' CIS *Issue Analysis* No 61 (Sydney: Centre for Independent Studies, 2005).

13 Ministers like to claim that a worker with dependent children does not pay as much tax as a single worker with no dependants because the former receives a generous Family Tax Benefit. However, FTB is in all but name a welfare transfer, not a tax cut. A worker with a family has tax deducted from his/her wages and then receives a fortnightly FTB payment to compensate. The net result may be the same as a tax cut, but the marginal effect is very different, for FTB is reduced at a rate of 20 or 30 cents in the dollar at the same time as income tax is paid at 30 cents or more. It is this that creates the high effective marginal tax rates that do so much to undermine work incentives. Moreover, the psychological value of a dollar earned and retained is very different from that of a dollar lost in tax and then returned through the welfare system. The former encourages an attitude of self-reliance; the latter an attitude of dependence on government hand-outs.

14 Against this, of course, it can be argued that welfare is intended to meet households' basic needs, and that taxpayers should not be required to give couples more than they need in order to cover their shared living costs.

15 One of the principal tax expenditures in his sights is the concession on super contributions. Currently, super contributions are taxed at a concessionary rate of 15%, but under his proposals, contributions would be made out of post-tax income (that is, after the 30% flat tax has been deducted on earnings over $30,000). Fund earnings would also be taxed at the full 30% rate (again contrasting with today's concessionary rate), although superannuation would not be taxed when it was finally withdrawn, for this would represent double taxation of the same money. Under Humphreys's proposed arrangements, anyone earning less than $60,000 per year would actually end up paying less tax on his or her super contributions than they do now, but those earning above this would pay more (today, on a salary of $60,000, they pay 15% on the 9% of their income contributed to super; under the Humphreys's scheme, someone earning $60,000 pays $9,000 income tax on the whole $30,000 of taxable income, which works out at a rate of 15%, and they pay their super contribution out of this taxed income. Below $60,000, the average tax rate is lower than 15%; above it, it is higher). However, there is also the problem that, by taxing fund earnings at the full 30%, people's funds will grow more slowly than they do currently, for they will lose some of the beneficial effects of compounding over time. When they draw down their retirement savings, retirees will pay no further tax, but their capital will be smaller. The number of people saving enough to avoid any reliance on the government age pension may, therefore, remain higher than Humphreys would hope.

16 Peter Saunders, 'After the house price boom' *Policy* Vol.21, No 1, (Autumn 2005), 3–8

17 Elizabeth Coleman, '$2bn blowout in tax breaks prompts call for review' *The Australian* (22 December 2005).

18 Peter Costello has opposed base broadening on the grounds that voters would resent the loss of tax deductions for work expenses (Elizabeth Coleman, 'Treasurer backs plans that cut tax' *The Australian* (29 October 2005)). John Freebairn calculates that $10 billion of revenue could be saved by scrapping a range of exemptions involving work expenses, fringe benefit concessions, CGT concessions, etc (*Income tax reform: Base broadening to fund lower rates*, Paper to Melbourne Institute *Maintaining Prosperity* conference, University of Melbourne, April 2005. His ideas were taken up later in the year by Malcolm Turnbull (see Turnbull and Jeromey Temple, *Tax reform in Australia*, Paper presented at Wentworth Liberal Party Tax Forum (1 September 2005)), but have been resisted by Costello.

19 Neil Warren, *Tax: Facts, fiction and reform* (Sydney: Australian Tax Research Foundation, 2004)

20 George Megalogenis 'Nation's rich pay only 25pc tax' *The Australian* (6 September 2005).

21 Peter Costello told the Press Club he opposes reducing the top rate because it would hand wealthy individuals like the late Kerry Packer a tax cut worth $100,000 or more (David Uren, 'The model of a modern budget' *The Australian* (15 October 2005)). This same article reports a Treasury estimate that moving to a top rate of 30% would cost less than $9 billion in lost revenues. Turnbull and Temple (*Tax reform in Australia*) estimate the revenue cost of reducing the 47% and 42% rates to 40% would be around $5 billion, assuming there was no efficiency gain from increased output.

22 Even a small increase of $2,200 in the tax-free threshold has been estimated to draw 57,000 more people into the labour force—see Peter Dawkins, 'Welfare to work: Labour supply responses to work incentives', Paper to Melbourne Institute conference on *Maintaining Opportunity*, April 2005 (www.melbourneinstitute.com/conf/sp/sp2005). The Melbourne Institute estimates that increasing the TFT to $8,200 would attract 26,000 more men and 23,000 more women into jobs, but the biggest impact is on couples (only 7,000 more single parents would get drawn into work by this change). Raising the threshold by $7,000 would cost the government $9.5 billion, but we might expect $3 billion of this to be recouped in additional revenues from an expanded labour force. Dawkins calculates that increasing the TFT from $6,000 to $8,200 would initially cost $3.1 billion, but nearly $1 billion of this would be recouped through increased employment. Turnbull and Temple (*Tax reform in Australia*) calculate that raising the TFT to $13,000 would cost $9.5 billion, but extrapolating Dawkins's figures suggests that almost one-third of this could come back in increased revenue.

23 See Saunders, 'The $85 billion tax-welfare churn'; and '20 million future funds' CIS *Issue Analysis* No 66, (Sydney: Centre for Independent Studies, 2005).

Chapter One. How highly taxed are we?

1 Australia's Superannuation Guarantee Charge is not included as a tax in the OECD statistics. See the Technical Appendix for a discussion of this exclusion and of the inclusion of the social security contributions of OECD countries in the comparative data.

2 Reserve Bank of Australia.

3 Population grew from around 11.6 million in 1965 to around 20 million in June 2004.

4 Michael Keating, 'The Case for Increased Taxation', *Academy of Social Sciences Policy Paper 1* (2004).

5 ACTU, *A Fair Australia—Tax Background Paper*, Background Papers (ACTU Congress, 2003).

6 ACOSS, *Taxation in Australia: home truths and international comparisons*, ACOSS Info347 (Sydney: June 2003).

7 Keating, 'The Case for Increased Taxation', 6.

8 See also Neil Warren, *Tax: Facts, Fiction and Reform*, Research Study No. 41 (Sydney: Australian Tax Research Foundation, 2004), 50–54.

9 To some extent the changes in the unweighted averages over time reflect compositional differences as countries such as Korea, Mexico and the Slovak Republic have joined the OECD. The five non-European countries who were OECD members in 1965 (Canada, the United States, New Zealand, Australian and Japan) have ranked among the lower taxing OECD countries throughout the past 40 years or so.

10 The five largest OECD countries account for over 71% of the total GDP of all OECD countries. These are the US (36.7%); Japan (14.5%); Germany (8.2%); the UK (6%) and France (6%).

11 It is sometimes suggested that, when countries are running budget deficits, the higher level of future taxes implied by the accumulation of debt could be taken into account (see for example, Warren, *Tax: Facts, Fiction and Reform*, 54). It is, however, the current level and structure of taxation that is relevant to cost-competitiveness. In any case, deficits do not necessarily or even generally, imply higher future taxes as a proportion of GDP. Debt can be repaid with the proceeds of asset sales; its real level erodes with inflation and it can imply increased productive capacity (if invested in GDP-boosting transport infrastructure for example). Other things being equal, a lower level of debt would imply a lesser need for taxation in line with lower debt servicing costs. Countries such as Australia, with very low public sector debt levels could be expected to have lower levels of taxation than high debt countries.

12 New Zealand, which accounts for around 6% of Australian trade (its sixth largest trading partner in 2004) and with total tax to GDP ratio of 34.9%, is something of an exception.

13 John Hassler, and Mats Persson, 'The international mobility of tax bases: an introduction', *Swedish Economic Policy Review* 9 (2002), 3–8.

[14] See Organisation for Economic Cooperation and Development (OECD), 2005, *Revenue Statistics, 1965-2004* (Paris: 2005), 290–1 and the discussion in the Technical Appendix.

[15] See the discussion in Bernd Genser, *Corporate Income Taxation in the European Union: Current State and Perspectives*, Working Paper No.17 (Canberra: Centre for Tax System Integrity, 2001). There does not seem to be any clear relationship between the degree of relief from double taxation and the level of taxation on corporate income among OECD countries.

[16] This is complicated for direct investment by non-Australian multinationals when Australian income tax is recognised and credited against other global tax liabilities.

[17] This is particularly the case when credit for foreign tax paid is washed out on distribution to domestic shareholders of Australian multinationals.

[18] Genser, *Corporate Income Taxation in the European Union,* 2, 6.

[19] This section benefited from discussions with Geoff Carmody of Access Economics. See also Warren, *Tax: Facts, Fiction and Reform*, 50–54.

[20] OECD, 2003, *Revenue Statistics, 1965–2002*, 34.

[21] OECD, 2005, *Revenue Statistics, 1965–2004*, 18.

[22] Warren, *Tax: Facts, Fiction and Reform*, 52.

[23] OECD, 2005, *Revenue Statistics, 1965–2004*, 74.

[24] Data sources for the calculation of weighted average are summarised in Table 1.6 below.

[25] OECD, 2005, *Revenue Statistics, 1965–2004*, 290–1.

[26] As above, 105-202

Chapter Two. How high taxation makes us poorer

[1] It is worth noting that subsidies have a similar wealth-destroying effect to the costs that are described here. Subsidies drive down the prices that consumers are willing to pay below the prices that producers wish to receive. Thus, subsidies induce *too many* exchanges of subsidised goods, and drive resources away from higher valued uses. Thus, in this sense, the wealth-destroying effects of subsidies are no different from those of taxes, and must be added on to the costs of taxation to get a full estimate of the cost of both forms of government intervention.

[2] For example, in a recent paper ('The Case for Increased Taxation', Academy of the Social Sciences, Occasional Paper No 1 (2004), http://www.assa.edu.au/publications/op/op12004.pdf) Michael Keating argues that 'the Australian economy could tolerate a significant increase in the ratio of taxation to GDP without great difficulty.' While framed in terms of GDP, the major thrust and implication of Keating's paper is that increasing taxes by a significant amount would not create any substantial economic costs.

3 For example, the quote is chiselled in stone at the US Treasury Building in Washington DC. This somewhat schizophrenic view of taxation was also adopted in 1999 by the Commissioner of Taxation (without crediting Holmes). The Commissioner attempted to make the 'ethical' case in favour of paying higher taxes by conflating its costs with the alleged benefits of government spending. See 'Ethics and Taxation', Speech Delivered to the Edmund Rice Business Ethics Forum, Sydney, 28 October 1999. (http://www.ato.gov.au/corporate/content.asp?doc=/content/sp9907.htm)

4 All quotes below are from A Smith, *An Inquiry into the Nature and Causes of the Wealth of Nations* (1776) Liberty Fund Edition (Indianapolis: Liberty Fund, 1981) Book V, Chapter 2, 826-827.

5 Australian Taxation Office *Annual Reports* 2002-2003 and 2003-2004 http://www.ato.gov.au/default.asp?menu=98 .

6 The issue of complexity is discussed by Geoffrey Walker in chapter 3. See also: P. Schuck, 'Legal Complexity: Some Causes, Consequences and Cures', *Duke Law Journal*, 42 (1992),1–52, and R. Epstein, *Simple Rules for a Complex World* (Cambridge, MA: Harvard University Press, 1995). For a formal economic analysis of the effects of complexity and variability of regulations, see R. Quandt, 'The Welfare Effects of Complexity and Variability in Regulations', *Economics Letters*, 13:2–3 (1983), 259–261.

7 R. Vedder, 'Replace the Income Tax with Consumption Tax', Paper presented at the World Taxpayers Conference, Gold Coast (November 2004).

8 G. Tullock, 'The Welfare Costs of Tariffs, Monopolies and Theft', *Western Economic Journal* 5 (1967), 224–232.

9 The costs of rent-seeking activities are certainly large enough to concern welfare economists. Recent estimates by D. Laband and G. McClintock, *The Transfer Society* (Washington D.C.: Cato Institute, 2001) are available for United States in the year 1997, and amount to US$546 billion (at 1997 prices).

10 See A. Robson, 'Rent Seeking and the Presence of Existing Distortions', Working Paper in Economics and Econometrics, No 448 (Canberra: Australian National University, 2005).

11 See, for example, R. Gittins, 'The Real Secret to Happiness: Higher Taxes' *The Melbourne Age (*14 April 2005).

12 We will use these terms interchangeably throughout the paper.

13 More precisely, the deadweight loss is the excess of the funds that must be given to a consumer to restore him to his pretax indifference curve, over and above the additional tax revenue collected from him. See P. Diamond, and D. McFadden 'Some Uses of the Expenditure Function in Public Finance', *Journal of Public Economics* 3 (1974), 3-21.

14 Diamond and McFadden, 'Some Uses of the Expenditure Function in Public Finance'; A. Auerbach, 'The Theory of Excess Burden and Optimal Taxation' in A. Auerbach, and M. Feldstein, (eds) *Handbook of Public Economics*, Volume 1, (Amsterdam: Elsevier Science, 1985); A. Auerbach and J. Hines, 'Taxation and Economic Efficiency' Working Paper No 8181, National Bureau

of Economic Research (2001); and B. Salanie, The Economics of Taxation (Cambridge, MA: MIT Press, 2003). Some economists and commentators implicitly include income effects in calculations of the deadweight loss of taxation. This approach is problematic for a variety of reasons, most of which are explained in the sources noted above as well as R. Tresch, *Public Finance* (New York: Academic Press, 2002).

15 See P. Martin, 'Tax Cuts Don't Make us Work Harder' *The Sydney Morning Herald* (30 March 2005).

16 On the other hand, a common finding is that adult *female* labour force participation and hours worked are much more sensitive to changes in net wages. Davidson discusses some of these studies in chapter 3.

17 Interestingly, Gruber and Saez use their findings to argue that efficient tax systems should feature tightly targeted transfers to lower income taxpayers and a flat or even declining marginal rate structure for middle and high income taxpayers. J. Gruber, and E. Saez, 'The Elasticity of Taxable Income: Evidence and implications' *Journal of Public Economics* 84 (2002), 1–32.

18 Other recent evidence also suggests that labour supply may indeed be highly responsive to tax rates. For example, E. Prescott, 'Why Do Americans Work So Much More Than Europeans?', *Federal Reserve Bank of Minneapolis Quarterly Review* 28:1 (2004), 2–13, estimates that Americans on average devote 50% more work to the market sector than, for example, French workers. He argues that this is primarily due to differences in the tax structures in these economies.

19 L. Lindsey, 'Individual Taxpayer Response to Tax Cuts: 1982–1984, with Implications for the revenue maximizing tax rate', *Journal of Public Economics* 33 (1987), 173–206.

20 G. Auten, and R. Carroll, 'The Effect of Income Taxes on Household Behavior', *Review of Economics and Statistics* 81:4 (1999), 681–693.

21 M. Feldstein, 'Behavioural Responses to Tax Rates: Evidence from the Tax Reform Act of 1986' *American Economic Review*, 85:2 (1995), 170–174; M. Feldstein, 'The Effect of Marginal Tax Rates on Taxable Income: A panel study of the 1986 Tax Reform Act' *Journal of Political Economy* 103:3 (1995), 551–572.

22 J. Navratil, *The Economic Recovery Tax Act of 1981: Evidence on individual taxpayer behavior from panel tax return data* (Unpublished Harvard Thesis, 1995).

23 R. Carroll, 'Tax Rates, Taxpayer Behavior, and the 1993 Tax Act. Office of Tax Analysis' (US Department of the Treasury, mimeograph, 1998).

24 E. Saez, 'The Effect of Marginal Tax Rates on Income: A Panel Study of 'Bracket Creep', Working Paper No 7367 (National Bureau of Economic Research, 1999)

25 J. Gruber, and E. Saez, 'The Elasticity of Taxable Income: Evidence and Implications', 1–32.

26 C. Ballard, J. Shoven, and J. Whalley, 'General Equilibrium Computations of the Marginal Welfare Costs of Taxes in the United States', *American Economic Review* 75 (1985), 128-138.

27 D. Jorgenson, and K. Yun, 'Tax Reform and US Economic Growth', *Journal of Political Economy* 98:5 (1990), S151-193.

28 D. Jorgenson and K. Yun, 'The Excess Burden of Taxation in the United States', *Journal of Accounting and Finance* 6:4 (1991), 487–509.

29 All forms of government revenue (including non-tax revenue) amounted to $310 billion, or 38% of GDP. See the Australian Bureau of Statistics *Government Finance Statistics* (2005), 7.

30 As above, Tables 31, 41.

31 J. Hausman, 'Labour Supply' in Aaron, H. and Pechman, J. (eds) *How Taxes Affect Economic Behaviour* (Washington, D.C.: The Brookings Institution, 1981).

32 Ballard, Shoven and Whalley, 'General Equilibrium Computations of the Marginal Welfare Costs of Taxes in the United States', 128–138.

33 Jorgenson and Yun, 'Tax Reform and US Economic Growth'.

34 Jorgenson and Yun, 'The Excess Burden of Taxation in the United States'.

35 M. Feldstein, 'Tax Avoidance and the Deadweight Loss of the Income Tax', *Review of Economics and Statistics* 81:4 (1999), 674–680.

36 In Australia, personal income taxation is the major source (47.3% in 2003–04) of federal government tax revenue. See Australian Bureau of Statistics, *Taxation Revenue* (2005*)*, Tables 3, 12.

37 Australian Bureau of Statistics, *Government Finance Statistics* (1999), Tables 31, 41.

38 There are many subtleties in the correct definition and computation of the MCF which we are glossing over here. For a rigorous discussion of the issues, see C. Jones, *Applied Welfare Economics* (Oxford University Press, forthcoming).

39 References include C. Ballard and D. Fullerton, 'Distortionary Taxes and the Provision of Public Goods' *Journal of Economic Perspectives* 6:3 (1992), 117–131; D. Fullerton, 'Reconciling Recent Estimates of the Marginal Welfare Cost of Taxation' *American Economic Review* 81:1 (1991), 302–308; Ballard, Shoven and Whalley (op cit); E. Browning, 'On the Marginal Welfare Cost of Taxation' *American Economic Review* 77 (1987), 11–23; C. Stuart, 'Welfare Costs per Dollar of Additional Tax Revenue in the United States' *American Economic Review* 74 (1984), 352–362; H. Campbell, 'Deadweight Loss and Commodity Taxation in Canada' *Canadian Journal of Economics* 8 (1975), 441-447; B. Dahlby, 'Progressive Taxation and the Social Marginal Cost of Public Funds' *Journal of Public Economics* 67:1 (1998), 105-122; E. Diewert and D. Lawrence, 'The Deadweight Costs of Taxation in New Zealand', *Canadian Journal of Economics* 29:0 (1996), S658-673.

40 H. Campbell, and K. Bond, 'The Cost of Public Funds in Australia', *Economic Record* 73 (1987), 22-34.

41 C. Findlay, and R. Jones, 'The Marginal Cost of Australian Income Taxation', *Economic Record* 58 (1982), 253–262. In 1991 the US government modified its cost-benefit procedures to assign a cost of $1.25 to every dollar of expenditures raised out of tax revenues.

42 The Laffer curve of a tax shows how tax revenue responds to changes in the tax

rate. All taxes have Laffer curves which, when no other distortions are present, indicate that tax revenue must fall if tax rates are increased above a certain level. Despite the debate surrounding the Laffer curve in public discussions of taxation, the fact that revenue may fall following an increase in tax rates is perhaps one of the most uncontroversial and uninteresting propositions in all of economics. It is also an extremely old idea, having been discussed by the French economist Jules Dupuit over 150 years ago (see J. Dupuit, (1844) 'De la Mesure de L'utilitié des Travaux Publics', *Annales des Popnts et Chausśees*. Published in English in Jackson, P. (ed), *The Foundations of Public Finance* (Cheltenham: Elgar, 1996)).

43 M. Feldstein, 'Tax Avoidance and the Deadweight Loss of the Income Tax'.

44 J. Slemrod and S. Yitzhaki, 'The Costs of Taxation and the Marginal Efficiency Cost of Funds', *IMF Staff Papers* 43:1 (1996), 172–198 show how to estimate (but do not in fact compute) the MCF when avoidance costs, evasion costs, administrative costs and compliance costs are present.

45 P. Trostel, 'The Effect of Taxation on Human Capital' *Journal of Political Economy*, 101:2 (1993), 327–350 develops an endogenous growth model allowing for human capital accumulation. He argues simulations, that higher income taxes have a significant negative effect on human capital formation. Specifically, for plausible parameter assumptions, he finds that a one-percentage point increase in a flat income tax rate causes the long-run stock of human capital to decline by 0.97%.

46 R. Kleine, 'State and Local Tax Levels and Economic Growth—A Regional Comparison', *Proceedings of the Annual Conference on Taxation of the National Tax Association—Tax Institute of America* (1977), 162–173.

47 R. Grierson, 'Theoretical Analysis and Empirical Measurements of the Effects of the Philadelphia Income Tax' *Journal of Urban Economics* 8 (1980), 123–137.

48 R. Grierson et al, 'The Effect of Business Taxation on the Location of Industry' *Journal of Urban Economics* 4 (1977), 170–185.

49 L. J. Helms, 'The Effect of State and Local Taxes on Economic Growth: A Time Series—Cross Section Approach' *Review of Economics and Statistics*, 67:4 (1985), 574–582.

50 A. Mofidi and J. Stone, 'Do State and Local Taxes Affect Economic Growth?' *Review of Economics and Statistics* 72:4 (1990), 686–691.

51 The literature on the relationship between taxation, GDP and economic growth is briefly surveyed in A. Robson, 'Taxation, Individual Incentives and Economic Growth', Second Prize, IREF Essay Contest on Taxation and Economic Growth, February 2005.

52 Per-capita growth data are taken from the Penn World Tables data set, available at http://dc2.chass.utoronto.ca/pwt/.

53 Interestingly, performing the same exercise for transfers and subsidies using Fraser Institute data (not reported here) leads to the result that higher subsidies and transfers are associated with lower per capita economic growth, which supports the results of Barro's (1991) study and more recent evidence. R. Barro, 'Economic Growth in a Cross Section of Countries', *Quarterly*

Journal of Economics 106:2 (1991), 402–443.

54 The practice of counting costs as if they were benefits is widespread in many discussions of government spending projects, and is one of the primary reasons why 'pork-barrelling' is so widespread. For a detailed discussion and a recent Australian example, see A. Robson, *Sweet and Sour Pork Barrelling: The Case of Queensland Sugar*, Issue Analysis No 45, (Sydney: Centre for Independent Studies, 2004).

Chapter 3. Cut taxes to raise more revenue[1]

1 I would to thank Jonathan Boymal, Robert Brooks, Tim Fry, Peter Saunders and an anonymous referee all of whom have made suggestions that have substantially improved this chapter. Of course, I am responsible for all remaining errors.

2 At the 2004 federal election, 36% of voters supported reducing taxation, while 37% supported higher spending on social services (Australian Election Survey, Question E1). The AES can be accessed via the Australian Social Science Data Archive. Those who carried out the original analysis and collection of the data bear no responsibility for my analysis or interpretation of the data. The AES consists of a stratified systematic random sampling of the Commonwealth Electoral Roll. The sample is selected by population weights. Data are collected by mail. A total of 4,250 surveys were posted out. The final response rate was 42% with 1769 completed returns. Full details are available at http://assdu.edu.au.

3 Ross Gittins, 'Economists forget their model when it suits them', *The Sydney Morning Herald* (23 May 2005), 34.

4 'Work' in this context has a very specific definition. Work occurs in the formal economy where individuals earn a wage or fee. Housework is 'leisure' by this definition.

5 Gittins, as above.

6 Joseph Stiglitz, the 2001 Nobel Laureate, in his leading text *Economics of the Public Sector* writes, 'Research in this area has been extensive and has yielded important (but controversial) results.' Joel Slemrod, in his introduction to *Does Atlas Shrug? The Economic Consequences of Taxing the Rich*, writes, 'Taken as a whole, …, the evidence is more mixed on the question of how, and how much today's Atlases shrug.' (Cambridge, MA: Harvard University Press, 2000), 24.

7 Australian Bureau of Statistics, 'Forms of employment', Cat 6359.0 (November 2004), 3. This implies there are more owner-managers in Australia than trade unionists in the non-public sector of the economy.

8 Peter Martin, 'Tax cuts don't make us work harder', *The Sydney Morning Herald* (30 March 2005), 11.

9 Henry S. Farber, 'Is tomorrow another day? The labor supply of New York City cabdrivers', *The Journal of Political Economy* 113:1 (2005), 46-82.

10 Colin Camerer, Linda Babcock, George Loewenstein, and Richard Thaler, 'Labor supply of New York City cabdrivers: One day at a time', *Quarterly Journal of Economics* 112 (1997), 407-441.

11 Mark H. Showalter and Norman K. Turston, 'Taxes and labor supply of high-income physicians', *Journal of Public Economics* 66 (1997), 73-97.

12 The implications for rural Australia are obvious. To the extent this study is generalisable to Australia, high rates of taxation are partially responsible for poor medical coverage in rural and regional areas.

13 Purists may argue that this calculation is performed 'out of context' and is invalid. Perhaps. Oklahoma, however, had a 17% state income tax. If they were to abolish that state tax, the numbers would work out precisely as I have calculated here.

14 Edward C. Prescott, 'Why do Americans work so much harder than Europeans?', *Federal Reserve Bank of Minneapolis Quarterly Review* 28:1 (2004), 2-13.

15 As above, 8, (emphasis added).

16 Alberto Alesina, Edward Glaeser and Bruce Sacerdote, 'Work and leisure in the US and Europe: Why so different?' *NBER Macroeconomic Annual 2005* (Forthcoming). To be fair to the authors, my analysis is drawn from a working paper version. The final paper may differ from the version I have available to me.

17 Steven J. Davis and Magnus Henrekson, 'Tax effects on work activity, industry mix and shadow economy size: Evidence from rich-country comparisons', National Bureau of Economic Research Working Paper 10509 (2004) www.nber.org/papers/w10509.

18 Donald Bruce and Tami Gurley, 'Taxes and entrepreneurial activity: An empirical investigation using longitudinal tax return data', (2005) United States Small Business Administration, available from http://www.sba.gov/advo/research/rs252tot.pdf

19 Robert Carroll, Douglas Holtz-Eakin, Mark Rider and Harvey S. Rosen, 'Entrepreneurs, income taxes, and investment', In Joel B. Slemrod (ed). *Does Atlas Shrug? The Economics of Taxing the Rich* (Cambridge, MA: Harvard University Press, 2000).

20 Max Moser, 'A comment on the Laffer model', *The Cato Journal* 1:1 (1981), 23–44.

21 Arthur B. Laffer, 'Government exactions and revenue deficiencies', *The Cato Journal* 1:1 (1981), 1–21.

22 John F. Kennedy, 'Address to the Economic Club of New York', 14 December 1962, available at http://www.americanrhetoric.com/speeches/jfkeconomicclubaddress.html. James Buchanan and Richard Wagner describe the Kennedy tax cut as being 'purely Keynesian'. Irrespective of the debate between Keynesians and supply-side economics, the fact remains tax cuts lead to an increase in tax revenue. See Buchanan and Wagner, *Democracy in Deficit: The political legacy of Lord Keynes* (Indianapolis: Liberty Fund, 1977 (1998)),

50–52.

[23] See Bob Schwartz, 'Throwing an economic curve ball', *Australian Financial Review* (19 July 2005), 55. He argues the 'Laffer curve itself is a joke' yet also concedes 'his intuition was not wrong'.

[24] Don Fullerton, 'On the possibility of an inverse relationship between tax rates and government revenues', *Journal of Public Economics* 19 (1980), 3–22.

[25] As above, 20.

[26] Charles E. Stuart, 'Swedish tax rates, labor supply, and tax revenues', *Journal of Political Economy* 89 (1981), 1020 -1038.

[27] Laffer, Tables 1, 4 and 7.

[28] As above, 11.

[29] As above, 11.

[30] As above, 3.

[31] 'The notion that governments could raise more money by cutting rates is, indeed, a glorious idea. It would permit a Pareto improvement of the most enjoyable kind. Unfortunately for all of us, the data from the historical record suggest that it is unlikely to be true at anything like today's marginal tax rates. It seems that, for now at least, we will just have to keep paying for our tax cuts the old-fashioned way.' Austan Goolsbee, 'Evidence on the High-Income Laffer curve from six decades of tax reform', *Brookings Papers on Economic Activity*, 2 (1999), 44.

[32] This was after George H. Bush had increased to the top marginal tax rate in 1991.

[33] General Government Accounts (OECD, 2004) available at http://www.oecd.org/dataoecd/42/47/33784603.xls.

[34] Prescott points out that US government debt continued to increase until the late 1990s when, as a consequence of the high-tech boom 'people worked more, output increased, incomes climbed, and tax revenue followed suit. You cannot tax your way to that sort of prosperity' (127).

[35] Data from the Cato Institute, available from http://www.cato.org/research/fiscal_policy/2003/images/int1-big.gif.

[36] General Government Accounts (OECD, 2004), as above.

[37] A (one sided) t-test for the equality of means returned a p-value of 0.4084. In other words I am unable to reject the hypothesis that tax cuts across these two groups of economies were equal.

[38] Stephen Moore, 'Laffing to the bank', *Asian Wall Street Journal* (14 June 2004), A13.

[39] Unfortunately, the equivalent one percent figure for Australia is not public knowledge. Those Australians, in 2003, who earned above $500,000 made up 0.12% of the taxpaying population, had 2.73% of the total taxable income, contributed 5.01% of total net income tax and faced an average income tax rate of 45.82 percent.

[40] James D. Gwartney and Richard L. Stroup, *Economics: Private and Public Choice* (Fort Worth: Dryden Press, 1997).

[41] Ross Gittins, 'Work: Less an ethic, more an order'. *The Sydney Morning Herald* (8 June 2005), 17.

42 Jon Gruber and Emmanuel Saez, 'The elasticity of taxable income: evidence and implications', *Journal of Public Economics* 84:1 (2002), 32.

43 Gerald W. Scully, 'Tax rates, tax revenues and economic growth', National Center for Policy Analysis, NCPA Policy Report No 98 (March 1991). Scully used a similar technique when advising the New Zealand government. This lead to substantial controversy in the late 1990s.

44 James M. Buchanan and Dwight R. Lee, 'Tax rates and tax revenues in political equilibrium: Some simple analytics', *Economic Inquiry* 20 (1982), 344-354. James M. Buchanan and Dwight R. Lee, 'Politics, time, and the Laffer curve', *Journal of Political Economy* 90 (1982), 816-819. A simple version of these papers is set out in Geoffrey Brennan and James M. Buchanan, *The Reason of Rules: Constitutional Political Economy* (Indianapolis: Liberty Fund, 1985 (2000)), 94–101.

45 Stuart, 1034.

46 Robert Breunig, Deborah Cobb-Clark and Xiaodong Gong claim that the 2005–6 budget cuts will have substantial effects on work incentives, particularly for women and for lower income workers (Improving the modeling of couples' labour supply, 2005, IZA Discussion Paper available at http://ssrn.com/abstract=809984). See also John Garnaut, 'Tax cut jackpot for hard workers' *Sydney Morning Herald* (11 August 2005).

Chapter 4. Who's not paying their fair share of income tax?

1 I wish to thank Robert Brooks, Mark Stewart and two anonymous reviewers for comments that have substantially improved this chapter. Some of the results here have appeared in an opinion piece published in *The Weekend Australian Financial Review* (February 21–22, 2004).

2 James Buchanan, 'The Icons of Public Debt', in *Debt and Taxes: Volume 14, The Collected Works of James M Buchanan* (Indianapolis: Liberty Fund, 1999–2002), 362.

3 Wayne Swan, 'Flat taxes sabotage level field', *The Australian* (9 January 2004), 11.

4 D. Uren, 'Income Tax Overhaul Urged', *The Australian* (18 March 2004).

5 The Greens National Economic Policy, www.greens.org.au/policies/economics/taxandrevenue

6 See www.ato.gov.au listed under 'Booklets & Publications.' This data is available free online for the years 1996–7 to 2000–1. Data prior to 1996–7 is available, but cannot be downloaded.

7 The data are not precisely comparable across years because the number of individuals in each quantile varies by year due to data collection dates varying and the number of returns at that date. However, the source of variation is small and is unlikely to bias the results of the analysis

[8] The ATO define 'net tax' as gross tax less rebates and any other credits plus the Medicare levy and Medicare surcharge. These credits may vary from year to year.

[9] According to some 'back of the envelope' estimates for the 2000–1 Superannuation Surcharge Tax the top 25% of income earners would have paid about 64.6% to 65.5% of taxes, a small but potentially significant increase on current estimates.

[10] See the transcript at <www.treasurer.gov.au/tsr/content/transcripts/2004/042.asp>.

[11] One of the most famous critiques of progressive taxation is Walter J Blum and Harry Kalven Jr (1953) *The Uneasy Case for Progressive Taxation* (Chicago and London: University of Chicago Press, 1978).

[12] Swan, 'Flat taxes sabotage level field'. Similarly, in a 2003 address to the Fabian Society, then-Shadow Treasurer Bob McMullen listed 'Progressivism and Equity' as his first (of six) principle of taxation. See www.bobmcmullan.com/Releases%20&%20speeches/Speeches/20030531%20-%20Fabian%20Society%20in%20Melbourne%20.htm>.

[13] Henry Simons, *Personal Income Taxation* (Chicago: University of Chicago Press, 1938), 19, for example, thought income inequality was 'distinctly evil'.

[14] L. Mises, *Human Action: A Treatise on Economics*, Fourth Revised Edition (San Francisco: Fox & Wilkes, 1949), 858.

[15] Mises, 739.

[16] F. Hayek, *The Constitution of Liberty* (Chicago: University of Chicago Press, 1960), 310–311.

[17] Hayek, 309.

[18] Paul A. Samuelson, *Foundations of Economic Analysis Enlarged Edition* (Cambridge, MA: Harvard University Press, 1947 (1983)), 227, fn. 26.

[19] J. S. Mill, (1848), *Principles of Political Economy* (New York: Augustus M. Kelley, 1989), 807.

[20] Arnold Jacob Cohen Stuart (1889), 'On progressive taxation', In Richard A. Musgrave and Alan T. Peacock, *Classics in the Theory of Public Finance* (Macmillan: London, 1958 (1967)), 60.

[21] Hayek, 309.

[22] J. Quiggin, *Taxing Times: A Guide to Australia's Tax Debate* (Sydney: UNSW Press, 1998), 21.

[23] As above.

[24] J. S. Mill, 805.

[25] J. S. Mill (1861) *Utilitarianism* (London, J M Dent .& Sons, 1962), 55.

[26] Frank Field, *The Ethic of Respect: A left wing cause* CIS Occasional Paper, No 102, (Sydney: Centre for Independent Studies, 2006).

[27] A. Harding and N. Warren, *Who Pays the Tax Burden in Australia? Estimates for 1996-97*, NATSEM Discussion Paper No 39 (1999). These results are based on an analysis of household income and expenditure. They do not investigate individuals per se. The Australian tax system has individuals as its unit of analysis.

28 Quiggin first made this argument in his book *Taxing Times: A Guide to Australia's Tax Debate*, 21, before the NATSEM study was published. He subsequently repeated the argument at his website, www.johnquiggin.com/archives/2004_06 (Fun and Fury, Part II).

29 When challenged on the validity of his claim that 36% is 'roughly proportional' to 51% Quiggin initially backed away from that statement. He, however, has subsequently repeated his 'roughly proportional' claim. It is possible that Quiggin confused the Australian and US evidence. The classic US study in this field found that the US tax system was 'essentially proportional for the vast majority of families'. J. Pechman and B. Okner, *Who bears the tax burden?* (Washington, DC: The Brookings Institution, 1974), 10.

30 Harding and Warren, *Who Pays the Tax Burden?*, 34.

31 Australian Bureau of Statistics, *Government Benefits, Taxes and Household Income 1998–99*. Cat 6537.0 (Canberra: ABS, 2001). By calculating the percentage of 'Total taxes allocated' to 'Gross Income,' the ABS 1998–99 data show the lowest 20% of households pay 26% of gross income in total tax, while the top 20% pay 33%. A problem in both the NATSEM and ABS studies is they include private income (that is, income earned from employment etc.) *and* benefits from the welfare system in calculating gross income. For low-income households, the welfare system contributes the bulk of all income (I estimate, using the ABS data, for 60% of households government benefits excluding health and education are greater than total tax paid. Only households in the top two quintiles pay more in tax than they receive in benefits. In other words, all public expenditure, net of welfare, is paid for by 40% of households.

32 NATSEM undertook an analysis of the likely impact of under-reporting by grossing up reported alcohol and tobacco expenditure and calculating total taxes including the grossed up 'sin' taxes. I have compared households that consume both alcohol and tobacco to those that consume neither alcohol nor tobacco. For those households that minimise their 'sin' taxes the Australian tax system is very progressive. Indeed, based on an analysis such as this one could almost claim that the only regressive component of the Australian tax system is the 'sin' taxes.

33 As James M. Buchanan has indicated, 'to the extent that value judgements enter the discussion, genuine "scientific" analysis comes to an end.' In *Public Finance in Democratic Process: Fiscal Institutions and Individual Choice* (Indianapolis: Liberty Fund, 1967 (1999)), 228.

34 This, of course begs the question, 'Why do economists argue in favour of progressive taxation?' The answer relates to techniques of economic method. Knut Wicksell described the approach as follows, 'Imagine how an enlightened and benevolent absolute ruler—one imbued, say, with the sense of equity of our modern educated classes—would organize the expenditures and taxes of his country.' (Knut Wicksell, 1896, 'A new principle of just taxation' In Richard A. Musgrave and Alan T. Peacock, *Classics in the Theory of Public Finance* (London: Macmillan, 1958 (1967)), 83). James M. Buchanan, the 1986 Nobel Laureate, has been quite scathing of this approach: 'Many

economists, along with other social scientists and social philosophers, enjoy playing God, by which I mean laying out in detail their own private versions of the 'good society' without being required to suggest ways and means of implementing their precepts or even to defend the consistency of these precepts with democratic political processes' ('Democratic Values in Taxation', In *The Collected Works of James M. Buchanan*, Volume 14 (Indianapolis: Liberty Fund, 1999), 36–37).

35 Hayek points out that the basis of public finance has been 'to raise the largest sums with the least resistance'. See F. Hayek, *Law, Legislation and Liberty Volume 3: The political order of a free people* (Chicago: University of Chicago Press, 1979), 52. See also Margaret Levi, *Of Rule and Revenue* (Berkley: University of California Press, 1988). Charles Adams in *For Good and Evil: The Impact of Taxes on The Course Of Civilization* (London: Madison Books, 1993) also contains an excellent discussion on the introduction of progressive taxes.

36 It is true that Adam Smith can be quoted in support of progressive taxes, 'It is not very unreasonable that the rich should contribute to the public expense, not only in proportion to their revenue, but something more than in that proportion' (1976, part 2, 368). This, however, is in the specific context of house rental taxation. Smith, apparently, did not approve of conspicuous consumption.

37 J.S. Mill, *Principles of Political Economy*, 807.

38 J.R. McCulloch, 'On the Complaints and Proposals Regarding Taxation', *Edinburgh Review* LVII (1833), 164.

39 Hayek, 313–323.

40 It is important to note the difference. The welfare system defines its operating unit as a household or family. The tax system defines its operating unit as an individual. This fundamental difference must be a source of some confusion and inefficiencies.

41 The AES can be accessed via the Australian Social Science Data Archive. Those who carried out the original analysis and collection of the data bear no responsibility for my analysis or interpretation of the data. The AES consists of a stratified systematic random sampling of the Commonwealth Electoral Roll. The sample is selected by population weights. Data are collected by mail. A total of 4,250 surveys were posted out. The final response rate was 42% with 1769 completed returns. Full details are available at http://assdu.edu.au.

42 Cathy Buchanan and Peter Hartley, *Equity as a Social Goal* (Wellington: New Zealand Business Roundtable, 2000), 183.

43 Following media comments it seems that some in the Revenue Lobby consider individuals with more than $52,000 as 'rich.' For example, *The Daily Telegraph* has 'Tax Cuts for All, Not Just the Rich' as its 14 May 2004 headline.

Chapter 5. The moral case for a flat tax

1 Robert E. Hall and Alvin Rabushka, *The Flat Tax* (Stanford: Hoover Institution Press, 1985) 5–6

2 It is worth noting that, if it really is the case that high marginal rates are an effective incentive to work even harder, then this could justify an argument for a deliberately regressive income tax system. With the highest rate of taxation at the bottom, then each bracket up the income scale taxed at a successively lower rate, one would have a powerful incentive to work one's way up the income scale as hard and as fast as one could, as one would keep more of each dollar earned in each successive bracket!

3 Adam Smith expressed this 'washing through' argument in relation to income tax in general in *The Wealth of Nations* (1776): 'A direct tax upon the wages of labour, therefore, though the labourer might perhaps pay it out of his hand, could not properly be said to be even advanced by him; at least if the demand for labour and the average price of provisions remained the same after the tax as before it. In all such cases not only the tax, but something more than the tax, would in reality be advanced by the person who immediately employed him. The final payment would in different cases fall upon different persons. The rise which such a tax might occasion in the wages of manufacturing labour would be advanced by the master manufacturer, who would both be entitled and obliged to charge it, with a profit, upon the price of his goods. The final payment of this rise of wages, therefore, together with the additional profit of the master manufacturer, would fall upon the consumer.' Adam Smith, *An Inquiry Into the Nature and Causes of the Wealth of Nations, Volume II* (Indianapolis: Liberty Classics, 1981), 864–865.

4 While some pricing is consumer income sensitive, seniors' discounts for theatre tickets are based in part on assumptions about the typical income levels of seniors, there are few products and services where prices are sensitive at the level of the individual consumer's income. Exceptions include some unions and professional associations, where membership fees vary relative to wage or salary level.

5 See, for example, Hall and Rabushka, *op.cit.*, Chapters 3 and 5, and John O. Stone, 'Australian Personal Income Tax System', Paper prepared for the Australian Travel Industry Association for consideration in relation to the Hawke government's so-called Australian Tax Summit (1985), for examinations of the rival implications for a proposed flat tax rate of allowing or disallowing a tax free threshold, with reference to the United States and Australia.

6 F. A. Hayek, *The Constitution of Liberty* (London: Routledge and Kegan Paul, 1960). 322.

7 J. S. Mill, *On Liberty* ed. R. B. McCallum (Oxford: 1946), 70.

8 F. A. Hayek, *The Constitution of Liberty* (London: Routledge and Kegan Paul, 1960), 93, and Robert Nozick, *Anarchy, State, and Utopia* (Oxford: Blackwell, 1974) 239–240.

9 Nozick, Chapter 7.

10 See Nozick's discussion of redistribution and property rights, 167–174.

11 Estonia is perhaps the most interesting case because, in relative terms, it is probably the most economically successful of the post-Soviet republics. According to the OECD, the Estonian tax system has been relatively stable since the present system was introduced in 1994. (OECD Country Report: Estonia (Paris: 2001), 12.)

12 There is a strong case for retaining a tax-free threshold, and a threshold that is much higher than it is at present. One reason is that it would on balance increase efficiency, thereby reducing costs, by cutting out the two-way traffic that involves all recipients of income below the threshold simultaneously paying income tax and receiving tax transfers to compensate them for their (further depleted) low income (see chapter 7). But are we justified in compromising the vertical equity involved in a pure flat tax to achieve this efficiency? Arguably we should conceive of an income as made up of two components, a basic entitlement which is not subject to tax, together with all income in excess of the basic entitlement which is taxable. This approach preserves vertical equity *among taxpayer incomes.* It also embodies a rhetorical advantage because it enables the flat tax to be defended as not merely non-regressive but mildly progressive relative to total incomes, for all incomes that exceed the threshold, that is, for all income recipients obliged to pay income tax. It might even make a flat tax politically saleable—eventually.

Chapter 6. Tax complexity and the rule of law

1 This paper was prepared at the invitation of the Australian Tax Research Foundation. The author wishes to thank the members of the foundation's board of governors for their comments and suggestions. The paper was written before the author was appointed to the Administrative Appeals Tribunal.

2 'The Rule of Law and Economic Vibrancy' (2003) 77 *ALJ*, 424, 425.

3 Roger Kerr, 'New Zealand's Flawed Growth Strategy', *Policy* (Autumn 2003), 3.

4 Michael J Graetz, 'Erwin Griswold's Tax Law—and Ours' *Tax Lawyer* 56 (2002), 173, 174.

5 James Buchanan, *Public Finance in Democratic Process*, (Chapel Hill, NC: University of North Carolina Press, 1967).

6 Charles Gustafson, 'The Politics And Practicalities of Checking Tax Avoidance in the United States' in Graeme S. Cooper (ed.), *Tax Avoidance and the Rule of Law* (Amsterdam: TBFD Publications/Australian Tax Foundation, 1997), 349, 352.

7 Charles Adams, *For Good and Evil: The Impact of Taxes on the Course of Civilization* (Lanham, MD: Madison Books, 1993), xvii.

8 Mark Latham MHR, 'Those Chains are Stifling Spirit', *The Australian* (18 November, 2003), 11; 'Tax Dodgers Thrive Despite GST Dragnet', *The Sydney Morning Herald* (26-27 July, 2003), 1. The ATO disputes the 15% estimate but offers no definite figure of its own: ATO Cash Economy Task Force, *The Cash Economy Under the New Tax System*, Report No 3 (September 2003), chapter 1.

9 D. G. Hill QC in Robin Woellner, Trevor Vella, Lee Burns, *Australian Taxation Law*, 5th edition (Sydney: CCH, 1994), Foreword to the first edition (v).

10 Geoffrey Walker, *The Rule of Law: Foundation of Constitutional Democracy* (Melbourne: University Press, 1988), 66. I will be referring to this and other publications of mine further, not as 'authority', but to incorporate certain lines of argument by reference for the sake of brevity.

11 (1942) 65 CLR 373.

12 Hill et al. *Australian Taxation Law*, see note 8.

13 Walker, *Rule of Law*, 192–93.

14 Graeme S. Cooper, 'Conflicts, Challenges and Choices: The Rule Of Law and Anti-Avoidance Rules', in Cooper, *Tax Avoidance and the Rule of Law* (Amsterdam: TBFD Publications/Australian Tax Foundation, 1997), 13, 18.

15 As above, 26.

16 As above, 21, 30; *Oxford Companion to the High Court of Australia* (Melbourne: Oxford University Press, 2001), 661.

17 Lord Oliver, 'Judicial Approaches to Revenue Law', in Malcolm Gammie, A. Shipwright (eds.), *Striking the Balance: Tax Administration, Enforcement and Compliance in the 1990s* (London: Institute for Fiscal Studies, 1996), 174.

18 *Commissioner of Internal Revenue v Newman*, 159 F.2d 848, 851 (2d Cir. 1947), J. Hand, dissenting.

19 James L. Payne, 'Explaining the Persistent Growth in Tax Complexity', in Donald P. Racheter, Richard E. Wagner (eds.), *Politics, Taxation and the Rule of Law: The Power to Tax in Constitutional Perspective* (Dordrecht: Kluwer Academic Publishers, 2002), 168, 171.

20 'Push to Simplify Income Tax Rules', *The Australian Financial Review*, (3 June 2003), 1.

21 Edmund Burke, 'Speech on American Taxation', F. Selby (ed.), *Burke's Speeches*, London 1930, 12-13.

22 Cooper, *Tax Avoidance and the Rule of Law*, 33. Complexity is also in part the result of an attempt at fairness: Payne, 'Explaining the Persistent Growth in Tax Complexity', 181.

23 Geoffrey Brennan, James M. Buchanan, *The Power to Tax: Analytical foundations of a fiscal constitution* (UK: Cambridge University Press, 1980), 191.

24 Payne, 'Explaining the Persistent Growth in Tax Complexity', 183.

25 L.W. Street , 'Judicial Law-making: Some reflections', (1982) 9 *Syd. L. Rev.* 535, 537.

26 Jeffrey Waincymer, 'The Australian Tax Avoidance Experience and Responses: A Critical Review', in Cooper, *Tax Avoidance and the Rule of Law*, 247.

27 Cooper, 'Conflicts, Challenges and Choices: The Rule Of Law and Anti-

Avoidance Rules', 49.

28 This is seen in the example of *FCT v Spotless Services Ltd* (1996) 96 ATC 5201, 5206; Michael D'Ascenzo, 'Part IVA and the common sense of a reasonable person', 37 *Taxation in Australia* (2 Aug 2002), 70, 76.

29 Malcolm Gammie, 'Tax Avoidance and The Rule of Law: A Perspective From the United Kingdom', in Cooper, *Tax Avoidance and the Rule of Law*, 181, 215.

30 Waincymer, 'The Australian Tax Avoidance Experience and Responses', 304.

31 As above.

32 As above, 305.

33 As above, 304. See *Vincent v FCT* 2002 ATC 4490, 4518-19 (FCA); 2002 ATC 4742, 4761 (FFC).

34 Sir Harry Gibbs, 'The Need for Taxation Reform', 11th National Convention of the Taxation Institute of Australia, 5 May 1993, 19-20.

35 *Fayed v Commissioners of Inland Revenue* (2003) SC 1; Hon LJ Priestley, 'The Commissioner's Powers of Settlement and Compromise', (2002) *Revenue LJ* 40.

36 Edmund Burke, 'Speech on American Taxation', F. Selby (ed.), *Burke's Speeches*, London 1930, 12-13.

37 A. L. Goodhart, 'The Rule Of Law and Absolute Sovereignty' (1958) 106 *U. Pa. L. Rev.* 943, 957.

38 For example, Income Tax Assessment Act 1936 (Cth), ss. 14ZAAA-AAM, 14ZAA-ZAZC.

39 Waincymer, 'The Australian Tax Avoidance Experience and Responses', 304.

40 *Federal Commissioner of Taxation v Firth* (2002) 50 ATR 1.

41 Neil Brooks, 'The Responsibility Of Judges in Interpreting Tax Legislation', in Cooper, *Tax Avoidance and the Rule of Law*, 93, 104.

42 As above, 99.

43 Waincymer, 'The Australian Tax Avoidance Experience and Responses', 304.

44 Ross Greenwood, 'Levy Heavies', *The Bulletin,* May 20, 2003, 62.

45 Walker, *The Rule of Law*, 40–41, 200–02, see note 9.

46 (1765) 19 St. Tr. 1030.

47 Brooks, 'The Responsibility Of Judges in Interpreting Tax Legislation', 99–100.

48 *FCT v Westfield Ltd.* (1991) 22 ATR 400; Graeme S. Cooper, 'The Political Economy Of Taxation and the Roles Of the High Court' (1993) 23 *WALRev.* 101, 115. The position does not appear to have changed significantly since the High Court's Westfield decision.

49 Hill et al. *Australian Taxation Law.*

50 Cooper, 'The Political Economy of Taxation', 101, 115.

51 Cooper, 'Conflicts, Challenges and Choices', 17.

52 *FCT v Westraders Pty Ltd* (1979) 11 ATR 24, 40.

53 Geoffrey Walker, 'Information as Power: Constitutional Implications of the Identity Numbering and ID Card Proposal', 16 *Qld L Soc J* (June 1986), 153.

54 Waincymer, 'The Australian Tax Avoidance Experience and Responses', 247–48.

55 Alan Lewis, *The Psychology of Taxation* (Oxford: Martin Robertson, 1982), 180.

56 G. T. Pagone, 'The General Anti-Avoidance Provisions in Australian Taxation Law', 27 MULR (2003) 770, 778, commentary on *FCT v Consolidated Press Holdings Ltd* (2001) 297 CLR 235.

57 Knut Wicksell, 'A New Principle of Just Taxation', (first published 1896) in R. A. Musgrave, A. T. Peacock (eds.), *Classics in the Theory of Public Finance* (London: Macmillan, 1958), 72, 82; Gary M. Anderson, 'Referendum, Redistribution and Tax Exemption: A Rent Seeking Theory of Direct Democracy', in Racheter and Wagner, *Politics, Taxation and the Rule of Law*, 81, see note.18.

58 D. C. Mueller, *Public Choice II* (New York: Cambridge University Press, 1991), 1.

59 Anderson, 'Referendum, Redistribution and Tax Exemption', 82.

60 Buchanan and Brennan, *The Power to Tax*, see note 22.

61 Anderson, 'Referendum, Redistribution and Tax Exemption', 81.

62 Brennan and Buchanan, *The Power to Tax*, 25; Alvin Rabushka, Pauline Ryan, *The Tax Revolt* (Stanford: Hoover Press, 1982), 21-26.

63 John G. Head, 'Tax Reform: A Quasi-Constitutional Perspective', in Cooper (ed), *Tax Avoidance and the Rule of Law*, 155, 178-80.

64 As above.

65 The inflationary results of the 1973 and 1974 budgets, coupled with a federal government-backed wages explosion at a time of low growth, were well understood even at the time: 'Oh, No—Not the 1973 Budget Again', *Australian Financial Review* (27 August 1974), 2; 'The inflation merry-go-round', *AFR* (27 August 1974), 1; 'Hyperinflation and Low Growth—The Two Threats', *AFR (*6 August 1974), 12. Even Bill Hayden's 1975 budget, touted by the government as reducing the tax burden on lower earners, led to the tax paid by those receiving less than average weekly earnings rising by 18% in a single year: R. J. Tanner, D. J. Collins, *Flat Rate Tax?* (Sydney: Tax Institute Research and Education, 1981), 4. Many countries suffered high inflation during that period as a result of the OPEC governments' monopoly pricing of oil. The Whitlam government lacked that excuse, however, because Bass Strait and Barrow Island crude made Australia self-sufficient in high-grade petroleum during the relevant period and government price controls prevented Australian oil producers from raising their prices to world levels: P. Walsh, *Confessions of a Failed Finance Minister,* (Sydney: Random House, 1995), 16; J. Nevile, Australian Inflation—Made at Home or Imported?' in *International Money—Experiments and Experience, Papers and Proceedings of the Port Stephens Conference, (ed.)* W. Kasper (Canberra: ANU Department of Economics, RSSS, 1976). In Switzerland, direct citizen control over government budgets via the referendum system kept inflation (and unemployment) in that country below 2% despite that country's exposure to the full effects of OPEC price rises. See Walker, *Rule of Law*, 340-41, see note 9. One must therefore conclude that the Whitlam government knew what it was doing when it opened the inflation floodgates without altering or indexing tax scales. Such a step would have served its goal of expanding the public sector, without the government's being seen to raise the necessary revenue by openly increasing taxes.

66 David R. Morgan, 'Personal Income Tax Indexation', in John G. Head (ed.), *Taxation Issues of the 1980s*, (Sydney: Australian Tax Research Foundation, 1983), 71.

67 Geoffrey Walker, *Ten Advantages of a Federal Constitution and How to Make the Most of Them*, (Sydney: The Centre for Independent Studies, 2001), 37-39.

68 Wolfgang Kasper, *Economic Freedom Watch* Report No 4 (Sydney: The Centre for Independent Studies, 2003),7; Allesandra Fabro, 'OECD Figures Could Herald Local Cuts', *Australian Financial Review* (23 October, 2003), 5.

69 Wolfgang Kasper, *EFW* Report No 5, (Sydney: The Centre for Independent Studies, 2003), 5.

70 'Experts Warn on Rising Number of Copycat Cheats', *The Sydney Morning Herald* (3 June 2003), 6. When the people have genuine control over the tax laws, as under Switzerland's citizen-initiated referendum system, taxpayers feel more of a moral obligation to comply with them: Mads Qvortrup, *A Comparative Study of Referendums: Government by the People* (Manchester: Manchester University Press, 2002), 66, 139; Bruno S. Frey, Alois Stutzer, *Happiness and Economics: How the Economy and Institutions Affect Well-Being* (Princeton, NJ: Princeton University Press, 2002), 139.

71 Head, 'Tax Reform: A Quasi-Constitutional Perspective', 180, see n. 62.

72 Peter Saunders, Kayoko Tsumori, *Poverty in Australia: Beyond the Rhetoric* (Sydney: CIS, 2002), 84–5.

73 Kasper, *EFW* Report No 4, 8.

74 Robert Gottliebsen, 'Taxing Issues of Brains and Ageing', *The Australian* (1 September 2003), 31.

75 Robert Gottliebsen, 'Risky Cocktail of Terror, Deflation and Dodgy US Dollar', *The Australian,* (20 May 20 2003), 24. See also: Peter Saunders, 'After the house price boom' *Policy* Vol. 21, No 1, Autumn 2005.

76 Wolfgang Kasper, *EFW* Report No 5 (Sydney: The Centre for Independent Studies, 2003), 5.

77 As above, 4. See also Alex Robson in chapter 2.

78 Kerr, 'New Zealand's Flawed Growth Strategy', 5,7, see note 2.

79 As above, 4.

80 'Bubble Trouble Frightens Investors', *The Australian* (19 September 2003), 20; Gottliebsen, 'Risky Cocktail of Terror', see note 74.

81 Wolfgang Kasper, *EFW* Report No 6 (Sydney: CIS, 2003), 6.

82 Sullivan, *Taxing the Family*, 15. Barry Maley, *Family and Marriage in Australia* (Sydney: CIS, 2001), 77-97.

83 Kasper, *EFW* Report No. 6, 7.

84 OECD, *Taxing Wages, Taxing Families*; at the time of writing the full text of the survey was unavailable, but its effect is summarised in Christine Wallace, 'Marginal Tax Rates in World's Highest', *Weekend Australian* (3–4 January 2004), 3.

85 Tax indexation should be a statutory, automatic mechanism similar to that introduced by the Fraser government, rather than a 'manual' process as in the United Kingdom, where thresholds are raised each year in the budget as a matter of practice and convention. Research shows that tax indexation, even on its own, measurably reduces non-compliance. Wehrner W. Pommereline, Hannelors Weck-Hannemann, 'Tax Rates, Tax Administration and Income Tax Evasion in Switzerland', Public Choice 88:1-2 (1998), 161, 168.

[86] Historically, except in 16th century Europe, inflation had been a local, temporary phenomenon: Irving S. Friedman, *Inflation: A Worldwide Diaster*, New (ed.), (London: Hamish Hamilton, 1980), 102, 88. Persistent, cumulative inflation of 1% to 2% has been regarded as tolerable (140), but 1% cumulates over 30 years to a rise of 35% in prices, and in 50 years, to 65%. In an industrial country, even 2% continuous inflation is disruptive: *id.,* 17, 139.

Chapter 7. Tax Reform To Make Work Pay

[1] Quoted in Elizabeth Coleman, 'Tax slug on poor singles' *The Australian* (14 January 2006). The net tax calculations include the Medicare Levy, the low income tax offset, Family Tax Benefit and childcare benefit, and are based on research commissioned by the federal Opposition and reported in *The Australian.*

[2] OECD *Taxing Wages 2004–5 Edition* Paris, OECD 2006, Table 4.

[3] John Humphreys discusses Negative Income Tax in chapter 9.

[4] Peter Whiteford, 'The welfare expenditure debate' Paper to the Social Policy Research Centre conference, *Looking back, Looking forward* (Sydney: University of New South Wales, 2005), 14.
Elsewhere, Whiteford calculates total welfare spending is the third-lowest in the OECD, but the value of net transfers to the poorest 30% of the population is the third-highest, greater even than Sweden and exceeded only by Norway and Finland. In P. Whiteford and G. Angenent, *The Australian System of Social Protection*, (FaCS, 2001) 50.

[5] This is mainly because, since 1975, Australia has provided family support through welfare payments rather than through tax allowances. Peter Whiteford, 'The welfare expenditure debate', 6.

[6] The following figures are derived from Centrelink, *A Guide to Australian Government Payments 1 January–19 March 2006* Australian Government.

[7] With a pre-school child they will probably also have to pay for child care, although part of this cost will be subsidised by even more means-tested government payments (the Child Care Benefit and Child Care Allowance).

[8] The usual term expressing the combined impact of tax plus benefits withdrawn is 'effective marginal tax rate', but this is arguably misleading, for loss of benefits is not a 'tax' as such. A better term might therefore be 'equivalent marginal tax rate'.

[9] On the issue of work requirements for single parents, see Peter Saunders, *Australia's Welfare Habit, and how to kick it* (Sydney: Duffy and Snellgrove, 2004), chapter 9. In 2005 the government announced that single parents whose children were aged 6 or more would in future be expected to find part-time employment (and would be eligible for Newstart, rather than Parenting

Payment, if they failed to find work). Following a predictable hail of criticism from the welfare lobby, this requirement was subsequently relaxed with the age cut-off extended to 8.

10 The government has tried to ameliorate this problem with the Working Credit which allows claimants to retain more of their benefits for a period after they begin work (the precise allowance depends on how many credits they have accumulated, which itself reflects the time spent unemployed). This does not solve the problem, however--its simply delays its impact

11 G. Beer, ''Work Incentives Under a New Tax System', *The Economic Record* Special Issue 79 (Canberra: NATSEM, 2003), S14–S25. A report prepared by the Office of Status of Women in 2003 estimated that almost 1 million people were losing at least 60 cents in the dollar of additional earnings (Sid Marris and Michael McKinnon, 'Howard Battler Tax Slog Revealed', *The Australian,* 18 September 2003).

12 Lachlan Chipman, 'A Just Society Repays Effort', *The Australian (*6 January 2004)

13 See Warren, *Tax: Facts, fiction and reform*, Table 2.12, based on ABS *Government Benefits, Taxes and Household Income 1998-99* Cat No 6537.0, August 2001. Peter Whiteford ('The welfare expenditure debate', 11) puts the share of welfare payments going to the top quintile even lower, at just 3%.

14 According to Peter Whiteford ('The welfare expenditure debate', 11) the middle 60% of households absorb 56% of all transfer payments. Warren's estimates put this higher, at 66%, with the bottom quintile getting 28% and top quintile 5%.

15 See Peter Saunders, 'The $85 billion tax-welfare churn' CIS *Issue Analysis* No 57 (Sydney: Center for Independent Studies, 2005). Peter Whiteford ('The welfare expenditure debate') takes issue with my analysis of churning, claiming that the problem is smaller in Australia than elsewhere. He estimates that just 6% of disposable income in Australia is churned, compared with an OECD unweighted average of 14%, and that 23% of direct taxes are churned (52% in the OECD). However, he also accepts that churning includes indirect, as well as direct, taxes, and welfare services in kind, as well as cash transfers. Defined more broadly in this way, churning is extensive in Australia (Whiteford cites a figure of 18% of disposable income). Whiteford then suggests that any attempt to substantially reduce this figure would alter income distribution patterns and create 'formidable' transition problems, but these are political objections, not social scientific ones. It is clear that, while churning is kept below European levels by the exclusion of top earners from the transfer payments system, as well as by a relatively large take-up of private health and education by higher earner families, it is still extensive, and it is very costly in both economic and sociological terms (see Peter Saunders, 'Six arguments in favour of self-funding', CIS Issue Analysis No 61 (Sydney: Centre for Independent Studies, 2005).

16 A. Duncan and M. Harris, 'Simulating the Behavioural Effects of Welfare Reforms Among Sole Parents In Australia', *The Economic Record* 78 (2002), 264–76. For those on lower incomes, this taper has subsequently been reduced even further, to 20%.

[17] H. Buddelmeyer et al, 'Bracket Creep', 20.

[18] '21% of those in the first income decile have EMTRs in excess of 50%, 19% have EMTRs in excess of 70%. The situation in the second income decile is even worse with 31% having EMTRs over 50% and 27% facing EMTRs in excess of 70%. Across all deciles about 16% have EMTRs in excess of 50% and only 8% are on EMTRs over 70%'. See H. Buddelmeyer et al, 'Bracket Creep', 18.

[19] For the original proposal, see Peter Dawkins, 'A plan To Cut Unemployment in Australia' *Mercer-Melbourne Institute Quarterly Bulletin of Economic Trends* 1/99 (1999) 48–59.

[20] P. Dawkins, A. Duncan and J. Freebairn, *Modifying Income Support in The Australian Tax and Transfer System,* Paper to the 'Pursuing Opportunity and Prosperity' conference (Melbourne: University of Melbourne, 2003)

[21] Peter Dawkins, *Welfare to Work: Labour supply responses to work incentives* Paper to Melbourne Institute conference on 'Sustaining Opportunity and Prosperity', University of Melbourne, March 2005. See also: H. Buddelmeyer et al, 'Bracket Creep', 22.

[22] The effect on part-time second earners in middle income households would be particularly sharp, and the architects of the EC proposal admit that the number of partnered women going out to work would actually fall as a result of the change. They argue that this is a price worth paying in order to encourage more people from wholly welfare-dependent households into work (Peter Dawkins, 'A Tax System for Workers', *The Australian Financial Review,* (29 January 2003)). The same effect of increasing disincentives higher up the income scale has been noted of both the American and UK tax credit systems. See Gary Burtless, 'Can Supply-Side Policies Reduce Unemployment?' *Australian Economic Review* 35 (2002), 3–28, suggests that the number of discouraged middle earners in the US far outweighs the number of welfare recipients who are encouraged to move into work. Philip Collins and Roger Wicks, 'Special Report on Means Tests and Tax Credits', *Prospect* (May 2003), 50–55 talk of a new 'middle income trap' in Britain, showing how a couple with two children earning £250 per week now gain only a 6% increase in net income from a 20% rise in earnings.

[23] Peter Dawkins, *Welfare to work: Labour supply responses to work incentives.*

[24] In absolute terms, every taxpayer benefits by exactly the same amount, but in relative terms, the lowest income earners gain the most. Increasing the threshold to $13,000 would represent an average 4% tax cut for top earners but a 50% cut for those on low and middle incomes (Malcolm Turnbull and Jeromey Temple, *Taxation Reform in Australia*, Table 4A).

[25] Turnbull and Temple, Table 4A.

[26] Peter Dawkins, *Welfare to Work: Labour supply responses to work incentives.* Buddelmeyer goes further, claiming that for half the cost, an Earnings Credit could generate twice the labour market impact (H. Buddelmeyer et al, 'Bracket creep', 22).

[27] Politically, it is certainly an advantage, for everyone gains and nobody loses. This should therefore be an easy policy to sell to voters. And as Lauchlan Chipman

suggests in chapter 5, delivering higher relative tax cuts to lower income taxpayers by raising the TFT could be the quid pro quo for reducing higher rates in a move to a flat tax.

28 Based on Melbourne Institute, *Poverty Lines Australia* September 2005, Table 4. Calculations are based on allowances, which are lower than pensions, and include rent assistance.

29 Under Dwyer's proposals, it would be for each family to choose how it wants to be assessed. Many working couples would probably prefer to continue filing separate tax returns so that each individual can retain his or her own tax-free threshold. They would be free to do so. Couples where there is only one earner, however (and especially those who also have dependent children) might prefer to transfer part of the threshold of the non-working partner to the working partner.

30 In recent years, the federal government has tried to counter some of the inequity in the tax treatment of individuals and couples by giving certain categories of families a welfare top-up. Family Tax Benefit, (Part B), for example, is paid to families where there is only one earner to try to compensate them for the disadvantages they suffer through the tax system. The result, however, is a tangle of money transfers in which people get tax taken from them only to have some or all of the cash returned in the form of welfare payments. This is not only costly, it is also wrong in principle. We should not be taxing families until they have secured their own subsistence—and a family's subsistence level will be higher than it is for single people or couples without dependent children.

31 ACTU, *Minimum Wages Case Fact Sheet* September 2005, www.actu.asn.au

32 This is a policy that has long been recommended by Barry Maley. For example: Maley, *Family and Marriage in Australia* (Sydney: The Centre for Independent Studies, 2001)

33 Total spending on Family Tax Benefits is $10,912,110,000. Maternity Allowance costs $216,634,000 and childcare support is another $1,692,371,000. We would also scrap the low income tax offset (a means-tested rebate aimed at raising the tax-free threshold for low income earners to $7,382) which costs another $392,020,884. Sources: 'Actual expenses 2002-03' *Budget and Additional Estimates 2003-04*; *2003-04 Budget paper No.1*, Part 3, Statement 5; Australian Taxation Office, *Taxation Statistics 2000-2001*. We are grateful to Caspar Conde for his work in producing these and subsequent calculations.

34 The cost of raising the threshold assumes current tax rates of 15% up to $21,600. In 2004 there were 8,343,000 individual income tax payers. We estimate that 967,681 of these would opt for the shared couple threshold of $21,000 (this includes all the 621,681 taxpayers currently receiving FTB (Part B), plus 346,000 couples where there is a single earner but no children). The remainder are assumed to opt for the individual threshold of $13,000. The total cost is therefore:

$(13{,}000-6{,}000) * 0.15 * (8343000-967681) + (21{,}000-6{,}000) * 0.15 * 967681$

= $8,760,150,000. In 2004 there were 3,984,178 children under the age of 15. A child tax credit worth $4,000 would therefore cost $15,936,712,000 per year.

35 L. Sullivan, *Taxing the Family,* Policy Monograph 50 (Sydney: CIS, 2001).

36 G. Walker, *The Tax Wilderness,* Policy Monograph 60 (Sydney:CIS, 2004), 9.

37 The survey was based on a sample of 5,721 Australian residents linked to the ACNielsen Australian Internet User Survey. Between 12 and 27 March 2003, people completing the internet user survey were also invited to do the CIS survey (4,369 people did so); in addition, a random sample of 4,369 respondents who had completed the user survey before 12 March were re-contacted, and 1,352 agreed to participate in the CIS survey. This is not a probability sample design, for it is based on self-selection, so inferential statistics (including standard errors) are inappropriate. There are reasons to believe that people who use the internet are a peculiar and specific section of the whole population—not a cross-section of it—and there is the normal survey bias problem that those in the target population who agree to participate in the survey may be quite unlike those who refuse.

These problems can be rectified to some extent by weighting. The final sample was weighted by gender, age, state of residence and annual income to bring it into line with population estimates by the Australian Bureau of Statistics. This is a standard survey procedure for correcting sample biases, but it is not ideal, for there is no guarantee that the sample will turn out to be representative on other, uncontrolled, characteristics. To check for this, we ran two tests of 'external validity'. The first compares our respondents' stated voting intentions and reported past voting behaviour with opinion poll data for the same period. This suggests there may be a small skew against Labor supporters in our final, weighted sample. The second compared our data on marital status with that recorded in the first wave of the Household Income and Labour Dynamics (HILDA) survey. The two surveys appear broadly consistent, although ours slightly overestimates those who had never been married and those who had been divorced/separated, and slightly underestimates those who are married. Overall, the weighted survey appears to generate reasonably valid population estimates, but the results should still be treated with some caution, for this is not as valid a survey as a more conventional probability sample would have been.

Chapter 8. The taxation of shared family incomes

1 This chapter is a revised and edited version of a paper 'Family Taxation, Participation Rates, and Unemployment: A Report for the Taskforce on Employment Opportunities' written by T. M. Dwyer and published in 1993 by the Commonwealth Taskforce on Employment Opportunities. The paper has since been updated. Commonwealth of Australia copyright material is reproduced by permission. Views expressed in this paper are those of the author. The paper owes much to many discussions with many people over many years, not least to the opinions of those who disagreed with me and forced me to refine my thoughts. It would be difficult to single out some and unfair to omit others.

2 Ordinary case law rights under a contract of service are not assignable at common law especially where to do so could interfere with the performance of a statutory office, see J. G. Starke QC, *Assignment of Choses in Action in Australia* (Sydney: Butterworths, 1972), 58–61. Lockhart, QC, now Justice Lockhart of the Federal Court, (see J. S. Lockhart QC, *The Assignment of Rights to Income*, Paper for the Taxation Institute of Australia, Convention Papers for the Sixth New South Wales Convention (June 1974), 6) states that 'there is something to be said for the view that the reasoning of the Courts and the Boards of Review in the cases that have involved attempts to alienate salary are inconsistent with *Shepherd's Case* and *Norman's Case*. If one applies the reasoning in *Shepherd's Case* and *Norman's Case* there is no present right to future salary at the date of assignment because the salary may never in fact fall due. For instance the employee may leave his employment or be dismissed, for example, for dishonesty but what of the case where there is an employment agreement for a fixed term and the agreement is so structured that the employer is obliged to pay the salary unconditionally. In such an instance it would be my view that the alienation would be effective, provided of course it was for consideration, or, if not, either complied with the *Conveyancing Act* or with the rules of Equity relating to voluntary assignments to which I have referred. Take for instance the case of a *retainer* which may be paid to an employee, consultant or agent of a company. If the *retainer* agreement is so structured as to impose an obligation upon the employer to pay the *retainer* so that it becomes payable unconditionally in the future, in my view, it could be the subject of a valid alienation of income. It is obvious that the implications of this could be far-reaching.' Bernard Marks, *Alienation of Income* First Edition (Australia: CCH, 1978), 210, argues that there is no clear authoritative principle on the tax effect of assignments of rights to future personal service income. He quotes McKay to the effect that 'insofar as the personal services principle rests upon the *Parkins v Warwick* decision and if it is to be found in the case law it must it possesses a legal foundation which is both shaky and of poor workmanship'. At 216, Marks goes on to suggest that Division 6A implicitly recognises the effectiveness of assignments of rights to personal service income.

Professor R. W. Parsons, *Asprey Proposals for Family Unit Taxation,* in Taxation Institute Research and Education Trust, Taxation and the Family Unit: Report of Proceedings of a Public Seminar (Sydney, May 1979), 5, observes there are many legal techniques to achieve income splitting. He also observes that he is not as certain as everyone else that a salary or wage earner could not assign any part of his income to anyone else. Professor Parsons (7) also suggests it might be possible for ordinary law to be amended to create methods of transferring salaries. He notes that there would be a constitutional problem, if the Commonwealth Government were to attempt to interfere in the ordinary law of the States. Capital gains tax in such an assignment situation might be an added complication today but could perhaps be avoided by a State law or Family Court order declaring joint rights of parties over contractual rights to wage or salary income.

3 The Commissioner of Taxation seems unhappy in 2004 with this situation and is apparently seeking to persuade the Courts to reverse their previous decisions, relying on Part IVA, the general anti-avoidance provision. But the then-Treasurer, now Prime Minister, the Hon John Howard assured taxpayers in his second reading speech that Part IVA would not strike at family arrangements or at husbands forming partnerships with their wives. As the courts are required to have regard to such aids to interpretation, it would be remarkable if the Commissioner succeeded in establishing the proposition that Part IVA effectively outlaws husband-and-wife income splitting, contrary to the expressed intention of the then-Treasurer.

4 This is the usual position. Undistributed income is taxed to the trustee at the top marginal rate and a trustee may pay tax on behalf of a child but the general principle is, and always has been, to trace income through to the beneficiary wherever possible. A similar policy applies to partnership income and was applied to companies in the first income tax law of 1915.

5 R. C. Gates, *The Effect of Taxation on Incentive,* Paper presented at First National Convention of the Taxation Institute of Australia (Canberra, May 1969), reprinted in John Dixon, *The Public Sector: Selected Readings* (Melbourne: Penguin, 1972), 223, quotes the 1966 Canadian Royal Commission on Taxation which declared: 'The tax system should ensure that the flow of goods and services is allocated among individuals and groups so that those who have little economic power or particularly heavy obligations and responsibilities are able to maintain a decent standard of living. With respect to the allocation of taxes this requires taxation according to ability to pay . . . and the recognition of the family, as well as the unattached individual, as a unit for tax purposes.'

6 It is sometimes suggested that tax equity for families does not matter because families can be 'assisted' through the Social Security system. However, attempts to compensate families for tax inequities through income-tested social security payments may be seen as undesirable because they extend the welfare net further.

7 This principle is clear when parents split up. There is obviously a transfer of income involved in maintenance payments—the person who earns the money is not the one who finally consumes it. But if the final recipient is the person who should be taxed when couples separate, why not when they remain together?

8 It is perfectly arguable that tax burdens should change upon marriage, just as they change when a person in a business takes in a partner and splits the income with that partner. The principle behind family law is that marriage is a partnership and that each partner to a marriage acquires a legal right to be supported by the other. Once this is recognised, one can argue that marriage neutrality means that the tax system *should* recognise the sharing of income with spouses and dependent children. Both the *Social Security Act* and *Family Law Act* assume and impose an obligation of income sharing between spouses. It may be argued it is hardly neutral for the tax system to ignore that fact.

9 Child endowment originated in the 1940s as a foregone wage increase allocated by all workers as payroll tax to those of their fellow workers with children, The wage restraint of workers in World War II was eventually repaid by payroll tax being given to the states as a 'growth tax' while child endowment was eroded away, the moral of the story being 'put not your trust in princes'.

10 The apparent exception of Family Tax Benefit Part B being income tested only on the secondary earner's income in two-parent families reflects its origins in the dependent spouse tax rebate. For sole parent families, the complete lack of income testing reflects the judgment in the former sole parent tax rebate that ability to pay is less. These apparent exceptions are therefore examples of implicit recognition of the need for taxing on the basis of equivalent incomes.

11 John J. Beggs and Bruce J. Chapman, *The Foregone Earnings from Child Rearing in Australia,* Discussion Paper No 190 (Canberra: Australian National University Centre for Economic Policy Research, June 1988), 4, note that most models of whether a married woman will or will not participate in the workforce assumes that women will work if their market wage rate exceeds their reservation wages. The reservation wage is the value placed on not working. It is determined by, among other things, husband's income and children. They find, in an empirical exercise, that the presence of children has a substantial negative effect on women's labour market participation. Moreover the younger the children and the more there are of them the lower is the probability of female labour force involvement. They also find (21) that the working hours of wage earning women are affected by the presence age and number of children. This is of course entirely consistent with Hakim's point about the variability of women's preferences relating to work, children and families.

12 It is wrong in economics, law and logic to refer to these as '*effective* marginal tax rates' as is commonly done. The withdrawal of a subsidy is not the imposition of a tax. To say a person on welfare facing a 100% income test is paying an *effective* marginal tax rate of 100% is hardly accurate when in fact that person

may be paying no tax but receiving several thousand dollars from taxpayers. What we are really talking about is equivalence only in terms of marginal loss rates from earning extra income. This may seem a pedantic point but it is necessary to dispel a looseness of thought that sometimes infects the reasoning of otherwise respectable economists.

13 Centrelink, *A Guide to Australian Family Payments, 1 January-19 March 2006* Australian Government Family Assistance Office.

14 Sometimes the argument is put that the second tax-free threshold enjoyed by two earner families is a compensatory offset for the non-deductibility of child care costs. This argument is not logical. The tax threshold exists not to cover costs of earning an income, but to cover the taxpayer's costs of subsistence. A taxpayer is not supposed to be taxed on an income so small that one could not live on it. If the tax threshold were related to otherwise non-deductible costs of earning an income it would be denied to income recipients such as pensioners or annuitants or persons living on income from property. But this is not the case.

15 Henry Simons, *Personal Income Taxation: The Definition of Income as a Problem of Fiscal Policy* (Chicago: University of Chicago Press, 1938), 136–137, admits that 'difficult questions arise here with regard to the family . . . our scheme would require that beneficiaries be taxed with respect to gifts without deductions on the part of the donors'. He then observes the question is raised as to whether such a scheme is grossly unfair to those who contribute to the support of others. 'It is a common criticism of our income taxes that they differentiate meagrely, especially within the upper income taxes, between families of different size.' At 138 he admits that concessions are necessary for families to obtain equitable relative taxation at persons with similar earnings and different family obligations. However, he fails to see that this admission really calls into question his whole idea of double taxing income transfers or gifts.

16 In setting out these options, budgetary considerations have been put to one side. Not only are they outside the scope of this paper, but any given net revenue result may be achieved through changes to the rate scale or by expenditure restraint. Therefore budgetary considerations are essentially irrelevant to the design of a neutral tax system. If revenue considerations are allowed to stand forever against removal of tax distortions or a more equitable tax system, tax policy has little meaning. Moreover, some options could involve offsetting savings on outlays. The extent or nature of those savings would depend on policy details, which may involve a re-ordering of other Budgetary priorities.

17 Meredith Edwards, *Social Effects of Taxation* in J. Wilkes (ed), *The Politics of Taxation* (Sydney: Australian Institute of Political Science and Hodder and Stoughton, 1980), 156, notes that if one were to abolish any recognition in the tax system of the sharing of income with a spouse, one would logically have to do the same with the social security system. In other words an unemployed married person would be entitled to unemployment benefit in the same way as every other unemployed individual, as was recommended by the Myers

Committee of Inquiry. While that approach has logical consistency in treating individual adults, it does raise questions. Taxpayers may generally wonder why an unemployment benefit should be paid to the wife of a millionaire or the husband of an heiress. Similarly, people might wonder why all social security benefits were not available for individuals under the age of eighteen. Why have ageism directed against young people?

18 McIntyre and Oldman, 'Treatment of the Family', 217, argue that 'since children are the beneficiaries of some fraction of the income received by their parents, the benefit rule suggests that the children rather than the parents are the appropriate taxpayers on a portion of the family income'. The family income really has to be allocated to those who really enjoy it. Elsewhere in Michael J. McIntyre and Oliver Oldman, 'Taxation of the Family in a Comprehensive and Simplified Income Tax', *Harvard Law Review* 90:8 (June 1977), 1573–1630, they observe that 'in the family context the special problem of determining the appropriate taxpayer is basically a problem of attributing an available pool of taxable income among family members . . . taxing the income to those who actually consume or accumulate it regardless of the source seems intuitively more equitable and provides a basic principle to govern how the tax system should take domestic sharing arrangements into account' (1577). William Andrews also argues that income tax should fall on the recipient of an income transfer rather than the donor, if one is to regard income as personal consumption plus accumulation. See William D. Andrews, 'Personal Deductions in an Ideal Income Tax', *Harvard Law Review* 86:2 (December 1972), 348–349.

19 But as Alan Tapper, *The Family in the Welfare State* (North Sydney: Allen and Unwin, 1990), 110, observes, two-income childless couples can be expected to enjoy very high equivalent incomes not just because they will both enjoy uninterrupted careers nor simply because they do not share their incomes with dependants; they also have the advantage of the economies of scale that come from shared living. Such couples are thus already taxed on a 'generous' per capita basis.

20 The same result could be achieved by allowing unlimited transfers of income but applying different rate scales to the recipient of such transferred income (for example, children could have half thresholds and half the range of lower marginal tax rates).

21 This idea was perhaps always charmingly naive in ignoring the fungibility of money. The idea that the Treasury could take money from the husband and put it into the wife's purse with no effect on any housekeeping allowance he might give her may perhaps have been an exaggerated claim in the first place. Again, reminding ourselves of Hakim's warnings on different preferences, such stereotypes forget the not entirely uncommon cases where a wife handles all the household finances anyway and hands the husband his weekly spending money.

[22] In the Draft White Paper on Reform of the Australian Taxation System (Canberra: Commonwealth of Australia, 1985), 62, it was suggested that the individual unit of taxation minimised distortion of the choice between paid employment and non taxable activity (especially for married women); and was consistent with a policy of promoting equal employment opportunity and of furthering of the independence of women. The first statement may be questioned, because, on a primary/secondary earner model of employment, the existing Australian tax system creates a distortion in favour of the second income instead of additional primary earner income. Secondly it may be argued that a neutral system, rather than a distorting tax system, is what is required to promote equal employment opportunity. A system of elective family income sharing would appear to give women greater choice and greater employment opportunity than the present system. Many women tend to have low paid, low status jobs. To the extent that tax recognition of family income sharing reduced their need for additional family income (the 'income effect'), their bargaining position in the labour market would be improved. They would not need to settle necessarily for jobs which they regarded as unsatisfactory.

[23] Mr Justice Asprey, in his reservation on the taxpaying unit in the Committee's report (see *Taxation Review Committee, Full Report* (Asprey Report) (Canberra: Australian Government Publishing Service, January 1975), 141), argued that a married woman should be treated under general law and the taxation system as an individual in her own right and, in relation to income which was morally and legally her own, should pay no more and no less tax than if she were a single person. However, a system of elective recognition of income transfers does not violate that principle. No one would be taxed on income she had not elected to receive as a transfer. Thus individual taxation can be reconciled with recognition of family income transfers and equity.

[24] Professor Parsons in his reservations in the Asprey Committee report on income splitting (see Taxation Review Committee (1975), 158) observed that it was odd that some people opposed recognition of family income sharing in the tax system yet were prepared to argue that, on death or divorce, a spouse should be regarded as having contributed equally to the accumulation of family assets and should be entitled to them. He also observes that an elective system of family taxation could not be said to be in any way inconsistent with the independent status of women.

[25] Ann Harding (21) remarks, 'One of the striking features of the last decade was the rise and rise of the 'dinkies' dual income couples without kids. In 1981–82 dinkies made up 29% of the richest 10% of the population. By 1989–90 this had increased to 36%. People living in two-income families both with and without children made up two-thirds of those individuals in the top decile by 1989–90, while those living in single income families dropped by 10% to 15% during the 1980s.' Similarly, Deborah Mitchell, *Taxation and Income Redistribution: The 'Tax Revolt' of the 1980s Revisited*, Paper presented at ISSA Conference, Comparative Research on Welfare States in Transition

(Oxford, 9–12 September 1993), 19, observes that over the US, UK, Sweden, the Netherlands, Germany, Canada and Australia, two income families are paying relatively less tax than in the past—where tax scales have been cut, they have gained twice. Similarly, the Population Issues Committee (see National Population Council, *Population Issues and Australia's Future: Environment, Economy and Society Final Report*, (Canberra: AGPS, December 1991), 90–91), observed that 'Increasingly, income has become concentrated in Australia in the hands of families with few or no children while those experiencing financial difficulty are increasingly those with children (both one- and two-parent families). There is a real danger that Australia will follow the path of the United States where it is now recognised that unless public policy offsets some of these trends there will be greater polarisation economically and psychologically among the young adults of the late 1990s and early 2000s.' The increases in family payments since the mid-1990s might be seen as a social reaction to these earlier predictions.

26 This is where Hakim's point on the sociological variability of women's preferences for children and families cuts deeply into economics. Suppose that in a non-tax world of 100 women, 50 want no children and 50 want five children. Leaving aside whether wishes are always fulfilled, one might expect mild population growth with a net reproduction rate below 2.5. If the tax system makes it more difficult for men to support families and forces women to revise downwards their desired family size to three children the net reproduction rate drops to 1.5. The result is demographic collapse of the fiscal base.

27 The efficiency costs of income-tested transfers are considerable. As Gary Burtless, 'The Economist's Lament: Public assistance', *America Journal of Economic Perspectives* 4 (Winter 1990), 75, observes, statistical experience suggests that it can be expensive to taxpayers to raise the net incomes of the working age poor by $1. Thus programs such as additional family payment which depend on tax financed, income tested, transfers may involve larger losses of output than what is transferred to the recipient.

Chapter 9. Rebuilding Australia's Tax And Welfare Systems

1 I would like to thank Sinclair Davidson, Alan Duhs, Terry Dwyer, Darren Kennedy and Peter Saunders for their helpful comments on earlier versions of this paper. I would also like to thank Duncan Spender for his earlier help in developing 'Reform 30/30'.

2 Information regarding federal government spending and tax rates are taken from www.budget.gov.au.

3 It is suggested that HECS repayments are also taken out of the tax system and instead administered separately as a government loan.

4 The exact details of how the NIT and TFT would be coordinated need not be finalised at this stage. One suggestion would be to tax all income at 30% initially with no TFT and then pay back the excess tax every fortnight along with the NIT payment. Such a payment would always sum to $9000. For example, with an income of $10,000 the worker would receive $3000 tax back and $6000 NIT. With an income of $25,000 the worker would receive $7500 tax back and $1500 NIT. The unemployed would receive $9000 NIT and those with incomes over $30,000 would receive $9000 tax back.

5 Milton and Rose Friedman, *Free to Choose* (Chicago: Harcourt, 1980).

6 John Humphreys, 'Reforming Wages and Welfare Policy: Six Advantages of a Negative Income Tax', *Policy* (Autumn 2001).

7 A recent expansion on the Five Economists' Plan was given by one of the five economists in Peter Dawkins, 'The 'Five Economists' Plan: The Original Idea and Further Developments', ANU Discussion Paper No. 450, (Canberra: Centre for Economic Policy Research, 2002).

8 As above.

9 Cited in Dawkins. Incidentally, the lower elasticity for employment compared with hours worked indicates that a higher income has a positive impact on hours worked for people already employed. This is consistent with the substitution theory of wages and the idea that tax decreases the incentive to work.

10 Robert Dixon, John Freebairn and G.C. Lim, 'An Employment Equation for Australia 1966–2001', Research Paper 892, (Melbourne: University of Melbourne, 2004).

11 In a frequently cited American study, Card and Krueger purported to find no relationship between minimum wages and labour demand, but there are a number of problems with this study. They used a short-term period when it is generally accepted that the link between wages and labour demand takes one to two years to be fully appreciated. They only considered one industry (fast-food restaurants) and therefore failed to notice that employment actually did fall following the increase in the minimum wage. And even if their findings were correct for America, the American minimum wage is significantly different from the Australian minimum wage (it is much lower, and fewer people are on the American minimum wage). Obviously, the more people on the minimum wage, the greater the impact of a change in the minimum wage. A better country comparison is France, where studies show a significant negative relationship between minimum wages and employment. See David Card and Alan Krueger, 'Minimum Wages and Employment: A case study of the fast-food industry in New Jersey and Pennsylvania', *American Economic Review*, 84, (1994), 772–93. Also Card and Krueger, *Myth and Measurement: The New Economics of the Minimum Wage* (Princeton: Princeton University Press, 1995). For further discussion of problems in the Card and Krueger study, see Alex Robson, 'A Labour Market Fable', *Policy* (Summer 2004–05)

12 Borland, 'Will Lowering Wages Reduce Unemployment?', *CEDA Bulletin* (July 1999), 16–18.

13 C. Richardson, 'Reducing Unemployment', in *Rebuilding the Safety Net, Proceedings of a Conference, 29 April 1999*, (Melbourne: Business Council of Australia, 1999).

14 P. Dixon and M. Rimmer, 'A Wage/Tax Policy to Increase Employment', (Melbourne: Business Council of Australia, 2000).

15 Peter Saunders, 'The $85 Billion Tax-Welfare Churn' (Sydney: The Centre for Independent Studies, 2005).

16 This idea shares a number of characteristics with the idea of 'earning credits' paid to low-income earners to offset their tax burden. This was one of the suggestions in the Five Economists' Plan. The primary difference is that Reform 30/30 has more benefits and fewer costs. Under a recent proposal for an earning credit in Australia, it was estimated that the EMTR for a jobless couple with two children would move from 69% to 65%. In contrast, under Reform 30/30 the EMTR for the same family would move from 69% to 30%. One complaint against earning credits is that they do not remove the work disincentive, but simply shift it up the income scale. A related complaint is that earning credits perpetuate the churning of money where a family is both taxpayer and welfare recipient. The NIT suffers from neither of these complaints as no taxpayer receives welfare and no welfare recipient pays income tax, and the EMTR is a constant 30% for every level of income.

17 These costings are taken from Malcolm Turnbull, *Taxation Reform in Australia: Some Alternatives and Indicative Costings* (Sydney: 2005), available at http://www.turnbullforwentworth.org.au/. Some costings had to be extrapolated.

18 Andrew Leigh, 'Simple Tax Means Many Happy Returns', *Canberra Times*, (27 October 2005).

19 Some of this evidence is summarised in Chapter 2 of Humphreys and Stoeckel, *Free Trade Areas*, (Canberra: RIRDC, forthcoming).

20 Further discussion of the links between tax and growth can be found at Alex Robson, *Taxation, Individual Incentives and Growth* (Brussels: Institute for Research in Economics and Fiscality, 2004), accessed at http://www.iref-europe.org/fra/irefdocs/irefdocs_RobsonEssay.pdf. Also see Daniel Mitchell, *The Impact of Government Spending on Economic Growth*, (Washington, DC: The Heritage Foundation, 2002).

21 Statistics for the current system (2004 data) taken from Saunders and Maley, *Tax Reform to make work pay*, does not take account of rent assistance or the Medicare Levy/Surcharge.

22 Only a flat consumption tax is truly proportional. A flat income tax double taxes savings because (1) interest on savings partly represents a payment in lieu of the time value of money (not an increase in wealth) and so taxing that interest is a tax on delaying consumption (that is, savings); and (2) capital return is double taxed because it is taxed itself and it is also lower due to expected future taxes (for example, future company tax liability decreases the share prices).

23 This problem was highlighted in my mind by an anonymous comment on the internet: 'In my case, I have sweated for every dollar, building a business from the ground up working 80 hour weeks for several years on a subsistence wage

and taking huge financial risk in the process (I have almost lost everything several times). Now that my business is better established and I can afford to increase my salary, that 48.5c marginal rate seems grossly unfair'.

24 Definition of tax expenditure according to the federal government: 'Tax expenditures provide a benefit to a specified activity or class of taxpayer. They can be delivered as a tax exemption, tax deduction, tax offset, reduced tax rate or deferral of a tax liability. The Government can use tax expenditures to allocate resources to different activities or taxpayers in much the same way that it can use direct expenditure programmes. For this reason, and noting their direct impact on the fiscal balance, these concessions are generally called tax expenditures.' http://www.budget.gov.au/2005-06/bp1/html/bst5-10.htm

25 It should be noted that there is an additional cost of tax returns for over-paying individuals in that they are effectively giving the government an interest-free loan from the time they pay tax until they receive their tax return.

26 Note the difference between tax avoidance and tax evasion is that tax avoidance is legal.

27 This estimate was derived in two ways. There are approximately 15.5 million adults in Australia of whom about 5 million are not in the labour market, 0.5 million are unemployed and 10 million are employed. If the NIT is paid to all non-working adults and the half NIT is paid to 4 million workers then the total cost would be about *$67.5 billion* ((5.5 million * $9000) + (4 million * $4500)). An alternative way to estimate the cost is to consider Reform 30/30 as a flat $9000 payment to all adults with no TFT. Under this estimate the total NIT payment would be about $140 billion (15.5 million * $9000) which is artificially inflated by treating the TFT as welfare. The value of a 30% tax on income under $30,000 is estimated at about $70 billion (extrapolated from Turnbull, 2005) and so the real cost of the NIT is *$70 billion.* This may be an overestimate of the cost of the NIT because it does not take into consideration the benefits from a larger economy or more employment.

28 It is worth noting the arguments of Davidson that Australia is on the 'wrong' side of the Laffer curve and therefore we would expect to see government revenue increase from the Laffer effect alone. However, evidence to suggest we are on the wrong side of the Laffer curve is not strong. Davidson points to the fact that Australia has high income tax rates but is a low tax country compared with others in the OECD and suggests that this is evidence that we are on the wrong side of the curve. However, Australia's relatively high level of *income taxes* does result in relatively higher taxes *from income.* Whether Davidson's comparison is a good proxy is a matter for debate. The estimates in this chapter do not support the proposition that Australia is on the wrong side of the Laffer curve.

29 I find it very hard to accept the argument that children are 'public goods' that need subsidising. Children are humans, and like all humans they bring benefits to people they interact with. If this is sufficient grounds for a subsidy, then there is nothing that would not be subsidised. Further, it is not true that we all benefit from child subsidies because we were all children—it is the parents

that pay for their children, the parents that benefit from child subsidies, and not everybody is a parent. The strongest argument for child subsidies is simply that we do not want any child to live in abject poverty.

30 Does not take account of rent assistance, childcare or the Medicare Levy/Surcharge.

Chapter 10. Why politicians aren't rushing to increase taxes

1 My thinking on this subject owes much to discussions with Richard Grant, his PhD thesis, and his archive of opinion polls. Christian Gillitzer provided valuable feedback on this and an earlier paper on the same subject. Peter Saunders offered useful suggestions for improvement. The usual disclaimers apply. So as not to clutter the text with footnotes, I have not referenced results from the Australian National Political Attitudes Survey, the National Social Science Survey, the Australian Election Survey, or the Australian Survey of Social Attitudes. These are all available from the Australian Social Science Data Archive at the Australian National University, http://assda.anu.edu.au/, along with full bibliographic details and information about sample sizes. Newspoll's results can be found at http://www.newspoll.com.au. More recent Roy Morgan polls can be found at http://www.roymorgan.com.au.

2 Surveying for The Australian, Newspoll found in January 2004 that 50% believed that the top tax rate of 47% for incomes over $62,500 was too high. Poll available at www.newspoll.com.au, first reported in George Megalogenis, 'Top rate too high, say half voters', The Australian (23 February 2004). Also, an ACNielsen poll conducted for the CIS found that large minorities (41% to 46%, depending on income group) thought that existing income tax payments were too high: Peter Saunders, 'What is Fair about a "Fair Go"?', *Policy* (Autumn 2004), 9. These results are explained in this paper.

3 Australian Council of Trade Unions, 'Government Services and Tax Resolution', ACTU Congress 2003, 1.

4 Shaun Wilson, 'The voters are getting restless, and government policy is yet to soothe them', *The Sydney Morning Herald* (3 May 2004).

5 John Quiggin, 'The social desirability of social democracy', http://www.johnquiggin.com/archives/001682.html, posted 8 May 2004.

6 Michelle Grattan, 'Are tax cuts losing their lustre?' *The Age* (5 May 2004).

7 Ross Gittins, 'Hip pocket nerve losing its appeal', *The Sydney Morning Herald* (26 May 2004).

8 Questions: 1967–1979 ANPAS survey; 1984–1986 National Social Science Survey; 1987 & 1993-2004 Australian Election Survey: If the government had a choice between reducing taxes or spending more on social services, which do you think it should do?

1974 Morgan Poll: If you had to choose between the Federal government increasing social services or reducing taxes which would you choose?

1990 Australian Election Survey: Some people think that the Federal government should reduce taxes a lot and spend much less on social services. Others think that the Federal government should increase taxes a lot and spend much more on social services. And others have opinions in between. Where would you place yourself on this scale?

AuSSA. Where grades of support for taxing and spending were available, in all polls from 1986–87 onwards, responses have been aggregated. Following the practice of other researchers, I have translated the 1984 and 1986 National Social Science Survey 'mildly for' more taxing and spending as equivalent to 'depends' in subsequent surveys. The argument for doing so is that there is a consistently large minority (20-32%) of equivocal respondents who choose this option, so including them in either lower tax or more spending overstates support for these options.

9 Results from 1984 onwards only record clear preferences; mild preferences or 'it depends' answers have been excluded. Earlier polls did not offer these options, and so produce larger numbers.

10 This result was probably boosted by express mention of health and education services, which are high priorities for Australian voters.

11 Mark Riley, 'Forget tax cuts, Coalition voters want health, education', *The Sydney Morning Herald* (20 May 2003), 6.

12 Shaun Wilson and Trevor Breusch, 'After the tax revolt: Why Medicare matters more to middle Australia than lower taxes', *Australian Journal of Social Issues* 39:2 (May 2004), 110.

13 The Newspoll was conducted 16–18 January 2004, details www.newspoll.com.au. It was first reported in George Megalogenis, 'Top rate too high, say half voters', *The Australian* (23 February 2004).

14 Wilson and Breusch, 'After the tax revolt', 110,

15 A 1992 AGB-McNair survey found a preference for less spending on the unemployed, despite the high number of jobless in the recession (Glenn Withers, David Throsby and Kaye Johnston, *Public Expenditure in Australia,* (Canberra: Economic Planning Advisory Commission, 1994), 32–34). A 1999 survey found no majority support for more government spending on the unemployed, except for people over 50 who could not find work (Peter G. Saunders, *The Ends and Means of Welfare: Coping with economic and social change in Australia*, (Melbourne: Cambridge University Press, 2002), 111). When an ACNielsen survey for the CIS told respondents extra money would be spent on 'on welfare and social services', only 12% were for higher taxes and spending and 36% were for lower taxes and spending (Peter R. Saunders, *A Self-Reliant Australia: Welfare Policy for the 21st Century,* (Sydney: CIS, 2003), 34).

16 The difference between the national and personal levels is exaggerated, since for the national question respondents are specifically asked for three issues, while no number is mentioned for personal replies (respondents can give more than one answer, but in practice few do). Newspoll's surveys also show that health has become a more important issue. See Richard Grant, 'Less tax or more social spending? Twenty years of opinion polling', Research Paper No 13 (Canberra: Parliamentary Library, 2004), 18.

[17] Question 1: Thinking about Australia as a whole. In your opinion, what are the three most important things the Federal government should be doing something about?
Question 2: What could the Federal government do that would be of most benefit to you and your family?
Source: Morgan Poll

[18] Riley, 'Forget tax cuts', 6.

[19] Similarly, support for spending was above 57% in other polls that referred to or assumed knowledge of the surplus. The January 2004 Newspoll, which specifically mentioned the surplus, came out 15 percentage points ahead of the 2003 AuSSA for spending on a comparable combination of services, and 31 percentage points higher if the money was to be split between spending and tax cuts. The May 2004 Taverner poll, also in the context of a Budget with a surplus but not directly reminding its respondents of it, found 65% for more spending on services rather than the tax cuts, and 14% for some of each. It had the lowest margin over the 2003 AuSSA, 8 percentage points, probably because it did not specify popular health and education spending.

[20] For discussion of loss aversion, see Daniel Kahneman and Amos Tversky, *Choices, Values and Frames*, (New York: Cambridge University Press, 2000), especially Chapter 8, 'Daniel Kahneman, Jack L. Knetsch and Richard H. Thaler, *'Anomalies: The Endowment Effect, Loss Aversion, and Status Quo Bias'.*

[21] Results with an article by Dennis Shanahan, 'Latham steals budget bounce', *The Australian* (18 May 2004), 2.

[22] Wilson and Breusch, 'After the tax revolt', 09.

[23] Question (Australian Election Survey 1998, 2001, 2004): Standard of health services since the (1996/1998/2001) federal election has... Question (Australian Survey of Social Attitudes 2003): Over the last two years (since 2001), do you think that the standard of health services, including Medicare, has... The increased and fallen responses have been aggregated, and all Figures rounded.

[24] Question (Australian Election Survey 1998, 2001, 2004): Quality of education since the (1996/1998/2001) federal election has... Question (Australian Survey of Social Attitudes 2003): Over the last two years (since 2001), do you think that the standard of public education has... The increased and fallen responses have been aggregated, and all figures rounded.

[25] For a more detailed analysis of these tendencies, including citations to relevant literature, see my 'Quality of Life and the Prophets of Gloom', *Policy* (Summer 2003–04), 12–18. In Australian and international surveys, people identify more serious problems when asked about others' situations than when they are asked about their own. ('I'm worried about education, but my kid's school is OK.'). Illustrating this phenomenon, Figure 10.2 shows that while only a small number of people nominate health services as something the Federal government can do that would benefit themselves or their families, a comfortable majority think the Federal government should do something about health services. Levels of concern differ partly because opinions about

systems as a whole come mainly from the media, which focuses on newsworthy shortcomings, rather than personal experience, which usually provides a more balanced view. Another factor is that accurate comparisons over time are very hard for non-experts. Bad memories fade faster than good, so past difficulties are forgotten while current problems remain fresh. The result is that people make comparisons which can be demonstrated to be false when measured against actual data from the two time periods.

26 Unlike the Morgan Poll of important issues (Figure 10.2), where respondents can choose any issue but are limited to three responses, Newspoll offers a restricted list of issues but allows any number to be nominated as 'important'.

27 Reserve Bank of Australia, Australian Economic Statistics 1949-50 to 1996-97, http://www.rba.gov.au/Statistics/op8_index.html

28 Morgan Result supplied by Richard Grant. There had been a House of Representatives election in 1966 and a Senate election in 1967. The question format differs from the later Morgan Polls in Figure 2, as respondents were asked about what would affect their vote rather than which issues the Federal government should be doing something about, and they were given a list of 11 issues to choose from, rather than being asked to nominate their own issues.

29 In a Morgan Poll conducted for the 1974 election, health was the second most important issue, with 42% nominating it as one of their top three issues. Inflation on 53% was the most nominated. It is however hard to interpret this as on-going concern about the quality of the health system, since division between the parties over Medibank's introduction made it an issue independent of concern about the current state of health services: Morgan Poll No 100, published in *The Bulletin*, (18 May 1974).

30 OECD, Revenue Statistics 1965-2002, pp.73-74.

31 Neil Warren, *Tax Facts, Fiction and Reform*, (Sydney: Australian Tax Research Foundation, 2004), 108.

32 Data on wages from the Commonwealth Treasury, http://www.treasury.gov.au/documents/562/XLS/Dec03.xls

33 Warren, *Tax Facts,* 108

34 McNair Anderson, *The Changing Australian,* (Sydney: Sentry Holdings/McNair Anderson, 1983)

35 Roy Morgan Research, 'In Australia Consumer Confidence Stable on 124.5', Article No 458, (11 February 2006).

36 A graph I constructed showing the decline of economic issues in the Morgan Poll of most important issues appears in Grant, Less Tax or More Social Spending, 32. From a peak of all issues mentioned of 71% in 1983, economic issues declined to 12% in 2003.

37 Question (Australian Election Survey 1998, 2001): Taxes since the (1996–1998) federal election have… Question (Australian Survey of Social Attitudes 2003): Over the last two years (since 2001), do you think taxes have… The increased and fallen responses have been aggregated, and all Figures rounded.

38 See: Peter Saunders, 'The $85 Billion Tax Welfare Churn'.

39 Michael Keating, 'The Labour Market and Inequality', *The Australian Economic Review* 36:4 (2003), 374–96.

40 Warren, *Tax Facts*, 110.

41 Commonwealth Treasury, 2004-05 Budget Paper No 1, Part 6, Table 2: http://www.budget.gov.au/2004-05/bp1/html/bst13.htm

42 Jennifer Buckingham (ed.), State of the Nation: An Agenda for Change (Sydney: The Centre for Independent Studies, 2004), 81–85.

43 Peter Costello, *Budget Strategy and Outlook* 2003-04, (Canberra: Commonwealth of Australia, 2003), 13–14. Two Liberal spending cuts appear in the Budget papers, but it is due to the classification of GST revenue and expenditure as 'state' revenue and expenditure. It was not to the Commonwealth's own-purpose outlays.

44 Michael Warby, 'Can votes be bought?', *Policy* (Spring 2004).

45 Australian Institute of Health and Welfare, *Health Expenditure Australia 2001-02,* (Canberra: AIHW, 2003), 20.

46 See Simon Kemp, *Private Goods and Public Wants: A Psychological Approach to Government Spending,* (Cheltenham, UK: Edward Elgar, 2002), chapter 8.

47 My calculation from original data available from Newspoll, www.newspoll.com.au

48 31 December 2005 Figure from the Private Health Insurance Administrative Council, http://www.phiac.gov.au/statistics/membershipcoverage/hosquar.htm

49 Australian Institute of Health and Welfare, *Health Expenditure Australia 2003-04,* (Canberra: AIHW, 2005), 22–23.

50 Ian Harper, 'Health Sense: When Spending Money Saves Lives', *Policy* (Spring 2003), 21.

51 Own calculations from Buckingham, *State of the Nation,* 46–48.

52 In the 2003 AuSSA, only 17% of respondents were prepared to pay 'quite a bit more' tax for spending on health, and 14% for schools. A further 58% (health) and 50% (education) were prepared to pay 'a little more tax', but a 'little more tax' is not enough for public services to be improved and to pay for any significant percentage of the people now using private health and education.

53 Question 1: Thinking about Australia as a whole. In your opinion, what are the three most important things the Federal government should be doing something about? Question 2: What could the Federal government do that would be of most benefit to you and your family? Until 1999, all tax responses were classified by Morgan as 'lower tax'. After that, 'no GST', 'tax reform' and 'other taxation issues were added. This creates difficulties in drawing trend lines. In that period 'lower tax' as a personal issue drops significantly, but taxation issues more broadly are stable. Pre-1999 some complaints about the tax system were probably coded as complaints about tax levels, though prior to the GST it is unlikely that this was a major factor. At least some of 'no GST' could probably be re-classified as a complaint about tax levels. Overall, the before 1999 'lower tax' Figures are likely to be slightly inflated, and after 1999 slightly deflated. The particular point of interest here, results from 2003 on, are unaffected by these changes.

54 Saunders, *Ends and Means of Welfare,* 204–05.

55 Wilson and Breusch, 'After the tax revolt', 108–109.

56 Those aged 50 and over are more likely to support spending: Wilson and Breusch, 'After the tax revolt', 104.

57 Grant, Parties, Press and Polls, 255–269.

Index

THE CENTRE FOR INDEPENDENT STUDIES

The Centre for Independent Studies is a non-profit, public policy research institute. Its major concern is with the principles and conditions underlying a free and open society. The Centre's activities cover a wide variety of areas dealing broadly with social, economic and foreign policy.

The Centre meets the need for informed debate on issues of importance to a free and democratic society in which individuals and business flourish, unhindered by government intervention. In encouraging competition in ideas, The Centre for Independent Studies carries out an activities programme which includes:

- research
- holding lectures, seminars and policy forums
- publishing books and papers
- issuing a quarterly journal, *POLICY*

For more information about CIS or to become a member, please contact:

Australia
PO Box 92, St Leonards,
NSW 1590 Australia
Ph: +61 2 9438 4377
Fax: +61 2 9439 7310
Email: cis@cis.org.au

New Zealand
PO Box 5529,
Lambton Quay, 3785
New Zealand
Ph: +64 4 499 5861
Fax: +64 4 499 5940

www.cis.org.au